Faulkner, Aviation, and Modern War

T0390436

Faulkner, Aviation, and Modern War

Michael Zeitlin

BLOOMSBURY ACADEMIC
NEW YORK • LONDON • OXFORD • NEW DELHI • SYDNEY

BLOOMSBURY ACADEMIC
Bloomsbury Publishing Inc
1385 Broadway, New York, NY 10018, USA
50 Bedford Square, London, WC1B 3DP, UK
29 Earlsfort Terrace, Dublin 2, Ireland

BLOOMSBURY, BLOOMSBURY ACADEMIC and the Diana logo are
trademarks of Bloomsbury Publishing Plc

First published in the United States of America 2022
This paperback edition published 2023

Cover design: Eleanor Rose
Cover photograph: Alfred G. Buckham; *Aerial View of Edinburgh*,
National Galleries of Scotland © Richard and John Buckham

Bloomsbury Publishing Inc does not have any control over, or responsibility for, any
third-party websites referred to or in this book. All internet addresses given in this
book were correct at the time of going to press. The author and publisher regret
any inconvenience caused if addresses have changed or sites have ceased
to exist, but can accept no responsibility for any such changes.

Library of Congress Cataloging-in-Publication Data

Names: Zeitlin, Michael, 1957- author.
Title: Faulkner, aviation, and modern war / Michael Zeitlin.
Description: New York : Bloomsbury Academic, 2022. | Includes
bibliographical references and index.
Identifiers: LCCN 2021027335 (print) | LCCN 2021027336 (ebook) |
ISBN 9781501356759 (hardback) | ISBN 9781501376054 (paperback) | ISBN 9781501356766
(epub) | ISBN 9781501356773 (pdf) | ISBN 9781501356780
Subjects: LCSH: Faulkner, William, 1897-1962–Criticism and interpretation. |
Faulkner, William, 1897-1962–Knowledge and learning. | Aviation. | Air pilots in
literature. | Flight in literature. | War in literature. | LCGFT: Literary criticism.
Classification: LCC PS3511.A86 Z9873 2022 (print) | LCC PS3511.A86
(ebook) | DDC 813/.52–dc23
LC record available at https://lccn.loc.gov/2021027335
LC ebook record available at https://lccn.loc.gov/2021027336

ISBN: HB: 978-1-5013-5675-9
          PB: 978-1-5013-7605-4
          ePDF: 978-1-5013-5677-3
          ePUB: 978-1-5013-5676-6

Typeset by Integra Software Services Pvt. Ltd.

To find out more about our authors and books visit www.bloomsbury.com
and sign up for our newsletters.

Denyse

Figures

Preface

William Faulkner's mother Maud was a proud woman and a strong force in the lives of her four sons. In *Every Day by the Sun: A Memoir of the Faulkners of Mississippi*, her granddaughter, Dean Faulkner Wells, remembers,

> I spent a great deal of time with my grandmother Maud, Nannie to me, during the war years. She was devoutly, even obsessively patriotic. During WWI, she had placed two stars on a piece of red, white, and blue felt and hung it in her window to show that she had sons serving in the armed forces—one for Jack, a marine who fought in the Argonne Forest in France—and one for William. (115)

On November 1, 1918, Jack was wounded, his helmet pierced by a shell fragment cutting deeply into his scalp. He kept the metal piece as a souvenir and gave it to his mother, as he recalls, "just as it was given to me, on a bloodstained piece of gauze. She kept it, along with my French Brigade citation, all the days of her life" (Murry Falkner 102). Of his brother William he writes,

> When this country entered the war in 1917, Bill was nineteen, I was seventeen, and John, fifteen. We all wanted to enter military service and each understood that the other was going to do so if possible .... With the country at war, Bill became as restless as I had ever known him to be. He was determined to enter military service, but hoped it could be as an officer .... Several years after the war was over I received at Oxford a small box and a big letter from Marine Headquarters. The one contained a Purple Heart (as everlasting evidence that I forgot to duck) and the other specified where my lack of presence of mind or memory, or both, had caught up with me–Argonne Forest, November 1, 1918 .... When I mentioned this unexpected, happy turn of events to Bill, he considered it a moment [and] smiled (after all, he had been in the war too). (88, 89, 103, 106)

After all, he had been in the war too. This is true, in ways this book seeks to understand more fully. Many myths and misconceptions about Faulkner's service in the Royal Air Force from July to December 1918 circulated among Faulkner's family and friends, and they circulate still. Had Faulkner first tried to join the U.S. Army Signal Corps as a pilot and was he rejected because he was "too short"? (No). Did he fly—or even ride in—an airplane while he was in the Royal Air Force in Toronto, Canada? (No). Did he ever crash in a training accident or Armistice Day joyride? Was he ever shot down in France or behind German lines? Was he ever physically wounded in the war? (No, no, no). Did he walk with a limp for a time after the war and claim he had a silver plate patched to his skull? (Yes). Did he wear RAF wings on the tailored pilot officer's uniform he wore home in December 1918?

The answer here is tricky. He did wear wings, but they were Royal Flying Corps wings, purchased in a Toronto pawnshop (Wells 59) and defunct as of April 1, 1918, April Fool's Day and Easter Monday both, when "the Royal Flying Corps and the Royal Naval Air Service in England were amalgamated and became the Royal Air Force, operating under one command" (Ellis 126). The RAF was "the world's first independent air force," founded to carry out "the long-range bombing of German industrial towns" in response to the German terror bombing attacks on London that had reached a climax on June 17, 1917 (O x). In wearing the wings of the old legendary service—the RFC—Faulkner was choosing to reflect the mystique of the aeronautical knight-errant over the reality of what modern aerial warfare *en masse* had become.

Faulkner did not fly Sopwith Camels or experience aerial combat in the First World War, but his military experience in the massive new service was real enough, both fascinating and alienating by turns. In addition to being marched, drilled, and, on occasion, sharply disciplined (as he notes in letters to his mother), he received a rigorous education in military aeronautics that he would draw from as a writer about aviation and modern war over the next four decades. Had the First World War continued into the spring of 1919, moreover, as most everybody in July 1918 believed, he would have been deployed as a pilot or gunner, most likely in an observation, strafing, or bombing squadron. Thoughts about what he would have had to face, and to do, overseas, and whether he would have survived the war at all, preoccupied him in 1918 and for years after. In words describing an RAF veteran in *Winged Victory* by V. M. Yeates, a novel Faulkner would come to value as "the best of the flying ones, and (to me) the best of the war books," Faulkner came home from the war "a very much more developed and dangerous personality than he went in" (To Harold Raymond, January 22, 1952, SL 327; Y 205).

Before and during his RAF service, Faulkner listened to the stories of war veterans and read about the war in the newspapers and magazines. After the war, he read histories and immersed himself in the war literature of the period—memoirs, diaries, stories, novels, letters, interviews. This book explores the writings of the pilots Faulkner names in his letters, stories, and novels: Jimmy McCudden, Mick Mannock, Billy Bishop, Norman Prince, Manfred von Richthofen, Eddie Rickenbacker, Victor Chapman, Raoul Lufbery, Victor Maslin Yeates, John MacGavock Grider, Georges Guynemer. Faulkner does not mention several others whose signatures are clearly legible in his work: Dana Carroll Winslow, James Norman Hall, Charles Biddle, Alan Bott, James McConnell, and James Warner Bellah. All these pilots have left us a living history of the air war as experienced by some of its most reflective and articulate witnesses, some as young as nineteen years old when they found they were objects of popular fascination at home. Their memoirs, diaries, and letters help us to visualize how the war in the air was fought. They offer insights into the pilots' martial psychologies and tactical philosophies and enable us to catch some stunning cockpit visions of the future of aerial warfare as it would play out over the next one hundred years.

In *The Real War 1914–1918* (1930), B. H. Liddell Hart reflects,

It was not easy for a conservative mind to realize that with the transition from a war of government policies into a war of peoples, the indefinite code of military chivalry must be submerged by the primitive instincts let loose by a struggle for existence .... in 1914, this "absolute" war was still only a latent conception. (76)

Through the first phases of the war it was as if "the mass of the people watched, from seats in the amphitheatre, the efforts of their champions" (Hart, *The Real War* 36). As the air war escalated in range, scale, and tonnage of bombs dropped, "the new reality that the war of armies had become the war of peoples" (80) became clearer:

> From January onwards, Zeppelin raids began on the English coast and reached their peak in the late summer of 1916, to be succeeded by aeroplane raids. The difficulty of distinguishing from the air between military and civil objectives smoothed the path for the development which, beginning with excuses, ended in a frank avowal that in a war for existence the will of the enemy nation, not merely the bodies of their soldiers, is the inevitable target. (Hart, *The Real War* 80–1)

One of the most fascinating ironies of the air war is that, in the tradition of "Ardant du Picq, a soldier-philosopher who fell in the 1870 war," the famous pilots themselves, grown weary of all the press they were receiving, "had stripped battle of its aura of heroic fictions, portraying the reaction of normal men in the presence of danger" (Hart, *The Real War* 45).

When Faulkner began his RAF service in July 1918, any residual imagination he might have had of himself as a solo *chasse* pilot, engaged in "a series of duels in which the skill and courage of the individual aces were displayed in all their brilliance .... as knights-errant of the air" (Douhet 43), was already becoming antiquated, historical, obsolete. During the course of his military service, and in the years of reading and writing that followed, Faulkner came to possess a profound understanding of the military institution, the realities of combat flying, the horrors of battlefield killing, and the First World War as "the great seminal catastrophe" of the twentieth century (Kennan 3). As an RAF veteran in the 1920s, Faulkner was also more than "a bit hipped on the subject of flying" (Basso 3), and he was hired in the 1930s and '40s on the basis of his military service and aviation knowledge to write screenplays for Hollywood movies. "In that sense," as Bruce Kawin has noted, "the work for these scripts began in 1918 in Toronto, where Cadet Faulkner trained at the RAF School of Aeronautics" (Kawin, *Faulkner's MGM Screenplays* xxi). Eventually Faulkner did learn to fly an airplane and he earned his pilot's license in 1933, though he was not considered a good pilot by his teachers and peers (see Bostwick for a summary of Faulkner's "rather mundane" [8] career as a civilian pilot). For a time in the mid-1930s, he flew as a "barnstorming" pilot or passenger until the death of his little brother Dean, the superior pilot, on November 10, 1935, in the Waco airplane William had given him. Faulkner helped to extract his brother's body from the wrecked machine and was present when the mortician tried to reconstruct Dean's face so that his mother could view her son one last time before he was buried. For his brother's gravestone, Faulkner selected the epitaph he had first used for "Lieut. John Sartoris, R.A.F., Killed in action, July 5, 1918" in *Flags in the Dust*: "I bare him on eagles' wings and brought him unto Me" (FL 870).[1]

I am hardly the first person to be fascinated by the theme of aviation in William Faulkner's life and work. The true "aviation pioneers" are Michael Millgate, Joseph Blotner, Robert Harrison, James G. Watson, Kenneth Weber, Gordon Price-Stephens, and Judith Bryant Wittenberg. In the course of researching this book, however, I discovered another scholar whose work should be acknowledged, Major Walter I. Bostwick (1933–84), whose unpublished Masters Thesis (Florida Atlantic University, August 1981), contains the lucid reflections of an experienced military aviator. I have not been able to find out much about Major Bostwick. He served in the USAF during the Korean War. He achieved a "Straight A" rating "while attending the Flying Safety Officers' Course at the University of Southern California" after the war when he continued to work on "improvement in aircraft accident prevention" as Director of Safety.[2]

He is buried in the Garden of Serenity at Daytona Memorial Park, Daytona Beach, FL. As Faulkner told Cynthia Grenier from behind his "epicanthic lids" in her fascinating interview of 1955, "What matters is at the end of life, when you're about to pass into oblivion, that you've at least scratched 'Kilroy was here,' on the last wall of the universe. Nothing else matters" (LG 227). Major Bostwick's "Kilroy" is here in this book in significant ways, as in his excellent summary of a story richly told by all the major biographers (including Blotner, Williamson, Sensibar, Parini, Weinstein, Rollyson): Faulkner's painful love affair with Estelle Oldham Franklin and its repercussions throughout his life and work. Estelle was "the girl next door" who ended up marrying another man, Cornell Franklin, in the spring of 1918. Faulkner went north to escape the scene of their wedding and found his way soon after into the Royal Air Force in Toronto. Bostwick gives the matter that concerns me most its essential perspective:

> In 1918, he was a smaller-than-average, not particularly attractive young man with few if any prospects for success in life. He was rejected by the parents of his teenage sweetheart, who preferred a wealthy young lawyer as a prospective son-in-law. His decision to join one of the most dangerous and certainly the most romantic parts of the military, and publicly risk death to seek fame and glory in the skies of France was not an unusual one for a young man in his position.
>
> When World War I ended before Faulkner had even started flying training, it must have been a bitter pill for him to swallow. The idea of ignominiously returning home in a shabby, government-issue Cadet uniform must have been appalling. He was probably far from the only person to exaggerate his military experience, although his exaggerations were somewhat extreme. A key point is that he deluded not only friends and acquaintances, but his family as well .... At some time in Faulkner's life he probably realized that he was trapped by the persona he had created. He could not repudiate it without causing shame and pain to his family, embarrassment to his friends and, to some extent, disapproval from critics and others in literary circles. He could not confirm the persona, however, because it was a complete fabrication which relatively simple research would reveal as a fraud. His 1950 letter to Professor Kohler is the only available document in which he denies seeing combat and being wounded, but even this letter does not deny

that he flew with the RAF in 1918 .... The fact that Faulkner created a mythical persona as a young man and maintained it relatively intact for the rest of his life is only one more complexity in the complex make-up of an inventive and creative author. (Bostwick 47)

The chapters of this book attempt to get further inside this story through Faulkner's own writing.

A Note on the Spelling of "Aeroplane"

I follow the Wright brothers, the British, the French, the First World War pilots, and Faulkner himself in spelling the word thus. The resonances of "aero" are also richly suggestive in a range of related terms that appear in the aviation literature that I explore in this book: aerodrome, aero-motor, aerodynamics, aeronautics, aerobatics, aeropoetry, aeropainting (*aeropitura* in Italian), the French Service Aèronautique, and so on. See also Robert Harrison's note on spelling in *Aviation Lore in Faulkner* (v).

Notes

1   "After Dean's death," writes Dean Faulkner Wells, who was born after her father's death and raised in William Faulkner's household, "William suffered from grief and guilt I imagine almost every day of his life .... It was as if William made a vow to Dean that November afternoon when he saw his unrecognizable body in the wreckage of the plane: He would tend to me in Dean's place" (Wells 2).
2   https://archive.org/stream/aerospacesafety19unit_1/aerospacesafety19unit_1_djvu.txt

Acknowledgments

Research for this book began in Toronto in 1974 when the great Mr. Gadsby, my grade 13 English teacher (yes, grade 13) at Jarvis Collegiate Institute, put *Light in August* on the reading list (the reading list is everything). My incomparable teachers at the University of Toronto also put Faulkner on their reading lists: Douglas Chambers, T. H. Adamowski, Michael Sidnell, Dennis Duffy, Michael Millgate. At some point I began to read Blotner's biography and learned, to my astonishment, that Faulkner, as a cadet in the Royal Air Force, lived at Wycliffe College between July and December 1918, right across the street from Trinity College on 6 Hoskin Avenue where I was enrolled. Apparently on certain nights Faulkner would march up and down that sidewalk in front of Wycliffe's gothic red bricks and chant out the rhythms of the day's military drill. Beer may have been involved, as it may have been involved for me too in those days. In any case, I stared down at that sidewalk on many a night and tried to discern Faulkner's tread. There never has been any plaque or marker at Wycliffe College to commemorate Faulkner's presence there, but I have asked my friend, Professor Paul Litt, a renowned expert in Canadian history, to begin to investigate what might be done.

The following admirable people have also helped me in all sorts of ways, mainly by taking an interest in what I was doing, sharing their valuable thoughts, giving me confidence that I could write this book. Their wisdom, kindness, and support have meant a lot to me, more than they can possibly know. Thank you Ira Nadel, Jay Watson, Peter Lurie, Robert Jackson, Kristin Fujie, Sarah Gleeson-White, John Duvall, Candace Waid, Julian Murphet, Stefan Solomon, Katie Kodat, Pardis Dabashi. Thank you Chris Rieger for reading the proposal and penultimate manuscript and for offering invaluable perspectives that helped me make a better book. Thank you John Wilson Foster, Paul Budra, Tom Carmichael, the Lava Men, Ian Grais, Sandy Tomc, Patsy Badir, Bo Earle, Jeff Severs, Jon Beasley-Murray, Rebecca Adelman, David Kieran, Jennifer Haytock, Les Marton, Montieth Illingworth, Paul Litt, Hugh Ker, Gavin Poolman, Kicking Horse Cliff Hanger Organic Espresso Beans, Sajeev Kanasanathan, Toby Hodgson, Matt Lorincz, Lori Kroeker, John Madden, Marina Kamimura, Alison Strobel, Phil Smith. Thank you Dream Teamers at Arts One: Gavin Paul, Brandon Konoval, Tom Kemple, and Carla Nappi. Thank you Paul Moore, Benjamin Hertwig, Lori Main, Mike Way, Joe Hall, Sean Glass, Jerry Lembcke, Dawn Trouard, Edwin "Chip" Arnold, Dr. Joseph Finkler, Dr. Jason Andrade, Dr. Matthew Bennett, Claire Lloyd, Soumya Bhattacharya, Doug Brigham, Leanne Koch, Keith Bunnell, and all the excellent UBC librarians. Thank you Greg Johnson and Lauren Rogers at Archives and Special Collections, J. D. Williams Library, the University of Mississippi. Thank you Stephen Railton and

Johannes Burgers. Thank you Elizabeth L. Garver and her colleagues at the Harry Ransom Center. Thank you Amy Martin, my superb and admirably patient editor at Bloomsbury. Thank you Katherine de Chant and Eleanor Rose for the cover design. I salute Dr. Bonnie Henry, Adrian Dix, and all the courageous health care workers of British Columbia. And in memory: Corey Copeland, Douglas Chambers, Noel Polk, James Watson, Michel Gresset, James Hart, Chris Lynch; Captain Jenn Casey, Snowbirds Demonstration Squadron, Royal Canadian Air Force; Dave Seraphim, Neil Peart, and Esther Zeitlin, my mother, who would have loved holding this book in her hands.

I thank my father, Irving M. Zeitlin, for the extraordinarily powerful influence of his love and scholarship, and my sisters, Ruthie and Bethie, my little brother Jeremy, and my sons, Isaiah Dunne-Zeitlin (hanging out at the YVR runways), Daniel, Jonathan, and Leo. I'm blessed to know you.

Most of all I thank Denyse Wilson, brilliant and supremely talented. This book is dedicated to her.

Abbreviations

A   John D. Anderson, *The Grand Designers: The Evolution of the Airplane in the 20th Century* (Cambridge University Press, 2018)

B   Joseph Blotner, *Faulkner: A Biography*. 2 vols. (Random House, 1974)

C   David T. Courtwright, *Sky as Frontier: Adventure, Aviation, and Empire* (Texas A&M University Press, 2005)

FA   William Faulkner, *A Fable* (1954). *William Faulkner, Novels 1942–1954* (Library of America, 1994)

FL   William Faulkner, *Flags in the Dust* (1928). *William Faulkner, Novels 1926–1929* (Library of America, 2006)

H   Samuel Hynes, *The Unsubstantial Air: American Fliers in the First World War* (Farrar, Straus and Giroux, 2014)

JY   Peter Jakab and Rick Young, *The Published Writings of Wilbur and Orville Wright* (Smithsonian Books, 2000)

LG   James B. Meriwether and Michael Millgate, eds., *Lion in the Garden: Interviews with William Faulkner 1926–1962* (Random House, 1968)

M   David McCullough, *The Wright Brothers* (Simon & Schuster, 2015)

NYT   *The New York Times*

O   Richard Overy, *The Birth of the RAF, 1918: The World's First Air Force* (Allen Lane, 2018)

PY   William Faulkner, *Pylon* (1935). *William Faulkner, Novels 1930–1935* (Library of America, 1985)

SL   Joseph Blotner, ed. *Selected Letters of William Faulkner* (Random House, 1977)

SP   William Faulkner, *Soldiers' Pay* (1926). *William Faulkner, Novels 1926–1929* (Library of America, 2006)

SU   Alan Sullivan, *Aviation in Canada 1917–1918* (Rous & Mann Limited, 1919)

TH   James G. Watson, ed., *Thinking of Home: William Faulkner's Letters to His Mother and Father, 1918–1925* (Norton, 1992)

Y   V. M. Yeates, *Winged Victory*. 1934. (Grub Street, 2004)

The Original Accident

Faulkner attempted to launch a homemade aeroplane in 1909, six years post–Kitty Hawk when he was twelve years old. He found the design in the spring issue of *The American Boy* magazine and supervised the craft's construction in an exciting neighborhood project. His little brothers Murry (Jack) and John (Johncy) and his cousin Sallie Murry were given key roles as builders and consultants but they let him take the maiden flight alone. Joseph Blotner tells what happened next, in two overlapping versions:

> "Let go!" shouted Billy from inside, and the crew gave a powerful heave. Airborne for an instant, the plane pitched as the tail rose. Then it swung through an arc in a half- revolution so that Billy was for a moment suspended upside down. Then the pilot and craft thumped down into the bottom of the ditch in a flutter of paper and bean poles. Billy silently picked his way out of the shattered fuselage as his crew looked on, dumb with disappointment. Finally they turned and walked back to the house for supper. (B 136)
>
> With a last lunge they launched it. It pitched as the tail rose and then swung through an arc and thumped upside down into the bottom of the ditch in a flutter of paper and beanpoles. Billy silently picked his way out of the shattered fuselage as Jack, Johncy, and Sallie Murry looked on, dumb with disappointment. (Blotner, *Faulkner*, one-vol. ed., 35)

Faulkner's brother John, however, tells us there were other participants too, offering another important angle on an event that frequent retellings kept alive in the Faulkner family lore:

> In unison the two Negroes heaved the machine out over the ditch. It went up for several feet and did the first part of a loop, minus the wing tips Mallory and Dooley had used for handholds, which remained in their hands. We saw Bill against the skyline, upside down, and then the ship began to come to pieces in the air. Stiff tatters of paper fluttered loose. The bean stickers began coming apart. And Bill fell in a shower of torn paper and scraps of kindling wood and landed on the back of his head in a pile of sand at the bottom of the ditch. (John Faulkner 100)

Contents

I will comment on Mallory and Dooley below, but for now, this collective memory contains all the major elements to be explored in Faulkner's aviation fiction: the passionate desire to fly, the brave testing of limits, the inevitable failure of the machine, the humiliating loss of control, the dumb gaze of the witnesses, the division of labor between pilot and ground crew. All this, for example, is at the heart of *Pylon* (1935), a novel about the mass spectacle of airplane racing in the modern technological age, a novel that tells "the furious, still, and legendary tale of what man has come to call his conquering of the infinite and impervious air" (PY 799).[1] The tone of *Pylon's* formulation, blending popular fascination, withering irony, and a deep identification with Icarus, is typical of Faulkner's overall aeronautical sensibility. In Faulkner's fictions, flying an aeroplane is always a daring exhibition, a scene performed before an astonished audience with "gaped and upturned faces" (PY 933). Sometimes the people on the ground chase after the airplane while shouting and gesticulating, as if the pilot has committed some terrible transgression. Sometimes a solitary watcher "feels her breath going out faster than she could draw it in again" (FL 597) as the pilot attempts to subdue an airship that seems animated by an uncanny will of its own. Sometimes the spectators watch as the pilot flies too high and then crashes to the ground. The dead are mourned as flowers are dropped from circling aeroplanes. Sometimes the pilot falls free from his machine, drops through the clouds, and vanishes into air, or water. A simple white panel, gravestone, or newspaper obituary commemorates him.[2]

Faulkner's pilots are "early" aviators in this sense, risking death with every flight, solo types that Dean C. Smith describes in his classic memoir *By the Seat of My Pants* (1961). Smith was an Army Air Service instructor at seventeen years old, an airmail pilot, a test pilot, and an Antarctic aviation pioneer. He reflects that, in the early days of aviation, "the only way one learned anything more advanced than a gentle turn was by trial and error." In this way one

> gradually discovered things that could and could not be done. Many were killed by getting into stalls and spins they had not learned how to control. If they survived, they would pass on their knowledge to others. The early art of flying developed not by our modern method of measured and controlled laboratory experiments calculated by results of earlier data, but by reckless enthusiasts, keen to know and to do, trying everything until they found something. (16)

As RAF historian Alan Sullivan noted in 1919: "it has been remarked that at the outset 'he [the cadet-pilot in training] has many opportunities for error and usually discovers them all'" (SU 103). The pilot learns by doing, struggling not only with the peculiarities of his flying machine but with his own instincts, reflexes, and impulses as they contend with aerodynamic forces that are never properly understood. Taking off on his first solo flight, many an embryonic military aviator immediately forgot what he thought he had mastered in the classroom, flying his aeroplane in "the blackest ignorance even of first principles" (D. V. Dodds, Directorate of Air Force History, Royal Canadian Air Force, qtd. in Weber 6). The early progress of aviation was soundly epistemological in this sense, for trainers and trainees alike. In Kenneth Weber's summary of "Canada's First Air Training Plan," "Canadian training philosophy had changed from a system picturing man as a member of a completely mechanistic universe where he was at the mercy of the whims of fate to a more optimistic system placing man in control of a universe in which he, through his intelligence and proficiency, could accomplish his desires" (Weber 7). The passage from fear and passivity to a more resolute aeronautical knowledge and confidence unfolds as a test of will and character.

> Character—that subtle union of temperament and disposition, the increasing air sense, the delicacy of control, the spontaneous response, the nameless faculty by which the pupil becomes, as it were, welded to the machine which in turn replies to the subconscious movement of hand and foot. (SU 212)

In Faulkner's aviation narratives, the relationship between the pilot and the machine is rarely as classical and composed, balanced or harmonious, as Sullivan ideally describes it. Faulknerian flight and character, rather, are realms of turbulence and contestation in which the pilot is invariably threatened with elemental terrors—"'loss of head,' 'brain fatigue' …. the stage in which the pilot has neither the power to reason, decide or act" (SU 226). The new field of aviation psychology responds by analyzing the pilot's mentality under the stresses of speed, altitude, disorienting motion, and fear—fear of injury, death, failure, humiliation. Sullivan appears to grasp the matter sympathetically:

> Under "loss of head," for instance, it is pointed out that the pupil in his new occupation of flying, especially for the first time, has every mental faculty on the alert at extremely high tension, and that the sense of danger, although not asserting itself, is also subconsciously present. It follows, therefore, that under the strain of an emergency the power of synchronized decision and act may lapse— this lapse resulting in what is known as "loss of head." … Then supervenes a state of mental inertia due to the swiftly repeated stream of impulses received in rapid succession by his brain. He begins to feel alone, and unable to assume control. Errors occur, and he becomes overwhelmed with the enormousness of the whole thing. Follows a state of brain fatigue and stupor, during which he awaits events and takes little part in the control of his machine. After such an accident, the pupil has generally no recollection of what has happened. His memory seems to be partially stunned. Under these circumstances, it seldom occurs that he resumes flying—his temperament as a general thing proving to be unsuitable. (SU 226–30)

First World War RAF pilot Captain Alan Bott observes in his memoir of 1917 that "if he gives way to unconsciousness the machine, freed from reasoned control, will perform circus tricks and twist itself into a spinning nose-dive" (Bott 243–4). The archetypal aviation scene in Faulkner is thus an essential site of what Thomas Mann, in 1938, called "the alpha and omega of all psychoanalytical knowledge": "the mysterious unity of ego and actuality, destiny and character, doing and happening … the mystery of reality as an operation of the psyche" (Mann 412). The aviator's psyche in Faulkner is never completely conscious and coordinated. It is always haunted by fear, susceptible to paralysis, and impelled by blind forces.

Such are the conditions, however, that make piloting an aeroplane (if one survives long enough) an opportunity for profound self-analysis, a chance, as one First World War pilot put it, "to find out the truth about myself" (qtd. in H 45). Eddie Rickenbacker, a hero for Faulkner and many others, recalls his feeling upon landing after his first solo flight over enemy lines:

> I forgot entirely my recent fear and terror. Only a deep feeling of satisfaction and gratitude remained that warmed me and delighted me, for not until that moment had I dared to hope that I possessed all the requisite characteristics for a successful war pilot. Though I had feared no enemy, yet I had feared that I myself might be lacking. (Rickenbacker 7)

Faulkner's pilots seldom get over this kind of fear that they "might be lacking" in some basic sense.

Flying in Faulkner is hard enough, an essentially oneiric and unreal form of machine-propelled movement generally "freed from reasoned control." This state of affairs is made exponentially worse when the aeroplane is a Sopwith Camel. The case of Johnny Sartoris in *Flags in the Dust*, "All the Dead Pilots," and "With Caution and Dispatch" is the central one. As Robert Harrison explains in "A Note on the Sopwith Camel," the Camel was "high-strung, skittish, easily 'spooked,' it called for a master's hand on the reins …. In level flight the torque of the 130-hp Clerget would roll the machine on its back unless the pilot kept both hand and mind constantly on the controls" (Harrison 43). These same dynamic and unstable characteristics, however, were also the machine's essential strengths in war:

> A Camel … had to be consciously held in steady flight, and came out of it in a flash. The very instability that made it a death trap for the mediocre pilot made it a darting, slewing, skittering gadfly in combat …. no attacker in fact could remain on its tail when it was turning to the right ….. it could outmanoeuvre any aeroplane ever built. (Harrison 44)

The richest and most realistic description of Camel flying, probably anywhere, appears in the novel Faulkner singled out for special praise, V. M. Yeates' *Winged*

Victory (1934). As the main voice of the novel explains, focalizing the narrative through the being and consciousness of British RAF pilot Tom Cundall, "A Camel hated an inexperienced hand, and flopped into a frantic spin at the least opportunity" (Y 25). "It would not fly straight for more than a second at a time" (Y 27). "A Camel might be going sideways or flat-spinning, or going in any direction except straight backwards. A Camel in danger would do the most queer things, you never knew what next, especially if the pilot was Tom Cundall" (Y 29). "But a Camel had to be flown carefully round with exactly the right amount of left rudder, or else it would rear and buck and hang upside down and flop and spin" (Y 30). "That was the worst of being in the flying service: you were always in the front line, even in England" (Y 31).

Yeates' signature is all over Faulkner's "With Caution and Dispatch." Flying through a rainstorm over the English Channel, Johnny Sartoris puts "his head well down in the office, one eye on his watch and the other watching the water between his left shoulder and the cockpit rim to hold his altitude and his course by the direction in which the chop was moving" (650). Suddenly he sees

> the side of a ship which looked as long as a city block and rose taller than any cliff. *I've already crashed*, he thought. He did three things as one: he slapped the throttle full on and snatched the stick back and shut his eyes; the Camel went up the side of the ship like a hawk, a gull up a cliff-face. (650)

In *Winged Victory*, Tom Cundall's commander, Mac, a flying virtuoso based on the Canadian Ace and master pilot Donald Roderick MacLaren (DSO, MC and Bar, DFC), does intentionally and with great skill what Sartoris only lucks into doing after he "shut his eyes": "Mac dived down past the cloud like a gull down the face of a cliff" (Y 320). Meanwhile Cundall, who is closer to Sartoris on the scale of proficiency, also flies through the rain with his head down. "The mist grew darker. He put his head in the office and flew by instruments" (Y 34). This habit nearly kills him on more than one occasion.

> He had to go all the way home through rain-mist just over house tops, and he opened full out to a hundred and ten miles an hour, keeping his head well in the office. A mountain suddenly looked up in front of him. The Camel shot up the side of it and staggered over the top. Christ, a slag heap. He felt shaky after the menacing instant. If he hadn't been going all out he'd never have zoomed it. The things he got away with. (Y 414)

The Camel's flying characteristics made a deep impression on Faulkner's understanding of the basic relationship between the pilot and his machine.[3] In fact it is hard to find a smooth landing by any aeroplane in Faulkner's world, or an aeroplane moving through Faulknerian airspace in the way the Wright brothers were first to achieve above Kill Devil Hills on December 17, 1903: "in sustained, powered, piloted, and controlled flight" (A 42).

"Uncle Willy"

The flight of the airplane in Faulkner is rarely straight or long sustained. Usually it follows an antic and absurd path, as in this scene from Faulkner's short story "Uncle Willy" (first published in *The American Mercury* in 1935):

> and we saw the airplane start, with Secretary still running after it, and jump into the air and duck down and then jump up again and then it looked like it had stopped high in the air above the trees where we thought Secretary was fixing to land that first day before it ducked down beyond them and went out of sight [....] (246)[4]

In this short story, too, the memory of "the two Negroes," "Mallory and Dooley," who do the heavy lifting in John Faulkner's account of the original childhood crash, seems to survive. One of the negro boys, this time, finds himself sitting in the cockpit of the toylike "little airplane with a two-cylinder engine. It was Secretary, in another new checked cap and goggles like Uncle Willy's" (241). Perhaps the other turns up as old Job, Uncle Willy's lifelong servant. This plane crashes too but not before it gets to fly around quite a bit, the young Black pilot's cap and goggles "synonymous with open-cockpit flying" (C 6) and that more romantic and individualistic era of aviation whose very visibility in Faulkner's work reminds us that flying was predominantly a white man's activity.[5] The typical congregation of pilots or the typical airport waiting room or grandstand crowd at the air races in the 1920s and '30s (as in the novel *Pylon*) "did not look like America" (C 11). Perhaps this is one of the realities that Faulkner's story attempts to surmount through the twists and turns of its plot. Secretary, the negro boy, must learn to fly the airplane so that he can teach the white man, Uncle Willy, how to do so (Willy is not allowed to fly on account of his addiction to heroine and alcohol). Yet the Black child who can fly is part of a dream "too fine to be true." The culture of moral proscription and racial surveillance that Uncle Willy briefly circumvents by putting Secretary into the cockpit ultimately prevails. But not before Uncle Willy, the ultimate rule-breaker, jumps into the cockpit himself and takes off alone, intent on going out his own way. The little airplane crashes and Uncle Willy dies, the freest and "the finest man I ever knew ... he wound up his life getting fun out of being alive and he died doing the thing that was the most fun of all" (225).

The narrator of the story remembers the scene he lived through as a fourteen-year-old boy, the youngest in this group of four and yet the one who was expected to be (but who actually was not in any sense) the responsible one: "Because I was the other white one. I was white, even if old Job and Secretary were both older than me" (242):

> Captain Bean at the airport wouldn't teach [Uncle Willy] to run it himself because he would need a permit from a doctor ("By God," Uncle Willy said, "damn if these Republicans and Democrats and XYZ's ain't going to have it soon where a man can't even flush the toilet in his own bathroom.") and he couldn't go to the

doctor because the doctor might want to send him back to the Keeley or tell Mrs. Merridew where he was. So he just let Secretary learn to run it first .... and he would stay there a week while Secretary taught Uncle Willy to run the airplane. Then we would head west. When we ran out of the house money we would stop at a town and take up passengers and make enough to buy gasoline and food to get to the next town, Uncle Willy and Secretary in the airplane and me and old Job in the car. "And by Christmas we will be in California!" I suppose I knew then that it wouldn't work, couldn't work, that it was too fine to be true. (242–2)

The federal "XYZ's" in their corporate-driven efforts to regulate the civil airways are putting the small barnstorming operators out of business. The major airlines are interested only in transporting paying passengers in straight lines from one city to another with the utmost "speed, safety, comfort, and economy," in the words of Donald W. Douglas, president and chief engineer of the Douglas Aircraft Company. The prototype of the Douglas DC-3 (Douglas Commercial-3) modern airliner first flew on July 1, 1933. This all-metal, streamlined airplane "had a maximum speed of 212 mph, which made it the fastest commercial transport of its day." It was propelled by "two powerful Wright Cyclone engines, each producing 1,100 horsepower. The Wright Cyclone was a 14-cylinder, air-cooled radial engine, with the cylinders arranged in two rows" (A 104–105).[6]

Uncle Willy could not compete with all this, nor would he have wanted to. Those of Faulkner's generation, born around 1900, grew up associating "flying with birdmen, dogfighters, and barnstormers, types disposed to crash and burn" (C 92). They were pre-Lindbergh types in this basic sense. After his spectacular solo flight across the Atlantic on May 20–21, 1927, Charles Lindbergh "became the great apostle of commercial aviation," making "safe and efficient operation the foundation of his message" (C 71). It was Lindbergh's "judgment, rather than any extraordinary piloting skill, that carried him safely across the Atlantic" (C 72).[7]

Naturally, all the careful judgment, planning, and checklists in the world cannot always prevent the collapse of airframes under extreme stresses or the failure of engines caused by flaws in design, the negligence of mechanics, the sudden arrival of violent weather, and so on (to say nothing, just yet, of the enemy's live ammunition). The wreck of the homemade airplane in 1909 is emblematic in this sense of the catastrophe that may always be latent in the attempt to fly, what French theorist Paul Virilio would call "the original accident" of Faulkner's childhood. "To get what is heavier than air to take off in the form of an aeroplane ... is *to invent the crash*, the air disaster" just as "to invent the train is *to invent the rail accident* of derailment. To invent the family automobile is to produce the *pile-up* on the highway" (Virilio, *Original* 10, his emphasis). Faulkner would have absorbed this elementary realization along with the ground's impact. "The destructive aspect of progress" (Horkheimer and Adorno xiii) "dogs the great discoveries and the great technical inventions like a shadow" (Virilio, *Original* 10). American combat pilot and volunteer in the Lafayette Escadrille, Dana Carroll Winslow, in a book Faulkner drew on for its richly textured description of aviation experience in war, captures the breathless irony of this "dialectic of enlightenment" in the opening lines of his memoir, *With the French Flying Corps* (1917): "In the last two years aviation has become an essential branch of the army organization of every country. Daily hundreds of pilots are flying in Europe, in Africa, in Asia Minor; flying, fighting, and dying in a medium through which, ten years ago, it was considered impossible to travel" (13).

The Wright Brothers' Original Accident

In their "Statement to the Aero Club of America" on March 12, 1906, the Wrights described their revolutionary achievement in direct and modest tones:

> In the past three years a total of 160 flights have been made with our motor-driven flyers, and a total distance of almost exactly 160 miles covered …. In operating the machine it has been our custom for many years to alternate in making flights, and such care has been observed that neither of us has suffered any serious injury, though in the earlier flights our ignorance and the inadequacy of the means of control made the work exceedingly dangerous. (JY 17)

They knew that an accident at some point was inevitable and that they would make history again with the first crash of their motorized machine. There had been many crashes of their "man-carrying gliding machines" at Kill Devil Hills in 1901 and 1902, but those had been on sandy ground from low altitudes and at relatively slow speeds. In the period of those early glider flights, "from mid-October to December 7, 1901, the Wrights tested over 200 different wing models, with different planform and airfoil shapes. These experiments produced the most definitive and practical aerodynamic data on wings and airfoils obtained to that date" (A 31). As one of their close associates recalled of them, "Those two sure knew their physics. I guess that's why they always knew what they were doing and hardly ever guessed at anything" (qtd. in M 86). Otto Lilienthal, from whom the Wright brothers learned a great deal about gliding and aerodynamics, was also a careful and exacting designer and tester who started experimenting with gliders in 1869. His death made a deep impression on the Wrights and everyone else in the aviation community. "On August 9, 1896, flying a favorite 'No. 11' glider, he crashed again, falling from an altitude of fifty feet. He died of a broken spine in a Berlin hospital the following day at age forty-eight" (M 28–9). The Wrights were renowned for their scientific methodology and meticulous planning before each flight, but they also knew, as an American airplane racer summarized the matter in the 1930s, that "if … any plane is flown enough, the odds are that it will eventually crash" (qtd. in Hull 183).

The first crash of a Wright Flyer occurred on September 17, 1908, more than five years after the first flight at Kitty Hawk. While Wilbur was demonstrating the Flyer before large crowds in Le Mans, France, Orville was at Fort Myer, Virginia (near Washington, D.C.) to begin "flight trials to fulfill the requirements of a U.S. Army contract for the sale of aircraft to the U.S. government" (JY 12). Orville "had not flown at all in two-and-a-half years" (JY 23). On September 17, 1908, Orville took off with U.S. Army Signal Corps representative Lieutenant Thomas E. Selfridge aboard.

> Those below watched in horror as the plane twisted this way and that, then plunged straight down, "like a bird shot dead in full flight," in Orville's words .... Orville and the lieutenant lay pinned beneath bloodstained wreckage, faces down. Orville was conscious but moaning in pain. Selfridge lay unconscious, a great gash across his forehead, his face covered with blood .... Orville was in critical condition, with a fractured leg and hip, and four broken ribs, but was expected to live. Lieutenant Selfridge, however, had died at 8:10 of a fractured skull without ever having regained consciousness. His was the first fatality in the history of powered flight .... "It seems to me that I am more or less to blame for the death of poor Selfridge, and yet I cannot account for the accident. Of course, when dealing with aeroplanes, or indeed anything mechanical, there is always the possibility of something breaking, and yet we imagined that we had eliminated all danger." (M 194)[8]

Orville brooded on this accident for years, obsessed with understanding the cause, eventually concluding that "the propeller caught in one of the wires connecting the tail to the main part. That also gave a pull on the wings and upset the machine" (Orville in the *Paris Herald*, September 19, 1908, qtd. in M 197). One can only speculate on the degree to which pilot error may have also been a factor in the crash: "the Wrights did not make a single flight from October 1905 to May 1908" (JY 34n). When he made the flight with Selfridge, Orville was relatively out of practice, but perhaps more practice would not have made any difference.

Trying to understand the cause of the aviation accident has a genealogy as long as the history of aviation itself. As 1930s air racer Joe Mackey recalls of one crash,

> Something fell off or fell apart. A cable broke or any one of a thousand things. You never knew for sure what had happened. Today, with all the sophisticated equipment, the voice recorders and all this junk, you may be able to find the cause, but you couldn't then. Whenever something drastic happened to a buddy in the air, we sat and tried to agree that it was something that couldn't possibly happen to us. (qtd. in Hull 40)

In 1918, the Royal Air Force, Canada, made an attempt to be comprehensive in its understanding of the causes of accidents. The following analytical categories emerged:

i. Aeroplane defect—
  (a) Breakage.
  (b) Engine failure.
  (c) Faulty rigging.
ii. Error of judgment—
  (a) Not due to poor instruction.
  (b) Probably due to poor instruction.

iii. Loss of head.

iv. Brain fatigue.

v. Fear.

vi. Physical illness.

vii. Unavoidable.

viii. Disobeying—

    (a) Rules of the air.

    (b) Instructions for that flight.

    (c) Standing orders.

ix. Weather (wing visibility, temperature effects) (SU 236)

As shown by the Boeing 737 Max fiasco that, at this writing, continues to unfold, classification systems continue to evolve. The Proceedings of The International Helicopter Safety Symposium, Montréal, Québec, Canada, September 26–29, 2005, concludes: "Prevention of accidents from material failure causes is a fairly mature process, whereas the ability to identify and correct specific human error in helicopters is still in its infancy."

Faulkner's fictional analysis of aeroplane crashes takes part in this evolutionary history. In *Pylon* the crowd comes out to watch the "8:00 P.M. Special Mardi Gras Evening Event. Rocket Plane. Lieut. Frank Burnham" (PY 793). A fiery crash is surely foreseen if not boldly promised by the air show's printed program and the pilot's very name. In its aftermath, some pilots and reporters gather to talk nervously about the "special" event they have just witnessed. The searchlights continue to hum and rove over the airfield:

> "Say, what do you suppose happened?"
> "Blinded, probably."
> "Yair. Blinded."
> "Yair. Probably couldn't read his altimeter at all. Or maybe forgot to watch it. Flew it right into the ground."
> "Yair. Jesus, I remember one time I was … ….." (877, Faulkner's ellipses)

The scene captures the terminal logic inherent in the aviation *dromology* (Virilio, *Speed and Politics: An Essay on Dromology*) as Faulkner understands it in *Pylon* and *A Fable*: "'to be tough and to endure until the flash, crash, whatever it will be, when he will no longer be anything and none of it will matter anymore, even the fact that he was tough and, until then, did endure'" (FA 854).

In the first decade of motorized flight, the Wright Flyer, patented, sold to the U.S. Army, and replicated in large numbers, continued to evolve, to fly, and to crash: "There were 148 accidents in 1909 and 1910, including 31 fatal crashes that claimed 34 lives. Six of the nine Wright exhibition fliers died in crashes, all but one of them before mid-1912. The military record was almost as dismal. Eight of the fourteen qualified pilots in the Army Signal Corps were dead by 1914" (C 34). As Virilio concludes, "the twentieth century did in fact swamp us with *mass-produced accidents one after the other*" (*Original* 5–6), an astonishing number of them photographed and filmed.

After the Wright Flyer exhibitions at Pau, France, in January 1909, the *Paris Herald* reported that the town had "simply gone mad about aviation. Nothing is talked about but mechanical flight, everyone is buying a new camera to snap aeroplanes" (qtd. in M 213). For the reporters, spectators, and photographers, as Virilio dryly notes, "the worst case scenario is sometimes a pretty safe bet" (*Original* 36).[9]

Training Accidents

In *High Adventure* (1918), a memoir of his experience in the Lafayette Escadrille, James Norman Hall describes the mentality that enabled most of the young flyers in his squadron to surmount their paralyzing fear of personal destruction. Training accidents were nearly daily occurrences. "An enterprising moving-picture company would have given a great deal of money to film that accident" (14), he recalls of one of them. Yet the pilots learned to accept the accidents as an operational necessity, for they "delayed the work of flying scarcely at all. As soon as a machine was wrecked, Annamites appeared on the spot to clear away the debris and take it to repair-shops, where the usable portions were quickly sorted out" (15–16) (see Chapter 7 in this book for more on the "Annamites"). The dead were buried with honors and the wounded removed to Casualty Clearing Stations or invalided home. Richard Overy notes that "Crashes and accidents were … routine occurrences" in the overall violence of the war. "British air forces lost 35,973 aircraft through accident or combat during the war, and suffered the loss of 16,623 airmen, either dead, or severely injured, or prisoners of war" (O 5–6). As Dana Caroll Winslow reported from the French Flying Corps in 1917, "Accidents occur every day, but we were here on 'active service' and our time was far too taken up with our work for anyone to pay much attention to the unlucky ones. That, at the front, is a duty reserved for the medical corps" (100).

Dean Smith reflects on the training accident carnage he witnessed as a young Army Signal Corps flight instructor:

> I shan't dwell on the horror of the experience, the assault it made on the senses. During the early years of my flying career I was exposed to many such scenes; all of them remain indelible in my memory …. Friends, close companions, men I had breakfasted with, were killed before my eyes; or I have gone to the place of a desolate crash and handled their torn and mutilated remains. I have dug gruesome hamburger from the twisted parts of engines that had smashed through a cockpit. I have helped to pick up mush that was a man before he fell thousands of feet without a parachute. (18)

Alan Bott remembers a sardonic ballad the nervous RAF flying cadets used to sing "to the tune of 'Tarpaulin Jacket,' handed down from the pre-war days of the Flying Corps":

> The young aviator was dying,
> And as 'neath the wreckage he lay (he lay),

To the A.M.'s assembled around him
These last parting words he did say:
"Take the cylinders out of my kidneys,
The connecting-rod out of my brain (my brain),
From the small of my back take the crank-shaft.
And assemble the engine again." (Bott 191)[10]

The era's dreamt of fusion of man and machine (what Marinetti called "the metallization of the human body" [qtd. in Benjamin 243]) is a hellish literalization in such examples.

Speed

Writes Liddell Hart in *The Real War 1914–18* (1930), "It is a truism that the war of 1914–1918 revolutionized all ideas of time, in a military sense, and especially in the duration of battles. For several thousand years of warfare, a battle, however great the scale, had been a matter of hours" (214). The stagnant prolongation of fighting along the trench lines of the Western Front was a "real change," and "of all the so-called 'battles' of the war, Verdun holds the duration record, extending from February 21 to December 15, 1916" (214). It is against the general condition of this "slow war" (Hertwig) that new conceptions of machine-driven speed and mobility were being grasped and described by the war's participants. The effects of the contrast could be dumbfounding.

In early November 1918, his service in the RAF rapidly coming to an end, though he would not know this for another two weeks or so, Faulkner continued to find his wings as an imaginary pilot within a training regime still largely confined to the classroom and the workshop (see Chapters 4 and 5). However, the cadets did get outside at the Long Branch aerodrome to watch the aeroplanes. Several more weeks away from actual flight training (the war ended well before he got to this phase), Faulkner is all anticipation in describing to his mother a beautiful new machine he has just seen at the aerodrome:

Sunday [November 3, 1918] [Toronto] They have a new 'plane at the flying field. It's a perfect beauty, lithe as a greyhound, one seater, with a 110 horse power Clerget rotary motor. Talk about your flying! You can turn it about in its own length, and at a 70-mile clip. Its small and has to go at least 60 m.p.h. to stay in the air. [FIGURE] [line drawing of a one-seater biplane]

It must be great handling one of them and I will certainly be glad when I am put in that squadron. A Curtiss lumbers along like a moving van beside it. Lieutenant-Colonel Bishop is in Canada, as you have probably seen in the papers. His home is in Toronto.

I can easily imagine my self freezing to death up here this winter. There is some talk of moving us all to California. no knowing, though, for there are so many rumors going around. (TH 124)

This new machine was probably a Sopwith Camel, or rather, a *photograph* of a Sopwith Camel, for, as Kenneth Weber has noted, "What can be definitely established is that absolutely no Sopwith Camels, a front-line fighter aircraft, were in Canada in 1918" (Weber 6). Robert Harrison also confirms that "All student pilots in Canada, even those at the School of Aerial Fighting at Beamsville, flew only one aeroplane: the Curtiss Jenny" (Harrison 24). Actual or illustrated, the new aeroplane Faulkner describes is striking in comparison with the "grossly underpowered" Curtiss JN-4 trainer, "a tandem two-seat biplane constructed in the conventional manner of the era." Propelled by a 90-horsepower OS5 engine, the "Jenny" was slow, boxy, unmartial, hardly an airplane to inspire the cadet's dream of speed and combat.

> Top speed was nominally 75 mph, though 65 was typical for a used specimen in average rig, and its climb rate was an anemic 200 feet per minute .... The Jenny lifted off at an airspeed of under 40 mph. Taking off into a 10 mph breeze, it would appear to an observer on the ground to be travelling only 30 mph. (Harrison 48, 151)

As Winslow observes of the early trainers in France, typically Blériots of about 35 horsepower,

> when making a landing against the wind, the force of the breeze blowing toward you will sometimes prevent you from coming down where you had planned. On many occasions I have seen aeroplanes remain practically stationary in the air, while descending, and sometimes even move backward in reference to the ground. (Winslow 97)

Faulkner's sense of the sometimes cartoonish motion of aeroplanes especially near the ground seems traceable to such observations on the flying field.

The new airplane, in contrast, has the look and the feel of the aerodynamic future. It "has to go at least 60 m.p.h. to stay in the air," an impressive minimum for an airplane's landing speed, the pilot's sensation of movement intensifying "with the vertiginous back-rush of the world" (Y 37) coming nearer. An American aviator in the Lafayette Escadrille at the Avord aerodrome describes the aeroplane landing from the groundling's point of view. "Around the school the air is buzzing continually like a giant beehive; there are at least thirty machines in the air at all times. You cannot imagine the speed with which the Nieuports land until you stand and watch them rush by you. It is almost incredible" (qtd. in Hall and Nordhoff vol. 2, 20). Speed, especially with respect to airplanes, "is a wholly new experience" (as Faulkner was beginning to really imagine it) in which "individual people were allowed to feel modernity in their bones: to feel its power as a physical sensation" (Duffy 4), if we may also judge from Faulkner's promise, two months earlier, "to write a better letter than this when my tooth stops, just now its going 60 an hour, on all cylinders" (TH 99).[11] To imagine what it would be like to "handle one of" these aerobatic new airplanes is also to imagine being trained in combat flying by the great Billy Bishop himself, who was sent home from the war in October as the greatest living British Empire Ace (with seventy-two official "kills") after the death of Mick Mannock on July 26, 1918. ("I saw Colonel Bishop the other day" Faulkner mentions in a letter two days later) (TH 126).

Faulkner's awakening to the new aesthetic epistemologies of airplane speed and flight is also traceable to the letters he wrote in the weeks before he enlisted in the RAF. These seem to have been Faulkner's first written descriptions of aeroplanes in aerial motion. From New Haven on April 24, 1918, he writes, "There was a plane over from Long Island today. It looked so short and small that I think it was French. It flipped and darted about a while, rolled over and dived and then went back" (TH 53). On May 27, from New Haven, he writes again about an aeroplane:

> A plane came over from the flying school at Marlin, and stayed over New Haven three hours, dropping propaganda and one $50.00 Bond. It came back just before it left and, just over the green, stood perfectly motionless on its tail for several seconds at about two thousand feet; then dived nose first, looped three times and finished about three hundred feet up, lying on its back.
>
> And we could see the pilot's face, pink as a peach blossom, as though we were looking down on him. Before he left, another came and they had a mimic battle, dipping and darting at each other, so low we could see the smoke from the exhausts. (TH 59–60)

The genealogy of Faulkner's fascination with spatial relativity ("as though we were looking down on him") is traceable, perhaps, to these early impressions of aeronautical speed, motion, and disarranging perspectives. In *Soldiers' Pay*, for example, lovesick George Farr lies out on the grass beneath trees at night waiting for a glimpse of his lover, Cecily Saunders:

> From this position the sky became a flat plane, flat as the brass-studded lid of a dark blue box. Then as he watched it assumed depth again, it was as if he lay on the bottom of the sea while sea-weed clotting blackly lifted surface-ward, unshaken by any current, motionless; it was as if he lay on his stomach staring downward into water through which his gorgon's hair clotting blackly sank straight and black and motionless. Eleven thirty. (SP 188)

In *If I Forget Thee, Jerusalem* (*The Wild Palms*), the tall convict looks across

> the River within whose shadow he had spent the last seven years of his life but had never seen before; he stood in quiet and amazed surmise and looked at the rigid steel-colored surface not broken into waves but merely slightly undulant. It stretched from the levee on which he stood, further than he could see—a slowly and heavily roiling chocolate-frothy expanse broken only by a thin line a mile away as fragile in appearance as a single hair, which after a moment he recognised. *It's another levee* he thought quietly. *That's what we look like from there. That's what I am standing on looks like from there.* (544)

Such dialectical exchanges are inherent in an imagination intent on transcending its bounded location (New Haven in the spring of 1918) in order to experience things from the pilot's seat, or the passenger's. Tom Cundall in *Winged Victory* imagines both perspectives in an account of "contour-chasing" that is one of the most vivid meditations on speed, stillness, "stunting," and spacetime relativity in the First World War era:

> There was no fun in flying comparable with the sport of contour-chasing. As soon as you got up a few hundred feet all the sensation of speed was lost. It was induced by the sight of objects whizzing by, and by this only, and the nearer they were, the more dizzy the feeling of speed. There was really no sensation at all in pure speed. Blindfold, you couldn't tell two miles an hour from two hundred miles an hour. It was the vertiginous back-rush of the world that was efficacious; and this was the one new sensation made possible by science. All the rest were known of old. Even the violent sensations of sudden acceleration and change of direction, such as were abundantly produced by stunting, were only intensifications of the antique pleasures of the swings and roundabouts, and they were too violent to be in themselves pleasurable, and stunts only gratified vanity. Everyone stunted and pretended to enjoy it, and it was a good way of working off surplus nervous energy. But Tom was sure in his own mind that no one really enjoyed stunting for its own sake; admittedly no one liked being taken up in a two-seater and stunted by someone else, in which case the vanity motive was absent. Ninety per cent of stunting was mere vanity and emulation. Intrepid birdmen, said the newspapers; fearless aviators. The young men jeered, but did their best to live up to it.
>
> But contour-chasing was pure joy, charging across country at a hundred miles an hour, flashing past villages where nervous old women swooned as you roared by their bedroom windows, jumping trees and telegraph wires, scattering troops on the march, diving at brass-hats in their expensive cars. (Y 37–38)

"Country Mice"

One of Faulkner's earliest fictional accounts of airplane flying represents the experience of passengers being "stunted by someone else," or of pilots who feel themselves to be little more than passengers aboard their self-willed machines. In the story "Country Mice," first published in the New Orleans *Times-Picayune* on September 20, 1925, a bootlegger describes his first flight as a passenger. When, afraid of being trapped in his seat, he questions the need for a safety belt, the pilot responds, "'Sure,' he says, 'she might buck you out like a horse'" (116). So "I shut my eyes and grabbed something" (116):

> "If you'd ask me how it looked from up there, I couldn't tell you. I don't know. But I looked out to the side once and seen the whole ocean before I could get my eyes shut again. The ground is good enough for me.

Anyway, after a while it felt like all my insides was falling out of me, and I shut my eyes tighter and held on. And then we bumped on the ground and after a while we stopped. Well sir, I sat in that damn thing for about ten minutes before I could move, and when I did get out it was like I had had a spell of sickness or something. We was in a big field on the edge of town, and the airplane fellow was walking about smoking a cigarette. And I lit one too, and felt a little better. I felt like taking a handful of that dirt and eating it." (117)

The passenger in that airplane now acts out the speed story again, only this time from the driver's seat of a fast "motor car … as long as a steamboat and the color of a chocolate ice cream soda" (108) so that he can work out his previously passive experience by aggressively subjecting somebody else to it. His passenger, the narrator of the story we're now reading, tries to listen and to hold on as best he can.

The road was straight and white as a swift unrolling ribbon, and Louisiana rushed by us in a fretful, indistinguishable green. Wind plopped at my ears and my eyelashes turned backward irritatingly, keeping me blinking.

"Yes?" I screamed [….]
"Yes sir. You can say what you …. 'member when …. what you call a hick cop …."
The wind tore the words from his tongue. I leaned toward him, clutching my hat.
"I can't hear you!" I screamed diffidently. "If you'd slow down a bit …." (109–10)

The passenger being stunted in the fast car observes of the driver that "when he goes anywhere he travels by a speed indicator" (109) and now "the speedometer began to climb" (110). The driver just likes to go fast, to go

"airing off"; i.e., to take the shortest way out of town and then to go somewhere, anywhere, at between forty and seventy miles an hour. He never drives faster than seventy because for some reason his car will not go any faster than seventy miles an hour. I am constantly uneasy over the expectation that some day someone will show him how to make it go eighty miles an hour. (108)

She was only doing sixty-six.

"Yes?" I screamed. He stared ahead frowningly, preoccupied. His car was practically new, but I knew that he already dreamed of a car that would go seventy-five miles an hour, or even eighty. It was not seventy miles an hour he wanted, it was five miles an hour for which he pined. But such is the immortal soul of man. (110)

The story ends, "My friend the bootlegger turned a corner viciously. The pedestrian, however, escaped" (120). We'll encounter driving like this again with ex-RAF pilot Bayard Sartoris in *Flags in the Dust*.

Seventy-five miles an hour, or even eighty. Further perspective on the machine-powered speed increment is given in a table arranged by Laurence La Tourette Driggs in *Heroes of Aviation* (Boston: Little, Brown, and Company, 1919), a popular book that I'll also engage more closely in the following chapter.

Table of Comparative Speeds

Man walking	4 miles per hour
Man racing	20 " " "
Horse racing	30 " " "
Bicycle racing	32 " " "
Steamship	42 " " "
Motor boat	62 " " "
Railroad train	90 " " "
Automobile	120 " " "
Aeroplane	150 " " "
Pistol bullet	600 feet per second
Machine-gun bullet	1000 " " "
Sound	1100 " " "
37-millimeter gun	1600 " " "
Largest gun	3000 " " "
Light ... ..., ...	186,300 miles per second. (Driggs 65)

Driggs' table of comparative speeds invites a manifold expansion at "Aeroplane" in light of its "exponential change over the past 100 years" (A x). For Italian general Giulio Douhet (1869–1930), who published *The Command of the Air* (1921) while serving in Benito Mussolini's Ministry of War, "the ever-increasing speed of airplanes" (38) was already beginning to dominate the future. He could not know how fast they would eventually fly, but R. J. Mitchell, designer of the Supermarine Spitfire which first flew on March 5, 1936, felt that "it would be presumptuous ... to assume that speed has reached its finality; continuous development will lead to further progress. Speeds which amaze us today will be commonplace tomorrow" (qtd. in A 116). We can now look back at the future Douhet and Mitchell were attempting to foresee. "Just compare," writes John D. Anderson, Jr., "the image of the 1903 Wright Flyer, flying at 30 mph at about a 10-foot altitude, with the image of the spectacular Lockheed SR-71 Blackbird flying at Mach 3 plus, at 90,000 feet [in 1964], or even the image of the Airbus 389 [from 2005] carrying over 600 passengers at near Mach One at 40,000 feet" (A x)—to which Virilio, no doubt, would reply, "the fact of wanting to fly thousands of passengers at the same time in one and the same air carrier is already an accident or, more exactly, sabotage of prospective intelligence" (Virilio, *Original* 22).[12]

At Rheims, France, in September 1909, competing for the prize of $37,000, "little known Glenn Curtiss astonished the crowd by flying at forty-seven miles per hour to win the Gordon Bennett Trophy Race" and the "exquisite silver trophy ... a beautiful model of the Wright biplane mounted by a nude goddess, a trophy symbolic of everything thrilling to the male imagination" (Hull 15). Perhaps, then, aviation's "original accident" is traceable to "everything thrilling to the male imagination" when it believes that flying faster and faster is a way of satisfying or "impressing some woman .... Well, maybe she ain't always a flesh and blood creature. She may be only the symbol of a desire. But she is feminine" (Faulkner, *Mosquitoes* 460).

In 1916, the Bristol F2A fighter, powered by an 80 horsepower Gnome rotary engine, flew at a top speed of 97 mph. Races continued to be won at record-breaking speeds year after year in the 1920s: 155 mph in 1920; 224 mph in 1922 in a plane flown by Billy Mitchell, "father" of the United States Air Force; 232 mph in 1925 (in an airplane flown by Jimmy Doolittle); 282 mph in 1927 (for details see Hull, Anderson, Montross). On September 13, 1931,

> The Supermarine S-6B was powered to victory in the final Schneider Cup race ... by a point-designed Rolls-Royce R liquid-cooled engine that produced 2,300 horsepower for limited durations; the S-6B averaged a winning speed of 340.1 mph. Later that month, the world's speed record of 401.5 mph was set by the same S-6B .... on September 28, the S.6B went on to set a new world speed record of 407 mph. (A 77, 132)

By the mid-1930s, however, "the speed limitations of propeller-driven aircraft were well understood" (A 194). In 1936, T. P. Wright, vice president for engineering at the Curtiss Airplane Company, showed mathematically that a "'probable ultimate limit'" (A 195) would soon be reached. At the National Air Races in Cleveland for the Thompson Trophy after the Second World War, for example, modified P-51 Mustangs and Corsairs, in the words of one racer, "we knew damn well ... were running in the neighborhood of 450 to 460 miles per hour" (qtd. in Hull 50). They could go no faster. "To the present, no propeller-driven airplane has ever broken the speed of sound. Shock waves are the culprit" (A 195).

The major change "that dominated airplane design in the 1930s" (A 59) was foreseen by "Hugo Junkers who in Germany designed and built the first successful all-metal airplane, the Junkers J.I in 1915" (A 54). That machine was too heavy to be effective against the fastest wooden biplanes of the era, but Douhet in 1921 was convinced that airplanes in the future would be "built of metal and independent of hangars. The aerial machines of the last war look like toys in comparison .... made out of wood and canvas" (Douhet 183). In the 1930s "the all-vegetable airplane became a thing of the past" (A 84). All-metal airframes would embolden pilots to explore higher velocities, attempt steeper dives and more daring aerobatic maneuvers, with less fear of wings tearing off or of fuselages collapsing. "Streamlining, all-metal construction, the NACA cowl, retractable landing gear, variable-pitch propellers" (A 67) along with "flush riveting" and "the advent of high-octane fuels" (A 81) were all part of the airplane's radical transformation in the 1930s.[13]

Further impelling the movement toward metal airframes was "the growing shortage of wood suitable for aircraft manufacture" (A 55) and the crash, on March 31, 1931, of a TWA Fokker trimotor "in a Kansas wheat field, killing among the passengers the famous Notre Dame University football coach Knute Rockne" (A 91). "Fokker airplanes were of wood construction, and the TWA airplane's main wooden wing spar had delaminated, causing wing failure. The highly publicized event not only hastened the end of the wooden airplane, it suddenly brought new Fokker transport sales to an end" (A 162). In the design and construction of the First World War aeroplane, as Winslow points out,

> The greatest danger lies in the propeller. The slightest obstacle will break it, and if the motor cannot be stopped instantly the increased revolutions are certain to force the flame back into the carburetor and you are *grille* before you can land. Aviators are from the first instructed to leave nothing loose about the machine or their clothing. Many pilots have been killed because their caps blew off, caught in the propeller, and broke it. (96)

The need for a transition from wood to metal helped conjure the image of aeroplanes without propellers. "Jet propulsion for airplanes had been discussed as a possibility by the aeronautical engineering community since the 1920s" (A 248), while "the jet revolution, in reality, began in the 1930s" (A 192). The swept-wing concept to reduce supersonic wave drag "was first introduced by the German engineer Adolf Busemann in 1935 during the fifth Volta Conference held in Rome. The topic chosen for the conference was 'High Velocities in Aviation' .... The German Luftwaffe classified the swept wing concept in 1936" (A 196). Army Air Force General "Hap" Arnold liked to quote Ezra Kotcher, "then serving as the senior instructor at the Air Corps Engineering School at Wright Field, as saying 'it reached the point that you couldn't throw a whiskey bottle out of a hotel window at a meeting of aeronautical engineers without hitting some fellow who had ideas on jet propulsion'" (A 248). With the jet's dominant arrival after the Second World War, airplane racing was also essentially finished. As one racer put it, "The fastest planes are the jets but they shouldn't race" (qtd. in Hull 179). Another reflected, "you can't fly a supersonic jet close enough for a grandstand crowd to see it with any safety at all" (qtd. in Hull 171). So it goes, as "the old creatures of propeller-humanity" find themselves displaced by "the new ones of jet-humanity" (Barthes 104). In February 1944, "the XP-80 became the first American aircraft to exceed 500 mph in level flight (502 mph at 20,480 feet)" (A 189). "On October 14, 1947, the experimental rocket-powered Bell X-1 could reach an altitude of 36,000 feet and fly faster than the speed of sound" (A 7):

> Indeed, Chuck Yeager's flight in the X-1 on October 14, 1947, which achieved Mach 1.06, opened the world of supersonic flight; it was arguably the most significant event in the history of flight since the Wright Flyer successfully flew on December 17, 1903 .... the successful X-15 hypersonic airplane program which spanned the 1960s, and generated a large data base for hypersonic flight which was essential for the later design of the space shuttle. (A 277)

Chuck Yeager (February 13, 1923—December 7, 2020), RIP.

The line "from the era of the strut-and-wire biplane, through the era of the mature propeller-driven airplane, and into the era of the jet-propelled airplane" (A 66) thus leads directly to the Space Shuttle's original accident:

T+40   *There's Mach one.*
T+58   *Throttle up.*
T+60   *Feel that mother go. Woooohoooo.*
T+1:13   *Uhoh.*

—Challenger pilot Michael J. Smith (qtd. in C 172)

Notes

1   See Robert Wohl on the ubiquity of the military metaphor, "the conquest of the air," during the first decades of flight. "The conquest of the air followed naturally from the conquest of colonial peoples, the exploration of the earth, and the penetration of the seas by submarines. The urge to dominate, to master, to conquer" (Wohl, *Passion* 228).

2   Quentin Roosevelt (November 19, 1897—July 14, 1918) describes the classical funeral rites of the First World War air services in a letter to his father dated February 3, 1918: "We all went over to the funeral of those two fellows that were killed …. Then, flying just above, were two of the French pilots, in the larger machines. They are marvellous pilots, and it was really beautiful to watch them crossing and recrossing over the cortège in beautiful smooth right-angled S turns. Then, just as they were lowering the coffins, another Frenchman dropped down in a long swoop, his motor almost dead,—dropped a wreath on them, and then swung off …. and round them and over, the planes circling, paying a last tribute. It takes away some of the bare horror that the two little twisted heaps of wrecked planes and twisted motors leaves" (Roosevelt 111–12).

3   Johnny Sartoris flying with his head down "in the office" may reflect Faulkner's own preoccupation when he was being trained to fly by renowned aviator Vernon Omlie in 1933. "I had trouble with Bill," Omlie reported. "He had trouble getting the feel of the controls. He had to learn to use the instruments, not the seat of his pants" (B 797). More on Omlie and his wife Phoebe below.

4   In "Faulkner, the Silent Comedies, and the Animated Cartoon," D. M. Murray observes that "the visual elements of Faulkner's humor often resemble effects in film comedy and cartoon" (242). He also notes that the "oral tradition of yarning should not allow us to forget its powerful appeal to the eye" (247). Focusing primarily on *The Hamlet* and the role of animals in such stories as "Was," "The Spotted Horses," and "Shingles for the Lord," Murray gathers an inventory of "miracles" and "visual gags" that seem to come out of the "silent film comedy in the great days of the Keystone Kops and Charlie Chaplin" (241). Murray's list of such filmic conventions includes "Frantic action, which typically involves violence that does no harm and which is often organized into the plot patterns of futile endeavor or comic chase." "Comic distortion in description and characterization, which often compares human beings to animals or machines." "The kaleidoscopic or pinwheel image." "The sudden

appearance of a character." "Delayed gravity." "The freeze shot." And so on (247–9). The essay offers many suggestive ways to think cinematically about the path of the aeroplane in Faulkner's work: lifting off, soaring, cruising, looping, diving, spiraling out of control, crashing. Murray mentions Mickey Mouse's *Plane Crazy* (1928) in a footnote (255n) but does not address Faulkner's aeroplane narratives explicitly. Later chapters of this book address the culture of "hangar flying" and some of Faulkner's many virtuoso performances in the genre.

5   Fascinating exceptions include Hubert Julian, "The Black Eagle of Harlem," and Bessie Coleman, "the only negress aviatrix" (NYT, September 4, 1922) of her era. For Julian see a profile on him in *The New Yorker* (July 11, 1931) and Ann Douglas (457–61). See also Robert Jackson's discussion of the race film *The Flying Ace* in *Fade in, Crossroads* (219, 221f). David Courtwright notes that "There were twenty-one licensed black pilots in 1936, including only five with limited commercial or transport licenses" (C 244n). In 1962, the year of Faulkner's death, "only three in every hundred African Americans had flown" even as commercial passengers (C 163). In the 1930s, many women pilots flew as racers and barnstormers, parachutists, or wingwalkers. Some achieved fame by breaking endurance and speed records and quite a few died in terrible accidents. The names of these women include Arlene Davis, Helen Dutrieu, Mary Haizlip, Dorothy Hester, Marge Hurbert, Florence Klingensmith, Ruth Nichols, Gladys O'Donnell, Jane Page, and Betty Skelton. (See Robert Hull, *September Champions: The Story of America's Air Racing Pioneers*.) Faulkner was a close friend of renowned aerobatic pilot and instructor Phoebe Omlie, who was married to the pilot who would train him to fly, Vernon C. Omlie. (See later in this book.)

6   The DC-3 was designed "to meet stringent specifications set down by the Transcontinental and Western Air, Inc. (TWA)," founded in 1930 (A 68, 69). The first flight of the Lockheed Electra (Amelia Earhart's airplane) took place on February 23, 1934. As a local newspaper reported, "Soaring gracefully into the air on its maiden flight, the sleek all-metal airliner flew easily, making another great stride in commercial speed development of air transportation" (qtd. in A 220). It was in the midst of these rapid developments that Faulkner, "flying with George A. Wiggs, a Federal flight examiner … passed the flight check required for the issuance of the private pilot certificate on December 14, 1933, and he was subsequently issued certificate number 29788. This certificate authorized him to fly single-engine, land aircraft of from 0 to 150 horsepower. Technically, Faulkner was not licenced to fly his own aircraft" (Bostwick 5–6). Bostwick adds in a footnote, "Letter received from Mark Weaver, Federal Aviation Administration, April 29, 1981" (Bostwick 5n). He also notes that, "based on his pilot certificate number, less than 30,000 Americans were qualified as pilots" in the United States at that time (Bostwick 31–2).

7   "'Some people believe the most important thing Charles Lindbergh contributed to the field of aviation was not the flight in the *Spirit of St. Louis* but the safety checklist,' Reeve Lindbergh wrote in her memoirs" (C 73). Faulkner would make the safety checklist the centerpiece of a film scene he was especially proud of, the "death of Quincannon" in Howard Hawk's *Air Force* (1943). (See Solomon 128–30.)

8   "The Wrights returned to Fort Myer with a new airplane in 1909 and completed the trials. Their airplane exceeded the Signal Corps' minimum performance requirements, the contract was fulfilled, and the Wrights were paid $30,000 for their airplane" (JY 23–4n).

9   "On May 6, 1937, as the afternoon drew to a close the dirigible *Hindenburg* caught fire above Lakehurst not far from New York. It was the first great aeronautical catastrophe of the twentieth century and it counted thirty-four victims …. without radiophony and the newsreel cinema of Fox-Movietone, this major accident would not have had the mythical impact it has had" (Virilio, *Original* 21). Courtwright discusses the ways in which the aviation accident was "magnified by the newsreels, the silent (and after 1927, talking) cinematic tabloids that specialized in spectacles and disasters" (C 52). "Carnivalesque images of flight," he notes, were also displayed in films like *Wings* (1927), *Hells Angels* (1930), and *Sky Devils* (1932). The mediated repercussions of the airplane disaster are central to the meaning of aviation modernity, while *Pylon* is perhaps the most powerful expression of this meaning in world literature.

10 One encounters this ballad in a number of places in the aviation literature of the period, including in Yeates and a book that Faulkner adapted for a screenplay, *War Birds: Diary of an Unknown Aviator* (1926), by John MacGavock Grider (ghost-written, though, by Elliott White Springs) (53).

11 See Murphet's *Faulkner's Media Romance*, his chapter "A Folklore of Speed," and Watson's *William Faulkner and the Faces of Modernity*, his chapter "Faulkner on Speed," for especially illuminating discussions of this subject.

12 David McCullough notes, "On July 20, 1969, when Neil Armstrong, another American born and raised in southwestern Ohio, stepped onto the moon, he carried with him, in tribute to the Wright brothers, a small swatch of the muslin from a wing of their 1903 Flyer" (M 262).

13 *NACA cowling*: "a shroud wrapped around the cylinders of air-cooled radial engines engineered to reduce drag greatly and to increase the cooling of the engine" (A 92), designed by the National Advisory Committee for Aeronautics, Langley Memorial Aeronautical Laboratory, Hampton VA. *Streamlining*: "smooth elongated bodies made with gentle curves resulted in low aerodynamic drag. This was in comparison to the earlier high-drag box-like configurations with flat surfaces and sharp corners …. streamlining was adapted by many Art Deco artists in the design of furniture, household appliances, building, etc." (A 71). *Variable-pitch propellers*: "Through World War I, airplane propellers were single piece designs made of wood …. such fixed-pitch propellers provided maximum efficiency at only one flight velocity, and for all other speeds the propeller was operating at substandard efficiency. Clearly, a propeller with an adjustable pitch angle during flight was needed" (A 57).

2

New Haven, Spring 1918: The War and the Newspapers

[p.s.] Tell me about Estelle's wedding
    —Faulkner to his mother, Sunday, April 21, 1918, from New Haven (TH 52)

Escaping the dismal scene of Estelle's wedding to Cornell Franklin in Oxford, Mississippi, Faulkner came north for the first time in the spring of 1918. (Quentin, though, puts it this way: "When I first came east") (*The Sound and the Fury* 86). After a brief stay in New York City he lived with Phil Stone on the campus of Yale University and worked, from April through June, in the accounting office of New Haven's Winchester Repeating Arms Company, whose "chimneys," in the words of Joseph Blotner, "spewed smoke as the factories turned out munitions for the Allies" (B 202).

On April 14, in a letter to his mother, Faulkner writes, "Yesterday I went through the plant and saw the rifle and machine gun assembling rooms. They are making Browning guns. There are eighteen thousand people working there, probably half of them are women and girls, in the machine shops even" (TH 50). Ten days later he writes, "I saw them making the H.E. [high explosive] shells—five and six point ones, about a yard long" (TH 53). Here in the North, as Italian aviation theorist Giulio Douhet was also observing of the European munitions factories, "The prevailing forms of social organization have given war a character of national totality—that is, the entire population and all the resources of a nation are sucked into the maw of war" (Douhet 5–6).

Ruby Lamar experiences this gravitational pull in *Sanctuary*, recalling to Horace Benbow, "Then the war came and they let Lee out and sent him to France. I went to New York and got a job in a munitions plant" (278).

On the Yale campus and around the town of New Haven, Faulkner met many veterans of the fighting and listened to their stories, including, as he writes on April 7, one told by Nicholas Llewellyn.

He was in the boche army eight months, at Rheims, and was wounded in the Channel fighting at the first battle of Ypres. He had an iron cross and sent it back when we went to war. He and Lieutenant Todd, a Canadian officer, have some warm arguments as to whether or not the French were using the Rheims cathedral for an artillery observation post.

Figure 2.1 Winchester Repeating Arms Company Assembling Room ("probably half of them are women and girls, in the machine shops even").

There are two other English officers here, Captains Massie and Bland. Bland is suffering from shell shock. (April 7, TH 48)

At the Oneco hotel tonight there was a wounded British "Tommy" with a Distinguished Conduct Medal and a stiff leg. He looked American, perhaps was, but had evidently been in the "show." (April 28, TH 54)

I just had dinner with two British officers, Lieutenant Todd, who was wounded at Vimy Ridge last year, and a tall, taciturn Scotchman names MacIntosh. (May 19, TH 56-7)

"Ad Astra" and other war stories that Faulkner would write in the 1920s and '30s can trace their origins to such New Haven experiences (Collins, "'Ad Astra'").

New Haven was an important center of production and activity on the war's domestic front (munitions, textiles, recruitment, transportation, training) and the war was everywhere. In a letter to his mother on April 6, 1918, Faulkner describes "a newspaper here with a thing like an enormous stock ticker in the window, and as soon as anything happens they show it there, just headlines, of course. This morning it says a British counter-attack has regained the grounds the Germans took yesterday near Amiens" (TH 47). As Ludendorff's Spring Offensive rages on, Faulkner is caught up in the universal fascination with the air war:

The evening papers are full of the death of Major Raoul Lufbery, the New Haven aviator in the Lafayette Escadrille. So there's only one of them left now, Captain

Figure 2.2 First World War Flying Ace Raoul Lufbery.

William Thaw. Don't you know he's lonesome! All six of them were Yale men; enlisted in the French Foreign Legion in '14, then were transferred to the Flying Corps. First it was Kiffen Rockwell, then Norman Prince, then Victor Chapman was shot down over Le Caleau as he was carrying some oranges to Prince in the hospital, then Bert Hall about two weeks ago, and now its Lufbery. His picture in a photographer's window on Chapel Street. I imagine Thaw feels that he's been left holding the sack. (May 19, TH 56–7)

Faulkner's brief account contains a few inaccuracies. Chapman was bringing oranges to Clyde Balsley (see Chapters 5 and 7), Bert Hall still lived, Chapman and Prince were Harvard graduates, Rockwell was a graduate of Virginia Military Institute and Washington and Lee University, and Lufbery was not a university man.[1] But the letter shows Faulkner's fluency in the vernacular of a captivating international story. It also suggests his deepening identification with New Haven's special connection with Lufbery and the American Ivy League pilots flying for France. "First it was Kiffen Rockwell, then Norman Prince, then Victor Chapman." Then William Faulkner? He would write his mother on May 19th that he could probably "enlist [i.e. pass] as a second-year Yale man" (TH 63). As for these American flyers, the actual order of their deaths was Chapman, Rockwell, Prince, Lufbery, their stories reflecting the rapid escalation of an air war that, in May, Faulkner was close to entering into the line to join. No one in the spring of 1918 saw the war ending soon. In his memoir, *Sherston's Progress*, Sigfried Sassoon recalls, "Writing about it so long afterwards, one is liable to forget that while the War was going on nobody really knew when it would stop" (27). "In July 1918" (when Faulkner began RAF training in Toronto) "everyone took it for granted that we should hold on till the winter and then wait for the '1919 offensive'" (Sassoon, *Sherston's Progress* 123). The prospect of the war's prolongation into 1919 loomed over the general mood that spring as did the mourning for Lufbery and the other fallen champions.

The war's "ringing heroic catalogue" (FA 746) that sounded in the newspapers was an extension of the one Faulkner claimed he had already begun to hear as a boy in Oxford, Mississippi, when air-war fascination first took root in him and his little brothers. As he recalled in 1954, "This was 1915 and '16; I had seen an aeroplane and my mind was filled with names: Ball, and Immelmann and Boelcke, and Guynemer and Bishop, and I was waiting, biding, until I would be old enough or free enough or anyway could get to France and become glorious and beribboned too" (Faulkner, Forward to *The Faulkner Reader* x). Many of these pilots were only a few years older than Faulkner himself (born September 25, 1897). Some were very close to his age and some pretty much his own age exactly, each one an invitation to reflect on that pathway to glory he might also strive to follow should the right circumstances suddenly materialize, as they did, to his astonishment, that June, when he succeeded in joining the RAF.

The list of "all the dead pilots" (as Faulkner would title one of his stories ten years later) who had achieved international renown in the newspapers of the time includes British, French, German, American, and Canadian flyers. Focalizing the narrative at this point through the soul of young RAF Lieutenant David Levine in *A Fable*, Faulkner writes of them thus:

> In Valhalla's un-national halls the un-national shades, Frenchman and German and Briton, conqueror and conquered alike—Immelmann and Guynemer, Boelcke and Ball— identical not in the vast freemasonry of death but in the closed select one of flying, would clash their bottomless mugs, but not for him. Their inheritors—Bishop and Mannock and Voss and McCudden and Fonck and Barker and Richthofen and Nungesser—would still cleave to the earth-foundationed air [....] (FA 747)

Such a conception of aviation's international fraternity can be traced to Dana Carroll Winslow, whose signature can be discerned at a number of points in Faulkner's work: "I became conscious of the understood but inexplicable freemasonry that binds all aviators together" (Winslow 20). Floyd Gibbons' *The Red Knight of Germany: The Story of Baron von Richthofen Germany's Great War Bird* (Garden City Publishing Co., 1927) is also a primary source: "His life and death, his victories and his defeat, his loves, his hopes, his fears bring a new record to the halls of that same Valhalla in which rest the spirits of Guynemer, Hawker, Ball, McCudden, Immelmann, Lufbery, Quentin Roosevelt, and many others who fought aloft and died below with hearts that held emotions other than hate" (5). In a letter dated July 1, 1943, to his Jewish editor Robert Haas, whose son, a pilot, had recently been killed, Faulkner also wrote, "the blood of your fathers and the blood of mine side by side at the same long table in Valhalla, talking of glory and heroes, draining the cup and banging the empty pewter on the long board to fill again, holding two places for us maybe" (SL 175).[2] Valhalla's roster of dead champions includes:

Max Immelmann (September 21, 1890–June 18, 1916)
Victor Chapman (April 17, 1890–June 24, 1916)
Kiffin Yates Rockwell (September 20, 1892–September 23, 1916)
Norman Prince (August 31, 1887–October 15, 1916)
Oswald Boelcke (May 19, 1891–October 28, 1916)
James McConnell (March 14, 1887–March 19, 1917)
Albert Ball (August 14, 1896–May 7, 1917)
Georges Guynemer (December 24, 1894–September 11, 1917)
Werner Voss (April 13, 1897–September 23, 1917)
Arthur Rhys-Davids (September 26, 1897–October 27, 1917)
Manfred von Richthofen (May 2, 1892–April 21, 1918)
Raoul Lufbery (March 14, 1885–May 19, 1918)
John McGavock Grider (May 18, 1892–June 18, 1918)
James McCudden (March 28, 1895–July 9, 1918)
Quentin Roosevelt (November 19, 1897–July 14, 1918)
Mick Mannock (May 24, 1887–July 26, 1918)
Frank Luke (May 19, 1897–September 29, 1918)
Frank Granger Quigley (July 10, 1894–October 20, 1918)

A few others would defer their entry into the airman's "vast freemasonry of death" (FA 747) until after the war:

William Thaw II (August 12, 1893–April 22, 1934)
René Fonck (March 27, 1894–June 18, 1953)
Billy Bishop (February 8, 1894–September 11, 1956)
Elliott White Springs (July 31, 1896–October 15, 1959)
Eddie Rickenbacker (October 8, 1890–July 23, 1973)

Newspaper stories about these pilots constitute a fascinating historical archive (to say the least) while also being a nearly inexhaustible source of narrative imagery and dramatic excitement for any writer intent on writing fictions about the war (Faulkner was in fact one of the first in America to do so). Many of these aviators were also extraordinarily gifted writers themselves (sometimes, but not always, with the help of gifted editors too). What may be striking as one reads through this living history of the air war is how honest these pilots are in reflecting their own not infrequent failures as military aviators, the times they made mistakes or escaped dangerous situations by mere luck. They describe many scenes of hesitation and doubt, rage and fear, of depression, moral waste, and soul injury as the killing escalates in ever-more ruthless campaigns. Perhaps it should not be surprising that accounts of genuine courtesy or acts of mercy between enemy combatants (especially late in the war) are rare in these pilots' narratives, though expressions of respect for the enemy's courage and prowess are not. Raoul Lufbery's description of one such encounter is vivid in all these respects:

> It is a little one-seater biplane of the Fokker or Halberstadt type. A glance around assures me that he is alone .... If it only may prove to be a beginner, lacking experience .... I dive upon him, but with a remarkable skill he gets out of range of my machinegun. He has anticipated my maneuver and parried the blow before it was struck. I am now aware that I have to do with a master of his art. [Flak bursts from Lufbery's own lines signal the presence of approaching enemy planes]. A lucky chance! I had now an excuse for abandoning without loss of honor the match, which I confess I am not at all sorry to leave. Only before leaving my adversary I feel that I must show him that I appreciate that he is a valiant foe and respect him as such. Drawing my left arm out of the fuselage I wave him a sign of adieu. He understands and desires to show courtesy on his part, for he returns my farewell. (qtd. in Driggs 117)

In such narrative accounts of the birth of modern war, "chivalry" is more often an ironical and strained residual gesture. British ace James McCudden reports that when Rhys-Davids proposed a toast to Richthofen after he was killed on April 21, 1918, "we all drank with the exception of one non-flying officer who remained seated, and said, 'No, I won't drink to the health of that devil'" (McCudden 205). British ace Mick Mannock "walked out of the mess in disgust when somebody proposed a toast to the memory of the German ace" (Mannock 186).

As one reads their memoirs, letters, and interviews, and the stories about them in the newspapers, each of these famous pilots also comes to possess a kind of romantic halo that casts a light upon the darkness of a war dominated by massive conscript armies, industrial machinery, and muddy terrain. For Fernando Esposito the aviator as illuminated in the contemporary mass media was "a powerful weapon in the struggle to give the war a meaning .... the air war compensated for the horrors of industrial-technological warfare on the ground .... It was trench warfare that produced the aviator-hero" (Esposito 185–7). With eyes skyward, one might forget the war on the ground for a moment and give way to a fascination with the signatures the pilots draw with their aeroplanes in careers achieving dramatic narrative shape and coherence by spectacular exploits and, usually, spectacular ends. They fly in fast single-seaters, for example the famous Nieuport fighting machine, "the best type of *avion de chasse*" (McConnell 17), an aeroplane especially well-suited to expressing the pilot's "adroitness in maneuvering and accuracy of aim" (Driggs 86). "The famous aviators of whom we read in the daily communiqués, like Navarre, Nungesser,

Vialet, and Guynemer, all gained their reputation with the small, fighting Nieuports" (Winslow 45).

Flying the Nieuport, James McConnell experiences "the restoration of personality lost during those months in the trenches with the Foreign Legion" (McConnell 21). "The Nieuport is the smallest, fastest-rising, fastest-moving biplane in the French service. It can travel 110 miles an hour, and is a one-man apparatus with a machine gun mounted on its roof and fired by the pilot with one hand while with the other and his feet he operates his controls" (McConnell 18). The famous pilots are brilliant individualists when they fly such machines. (The bombers and observation aeroplanes, in contrast, carrying two men or more, are heavy and slow, designed for steady lines of flight offering less leeway for individual expression.) For the ultimate *chasse* pilot, French Captain Georges Guynemer, as he explains in one of the first interviews he granted to the press,

> hunting must be done according to the temperament and character of each individual hunter. If it shows itself as individual prowess, all the better. This must be cried out aloud, for many young men come to the squadron with false ideas and arrested wills .... He who has in him the quality of a champion is the pilot who has recourse to his own initiative, to his own judgment, to his own personal equation. (qtd. in Mortane xxvii–viii)

Notes American pilot Charles Biddle, who flew in Escadrille N. 73, Guynemer's Nieuport squadron, Guynemer "is small and very slight. He is 22 years old and without question the greatest individual fighter this war has produced" (Biddle 44). In the Royal Air Force, recalls decorated British pilot Captain Alan Bott,

> The outstanding pilots of my old squadron were all individualists in attack, and it was one of my hobbies to contrast their tactics. C., with his blind fatalism and utter disregard of risk, would dive a machine among any number of Huns, so that he usually opened a fight with an advantage of startling audacity. S., another very successful leader, worked more in co-operation with the machines behind him, and took care to give his observer every chance for effective fire. (Bott 177)

Bott singles out legendary RAF pilot Albert Ball for special recognition, "probably the most brilliant air fighter of the war ... the individualist *in excelsis*" (Bott 176).

Reading such accounts, one learns to interpret the main forms of combat flying as personal gesture. The great aerial "tacticians" (McCudden, Mannock, Boelcke, Richthofen), daring yet cool, attack only when they have the advantage of stealth or numbers. Those who fly with "reckless valor," typically the heroic novices, launch impetuous solo attacks into the midst of enemy squadrons (Roosevelt, Luke). Victor Chapman "always fought against odds and far within the enemy's country" (Hall and Nordhoff vol. 1, 23). All the pilots "fly alone" at some dramatic point in their legendary careers, in scenes that often occlude, at least for the purposes of dramatic narrative, the more prevalent reality, as the war ground on and on, of formation flying in ever larger bombing and strafing missions (see Ledwidge, Overy, Yeates, Douhet, Mitchell). All the dead pilots and those soon to be dead are "marked out," in Aristotle's language, for both good and "bad fortune" in the tragic plots that control their destinies: "anyone who hears the events which occur shudders and feels pity at what happens" (Aristotle 11, 22). Some die in preventable accidents or as a result of sudden and unaccountable lapses of judgment or attention (Mannock, McCudden, Richthofen), while others are caught up in "badly constructed plots," that is, in circumstances that are not truly tragic (in any aesthetic or poetic sense) but are "simply monstrous" (Aristotle 22). Such events are governed by the violence of dumb chance, by ineptitude or contingencies for which the pilot is not mainly responsible. Those thus "marked out for bad fortune" and absurd accidents are simply unlucky (Prince, Boelcke, Hobey Baker, and a young pilot named Armstrong who, as Charles Biddle relates, "had a bit of the hardest luck that it is possible for a flyer to have .... I suddenly saw his right wings and tail fly off while the rest of the machine fell in a cloud of black smoke, leaving the air filled with fragments of the plane. He had run squarely into one of our big shells on its way to Germany") (Biddle 267). Some die in almost unimaginably horrible circumstances (Lufbery, who foresaw the manner of his death). Some simply disappear, never to be seen again (Guynemer, according to legend). All win multiple medals, ribbons, and honors, some "possessed of every decoration that a grateful nation could officially bestow" (Driggs 84). And all—their corpses, coffins, or memorial stones—are covered in flowers, the pilots given magnificent funerals often elaborately described, photographed, sometimes even filmed (as in Richthofen's case: you can watch it on YouTube). A few, like Edward V. Rickenbacker and Billy Bishop, survive the war completely intact, at least physically. Reading Rickenbacker's memoir, *Fighting the Flying Circus* (1919), one is reminded, perhaps, of Colonel Kilgore in *Apocalypse Now*: "He had a weird light around him. You knew he would come out of this without a scratch." Billy Bishop had it too, the same weird light (see his *Winged Warfare*).

Faulkner's biographers report that in Oxford, Mississippi, Billy Falkner and his little brothers were fascinated by the war. "The pages of the [Oxford] *Eagle* often referred to major battles, and Billy and his brothers would get together in their bedrooms at night, spreading out maps of Europe, tracking battle lines" (Parini 35). "Each day he and Jack avidly read the dispatches from the war fronts in the Memphis *Commercial Appeal*" (B 164). But it was the air war that gripped them especially. Billy during his classes at school "carefully filled pages with pictures of goggled men and their fragile, angular machines" (B 140–1) in his notebooks.[3]

Stories about the American pilots flying for France in the Lafayette Escadrille appeared almost daily and were always boldly pronounced, as in these typical dispatches radiating a fascination that still makes the subject glow:

WITH THE FRENCH ARMY ON THE SOMME FRONT, November 3, 1916 (Correspondence of The Associated Press).—The little squad of American volunteer aviators with the French army has brought down twenty-one German machines since its formation into a fighting unit in May of this year, according to official figures. When the squad was organized there were fifteen members. Three of these, Sergeants Norman Prince and Kiffen Rockwell and Corporal Victor E. Chapman, have since been killed in aerial combats .... Adjutant Raoul Lufbery... has achieved the distinction of becoming a French "ace"—a destroyer of five German machines .... They soared and circled over the French lines ready to give battle to any German flier who might attempt to attack the French observation aeroplanes or kite balloons. The Americans are fighting purely, and take no part in technical observation work or dispatch carrying .... Their comfort is looked after by soldier servants. In one of these huts lives a six months' old lion cub, the mascot of the squad. He is named "Verdun." Verdun has an understudy in the form of a big wolfhound and the two are inseparable companions.

21 GERMAN MACHINES TOLL OF AMERICANS. Volunteer Fliers Have Brought Down Seven Times as Many Men as They Have Lost. (NYT, November 19, 1916)

"As one considers the historical significance of the Lafayette Flying Corps," writes James Norman Hall in 1919,

> it becomes evident that the outstanding accomplishment of the volunteers was their influence on public opinion in America at a time when we were neutral and under heavy pressure to maintain our neutrality .... The best element in America was already in open sympathy with France, and the French authorities, with ready understanding of our race, realized that the presence of a band of young Americans in French uniform, fighting the spectacular battles of the sky, would be certain to arouse a widespread interest and sympathy at home. (Hall and Nordhoff vol. 1, 3)

With Liddell Hart "it is worth remembering Foch's answer of 1910 when Henry Wilson asked what was the minimum military aid that would satisfy France: 'A single private soldier; and we would take good care that he was killed'" (Hart, *Europe in Arms* 206).

Victor Chapman and Oswald Boelcke

When the war began, Victor Chapman was one of the first Americans to volunteer, joining the French Foreign Legion on August 30, 1914. He was a founding member of the Lafayette Escadrille in March–April, 1916, serving at the front with Norman Prince, Elliott Cowden, William K. Thaw, Kiffin Rockwell, Bert Hall, James McConnell, James Norman Hall, and other American pilots. He was the first American pilot to die in the war, his death, and the resounding international reaction to it, much covered in the newspapers. He is forever linked in the reports to the German pilot who was initially said to have shot him down, Oswald Boelcke (the one who actually killed him was perhaps Walter Hödorf or Kurt Wintgens) whose fame in America is traceable to

American journalist Herbert Bayard Swope, a name that to our Faulknerian ears must sound quite uncanny.

In the first presentation of the Pulitzer Prize in 1917, Swope won the award for a "series of articles he had written in Germany and occupied France in the fall of 1916" for the *New York World* (Berg 254). In "Boelcke, Knight of the Air," Swope seems to trade on the latter-day chivalric codes that his portrait of the renowned German aviator also exposes as resolutely fraudulent. "Only among the aviators of the fighting armies," we are told, "is one certain to find that chivalry which once was never dissociated from war. Theirs is the special heritage of preserving the knightly tradition. The extraordinary bitterness of the other arms of the service makes the contrast all the sharper" (255). Swope, deadpan, then quotes Boelcke's description of his own fighting tactics:

> I use no special formula except to try to get my man before he gets me. Almost all fighting aëroplanes are similarly rigged, with a machine-gun fixed in front of the pilot. As the gun is stationary, to get it into position I must manoeuver my machine, and this is done best by outflying the enemy and coming into him from the rear … [I] outspeed and outsteer him, gaining the rearward position, where my shots go home while he has nothing to shoot at. (Swope 258)

In Faulkner's *A Fable*, American combat pilot Monaghan summarizes the matter in unanswerably colloquial terms: "Oh, I just ran up behind and busted the ass off the son of a bitch …. I'm trying to kill the son of a bitch. That's why I came two thousand miles over here: to kill them all so I can get to hell back home!" (FA 762). Still, Boelcke, small, trim, erect, *looks* like a knight, much as Faulkner does in the uniform he brought home with him (to be discussed later in this book):

> I found him to be a good-looking young chap, twenty-five years old, of the thin, wiry, quick, and graceful type usually associated with airmen …. Boelcke stood about five feet seven, clean-shaven and red-cheeked, with gray-blue eyes that never left the questioner. He had a thin Roman nose, a soft voice, and rather quick enunciation. He carried a cane of necessity because of a recent wound. (256)

"He always flew alone" (257). This is an essential claim of the air-war myth that Boelcke modernizes in his own practice. The airborne knight-errant roves freely but he actually cares nothing at all about chivalric duels and adventures. He is a stealthy hunter or ruthless assassin, doing his duty for his Kaiser without fear or pity. In fact, like his pupil, Manfred von Richthofen in his "Flying Circus," Boelcke was the quintessential squadron flier who always sought a numerical advantage. If he "flew alone," that was because he hovered above his squadron unseen, waiting to dive down on his unsuspecting prey. Bullets from his machine gun "exceeded five hundred shots a minute …. And with a wave of his hand Boelcke turned to his quarters to climb into flying-clothes. Three weeks later they dressed him in his shroud" (Swope 259, 260).[4]

He is survived by his immortal "Dicta Boelcke," the indispensable tactical manual of twentieth-century aerial combat:

1. Be sure you have the advantage before you attack (speed, height, numbers, position); attack out of the sun when you can.
2. Once you have begun an attack, prosecute it to the end.
3. Open fire only at close range, and then only when your opponent is square in your sights.
4. Don't let you opponent out of your sight.
5. In any type of attack, it is imperative that you approach from behind.
6. If your opponent dives on you, do not try to evade his attack—turn toward your attacker.
7. When over enemy lines, always keep in mind your own line of retreat.
8. [*nota bene*, Herr Boelcke]: When fighting in groups, it is best to attack in groups of four or six; when the melee begins, ensure that not too many of your own aircraft go after the same adversary. (qtd. in Ledwidge 31)

Victor Chapman, like Donald Mahon of *Soldiers' Pay* and Johnny Sartoris of *Flags in the Dust*, was shot from behind by a German pilot well schooled in the "dicta."[5]

BOELKE STILL FIGHTING, AMERICAN AIRMEN SAY. Victor Chapman Thinks He Fought Noted German Aviator on Saturday. (NYT, June 21, 1916)

"Last Saturday I had the narrowest escape to date. Coming home late from a reconnaissance alone, I was attacked from behind by a Fokker swooping from a great height. This, I think, was Boelke, as that is his invariable method of attack" …. Mr. Chapman added that his assailant was flying a black machine …. Americans say that Boelke's aeroplane is black with a huge skull painted under each wing. This, they think, is a deliberate attempt to unnerve the opponents upon whom he swoops.

Three days later Boelcke or one of his pupils shoots Chapman dead in his cockpit and the world, reading about it in the newspapers, watches as Chapman's airplane falls for two miles. He falls as does Johnny Sartoris in *Flags in the Dust*, "sublating this terrestrial rush into an aerial apotheosis" (Murphet, *Faulkner's Media Romance* 96).[6]

The overall story of Chapman's life and death is the Dicta Boelcke's "obverse reflection" (to use Quentin's formulation in *The Sound and the Fury*, 943) and it has continued to live as long. Chapman was killed "while on an errand of mercy":

CHAPMAN MET DEATH AIDING HIS COMRADES. French Statement Contains Remarkable Tribute to Aviator—Other Americans Honored. (NYT July 1, 1916)

Captain Bölke, the most famous of all German aviators, who up to that time had accounted for eighteen aeroplanes, sent Chapman to his death …. Sergeant Clyde

Balsley of San Antonio, Texas, wounded in a flight near Verdun and probably crippled for life, is in a hospital a few miles from the aviation camp to which Corporal Chapman was attached. The Sergeant asked for an orange, but there was none to be had at the hospital. Corporal Chapman heard of the incident and decided to gratify the desire of his comrade. He obtained a small basket of oranges and set forth in his aeroplane for the hospital .... Then Captain Bölke turned on the American, and caught him at such an angle that he was able to rake the aeroplane with machine gun fire. One bullet struck a vital spot, and Chapman plunged lifeless to the ground. He fell within German lines.

The story of Chapman, Balsley, and the small basket of oranges was oft retold by Chapman's contemporaries, including James McConnell, Kiffin Rockwell, James Norman Hall, and Dana Carroll Winslow:

Balsley had been wounded in an encounter with several Germans. He was doing well, when he was struck in the thigh by an explosive bullet which burst in his stomach .... Two fragments of the explosive bullet were removed from his intestines. These he kept wrapped up in a handkerchief as proof that the enemy, despite their denials do violate the rules of civilized warfare. For a long time the only nourishment he could take was the juice of oranges, and that was why Chapman was on this mission on that unfortunate day. (Winslow 160–1)[7]

It will be worth keeping the story of the oranges in mind as we consider the impulsive and frankly suicidal mission Faulkner imagines for Johnny Sartoris's brave and reckless forbear, Bayard Sartoris, killed more or less on a dare in the Civil War while solo raiding after some Yankee anchovies:

"No gentleman has any business in this war," the major retorted. "There is no place for him here. He is an anachronism, like anchovies. At least General Stuart did not capture our anchovies," he added tauntingly. "Perhaps he will send Lee for them in person?"

"Anchovies," repeated Bayard Sartoris who galloped nearby, and he whirled his horse [....] "And so," Aunt Jenny finished, "Mister Stuart went on and Bayard rode back after those anchovies, with all Pope's army shooting at him. He rode yelling 'Yaaaiiiih, Yaaaiiiih, come on, boys! right up the knoll and jumped his horse over the breakfast table and... into the wrecked commissary tent and a cook who was hidden under the mess stuck his arm out and shot Bayard in the back with a derringer" [....] and Bayard Sartoris' brief career swept like a shooting star across the dark plain of their mutual remembering and suffering, lighting it with a transient glare like a soundless thunder-clap, leaving a sort of radiance when it died. (FL 555–6)

Two generations later, RAF pilot Johnny Sartoris flies solo across enemy lines in bad weather, looking for trouble. His twin brother Bayard had tried and failed to prevent him. "'He was drunk .... Or a fool .... any fool could a known that on their side it'd be

full of Fokkers that could reach twenty-five thousand, and him on a damn Camel ....
I couldn't keep him from it. He shot at me,' young Bayard said; 'I tried to drive him
back, but he gave me a burst'" (FL 576). Murphet observes, "It is, then, the suicidal
romanticism of the first Bayard, whirling his horse around to recover the forgotten
anchovies, that finds its belated and now fully technological echo in the late John's
death in the skies over France" (*Faulkner's Media Romance* 53). Johnny Sartoris,
however, was shot down by no commissary cook:

> "It was Ploeckner," [Bayard] added, and for the moment his voice was still and
> untroubled with vindicated pride. "He was one of the best they had. Pupil of
> Richthofen's."

> "Well, that's something," Miss Jenny agreed, stroking his head. (FL 575–6)

Ploeckner is a fictional name but "him and his skull and bones" is Boelcke's
unmistakable signature, as are the ruthless tactics Bayard imitates in setting his own
aerial trap:

> "There was one I had to lay for four days to catch him. Had to get Sibleigh in an old
> crate of an Ak. W. to suck him in for me. Wouldn't look at anything but cold meat,
> him and his skull and bones. Well, he got it. Stayed on him for six thousand feet,
> put a whole belt right into his cockpit. You could a covered 'em all with your hat.
> But the bastard just wouldn't burn" .... and young Bayard's voice went on and on,
> recounting violence and speed and death. (FL 575–6)

Boelcke, in turn, was not shot down by an enemy worthy of his arrogance. He died
absurdly, as surely he would have felt. Perhaps, in his mentality as a commander, he could
not have foreseen his own failure to heed point #8 from his own *dicta*: "when the melee
begins, ensure that not too many of your own aircraft go after the same adversary."

BOELCKE, DESTROYER OF 40 ALLIED AEROPLANES KILLED IN COLLISION IN AN OPEN AIR BATTLE. (NYT October 30, 1916)

As Boelcke's group descended upon a lone British plane, the upper left wing of Boelcke's
machine contacted the undercarriage of an Albatros aeroplane being flown by a young
pilot in his own squadron. The collision tore the wing's fabric and sent Boelcke's plane
spiraling down to earth.

As in the case of Hobey Baker, Norman Prince, and countless others, Boelcke,
unrestrained by cockpit harness and unprotected by a crash helmet, died of a fractured
skull (it was probably the butt end of his own machine gun that killed him), the "huge
skull painted under each wing" ("Boelcke Still Fighting," NYT, June 21, 1916) his own
death's-head portent and seal.

Bayard Sartoris, meanwhile, keeps the reckless Sartoris legacy alive by dying as a
test pilot after the war. He probably knew the experimental aeroplane was nothing but

a badly designed lethal contraption (FL 863–4) but it served his purposes in getting himself his own headline. His aunt, Miss Jenny Du Pres,

> took the folded paper [Dr. Peabody] offered. **MISSISSIPPI AVIATOR** it said in discreet capitals, and she returned it to him immediately and from her waist she took a small sheer handkerchief and wiped her fingers lightly.
> "I dont have to read it," she said. "They never get into the papers but one way."
> (FL 866)

Chapman, Guynemer, and the Warrior's Knowledge

In *Victor Chapman's Letters from France* (1917), Chapman's father, John Jay Chapman, tells us he followed his son's exploits in the papers and sent him the clippings:

> They were high-colored, journalistic sketches, in which Victor invariably appeared as the hero, the rescuer, the resourceful stage person. They had about them that false glare of literature which the public loves, and which the soldier hates; and I used to forward them to Victor in order to annoy him. He could not be expected to understand that the glamor, limelight and bad taste in them were the conventions of a certain kind of newspaper work. (98–9)

The "the lived reality of actual warfare" (Gibson 468) isolates the pilot beyond the newspapers' glare and the public's comprehension, a modernist theme that works its way through all of Faulkner's writing about war while also appearing in the various modes of his public self-presentation as a nerve-shot war veteran (see later in this book).[8]
 Captain Georges Guynemer ("Knight of the Air," "Eagle of France," "King of the Aces"), acknowledging "that mysterious atmosphere which serves as an aureole to the Ace," also expresses impatience with his own publicity and is at pains to explain basic matters to readers of the first book being written about him (he would not live long enough to read it himself), Jacques Mortane's *Guynemer: The Ace of Aces* (New York: Moffat, Yard & Company, 1918). In a foreword bluntly titled "Advice to Boche-Hunters," Guynemer declares,

> The public as a rule has a false idea of hunting and the hunters ....
> I can not express in words the enervation which I feel sometimes while listening to the inept remarks addressed to me, in the form of compliments, and which I am compelled to accept with a smile, which is almost a bite. I want to shout out to the speaker: "But, my poor fellow, you ought not to speak about this subject, for you know nothing whatever about it. You do not understand the first word of it all, and you can hardly believe how little your eulogies please me, under the circumstances ...." If the layman were to become competent to judge, he would possibly no longer hold the same admiration for the hunters .... we are interesting to them only because they know nothing about our work. (Mortane xxi–xxiii)

Figure 2.3 Captain Georges Guynemer.

What Guynemer wants you to understand above all else is that he is a ferocious killer on your behalf. Air-war hunting is not a sport. When he locates an enemy machine, he approaches as closely as he can in order to fire upon it at "point-blank distance" (Mortane xxvi): "I stayed close to my adversary, as if I were mad. When I held him, I would not let him go" (xxvii). "'My aeroplane,' he said one day, 'is nothing but a flying gun'" (Driggs 100). What sets Guynemer, Bishop, McCudden, Mannock, Lufbery, and Rickenbacker apart is their ability to fly their planes "through their gunsights" even when all hell is breaking loose. They were renowned for the meticulousness of their technical preparation, the relentlessness of their shooting practice, and the formidable tranquility of their minds in combat. With Michael Herr in *Dispatches* we can say of each one, "He was a good killer, one of our best" (14). Second World War Battle of Britain pilot Robert Doe clarifies the central challenge of combat flying in both the world wars: the pilot must always keep a sharp lookout all around him while flying his plane solely along the line of aim once the enemy is in sight. "I really concentrated on learning how to shoot, and when you're flying an aeroplane through the gunsight, you do what's needed to keep the gunsight where you want it" (qtd. in Kaplan and Collier 116).

After Guynemer had achieved his fiftieth kill a few weeks before his death, "He became nervous, sick and irritable. The most envied man in France found himself discontented and unhappy" (Driggs 95–6). Mourning lost companions, exhausted, depressed (as we would now say), he refused nonetheless to go on leave. Whatever the reasons for Guynemer's unravelling near the end, his story is also, finally, that of a soul destroyed by the war. After three more victories, he went missing in action over Poelcapelle, Belgium on September 11, 1917, and neither his body nor any grave or memorial marker was ever found in the muddy fields of Flanders where he fell. Driggs summarizes the contemporary speculation about the wasting of Guynemer's soul:

> Was it because he had attained his mark of fifty? Because he had seen the fulfillment of his desires in his new fighting plane which he had proved to be a success? Because the pent-up passion and determination which had so miraculously carried a human body safely through so many almost inevitable annihilations was at last beginning to devour the slight vessel which contained it? Such was the opinion of Commander Brocard, his early mentor and close friend. (Driggs 95–6)

Victor Chapman also wished to explain something of his truth as a war pilot, at least to his father. Explanation here broaches upon confession as Chapman describes a bombing mission against "the town of Dillingen where there were said to be huge casting works …. I still have scruples about dropping on dwelling houses—they might be Alsatians" (148). He drops the bombs as ordered from a great height and sees clouds of black smoke far below, not knowing whether any primary targets were hit: "From a good altitude the country looks like nothing so much as a rich old Persian carpet" (150) and, besides, "we did not have unity or concentration of attack enough to get them" (185), a frank admission that the era of aerial dueling is in the process of being fully transformed by the tactics of mass bombing formations. Even in smaller-scale bombing raids, the pilot can only hope that whatever his bombs hit in their random diffusive patterns will be the legitimate targets. (The realities of high-altitude bombing will simply mean that anything the bombs strike on the ground will be "legitimate targets" by definition.) The Germans retaliate, French civilians are killed, the bombing war escalates another bloody increment, and the newspapers become the pilot's curse:

> June 1, 1916: The Boches had come over Bar-le-Duc and plentifully shelled it …. The town, the station, the aviation field all shelled—40 killed, including ten school children…. Yes, this is what comes of getting notoriety. There were disgusting notices about us in the papers two days ago,—even yesterday. I am shamed to be seen in town today if our presence here has again caused death and destruction to innocent people. It would seem so. (183)

On June 6, 1916, in one of his last letters to his father, Chapman writes: "It was all rot and rotten from beginning to end" (186). His father concludes, "Victor was quite aware that he was going to be killed, and three days before his death he said in an off-hand way to his Uncle Willy, 'Of course I shall never come out of this alive'" (186).

Notes

1   American pilot Carroll Dana Winslow, in *With the French Flying Corps* (1917), a book Faulkner clearly read, identifies three general classes of air men: "The first and predominating class is that composed of 'gentlemen.' By gentlemen I mean gentlemen in the English sense—men who in private life have the leisure time to be sportsmen, and who in war have chosen aviation because it is a more sporting proposition than fighting in the trenches" (103). The Ivy Leaguers clearly belong in this class. "The second class comprises those who before the war were professional pilots or aviation mechanics" (103), pilots like Glenn Curtiss, Eddie Rickenbacker, and Howard Hawks (Curtiss raced motorcycles and Rickenbacker and Hawks motor cars before the war). "In the third class one finds men who were mechanics or chauffeurs by trade and who were accepted because their knowledge of machinery would ultimately help them to become pilots" (103–4): Raoul Lufbery, *par excellence*.

2   See Kartiganer on this awkward scene in "'So I, Who had Never had a War.'"

3   The sketching habit was lifelong. With Joan Williams in 1953, Faulkner one evening in her apartment picked up a pencil and made a few sketches, including one of himself "attired in dress in RAF uniform with boots and cane [and] a drawing of a Sopwith Camel" (B 1474). With Jean Stein a couple years later, "Faulkner was grateful for the devotion Jean gave him and he showed it in different ways, letting her see the new work he was doing and sometimes drawing a sketch for her: himself in the RAF uniform, in profile with large nose and pipe ... " (B 1595).

4   "Early in 1915 the machine gun was introduced as an aerial weapon, the first types being fired backwards over the pilot's head, so that the plane had to fly away from its target. Next came a swivel mounting, and that summer the Germans brought out the Fokker monoplane [this was the plane Boelcke flew], equipped with a synchronizing gear which allowed the gun to be fired through the propeller blades" (Montross 705–6).

5   Artistic types prone to deep meditation, perhaps, Chapman, Mahon, and Sartoris failed to "Beware the Hun in the Sun." Sartoris, we are told, was a poet. "Were they poets?," Horace Benbow asks of the Sartoris twins. "'I mean, the one that got back. I know the other one, the dead one, was'" (FL 694). So too was Victor Chapman, in prose:

> June 1, 1916: *Dear Papa*: This flying is much too romantic to be real modern war with all its horrors. There is something so unreal and fairy like about it, which ought to be told and described by Poets, as Jason's Voyage was, or that Greek chap who wandered about the Gulf of Corinth and had giants try to put him in beds that were too small for him, etc..... Yesterday afternoon it was bright but full of those very thick fuzzy clouds like imaginary froth of gods or genii .... Then it was marvelous. At 3000 metres one floated secure on a purple sea of mist. Up through it, here and there, voluminous clouds resembling those thick water plants that

grow in ponds; and far over the ocean, other white rounded ones just protruding, like strands on some distant mainland .... Everyone says they get tired of flying, "It's monotonous." I don't see it, but on the contrary, an infinite variety is this, when there is a slight sprinkling of clouds. Clouds are not thin pieces of blotting paper; but liquid, ceaselessly changing steam. I played hide-and-seek in and out them yesterday; sometimes flat blankets like melting snow on either side below me, or again, like great ice floes with distant bergs looming up, and "open water" near at hand, blue as a moonstone cloud, floating full, for all the world like a gigantic jelly-fish (those that have red trailers and a sting) .... Some have many feathery, filmy points and angles, others are rounded and voluminous, with cracks and caverns in them. These are all the fair-weather, fleecy clouds; for there are the lower, flatter, misty ones, and the speckled, or mare's tail clouds, above which one never reaches. There are such a lot of trumpet-shaped and wind blown clouds this evening that I should like to go out and examine them; but it's a bore for my mechanic, and I doubt if I could go high enough to warrant crossing the lines. (Chapman 181–6)

Boelcke's mind might have been more like Ted Hughes' "Hawk Roosting" (1960), a predator careful to note that "The sun is behind me." Rickenbacker reports that the imperative to be aware of one's surroundings in all 360 degrees produced his chronic ear and neck trouble: "The constant twisting of my neck in air, turning my head from side to side to watch constantly all the points of the compass had affected in some mysterious way my former malady" (Rickenbacker 227). It is hard to imagine Chapman or Faulkner's pilots concentrating so relentlessly on the here and now.

6   Edward Jablonski describes Chapman's fall: "The Nieuport jerked into a nose-down attitude and then from 10,000 feet plunged straight down. About halfway the wings ripped from the fuselage, fluttering end over end in the brilliant blue sky" (93). See James McConnell, who was shot down and killed by two German planes on March 19, 1917: "Next to falling in flames a drop in a wrecked machine is the worst death an aviator can meet. I know of no sound more horrible than that made by an airplane crashing to earth. Breathless one has watched the uncontrolled apparatus tumble through the air. The agony felt by the pilot and passenger seems to transmit itself to you. You are helpless to avert the certain death. You cannot even turn your eyes away at the moment of impact. In the dull, grinding crash there is the sound of breaking bones" (86–7). Alumnus of the University of Virginia and flyer in the Lafayette Escadrille, McConnell is memorialized in Gutzon Borglum's statue, "The Aviator," which stands, or rather flexes, about to leap, in front of the Clemons Library (https://news.virginia.edu/content/uva-honors-inspiration-winged-aviator-statue-100-years-after-his-death). McConnell's memoir, *Flying for France: With the American Escadrille at Verdun* (1917), is one of the classics of the war.

7   Jablonski (88–91) offers a more recent dramatization based on Balsley's own account (as I discuss it in Chapter 7 in this book). Kiffin Rockwell, the second American pilot to die in the war, was killed by an explosive bullet that tore through his chest. The British used incendiary bullets to shoot down Zeppelins and observation balloons. American pilot Major Charles Biddle is frank about the use of incendiary bullets to shoot down aeroplanes with his "special gun" (Biddle 265–6), modeled on the one Guynemer had also used (see below). In his report on Boelcke, Swope discusses the "matter of ammunition that, after two years of chivalry among the knights of the air,

threatened to lead to great bitterness. The Germans accused the English fliers of using incendiary bullets in their machine-guns. These cartridges, slightly larger than the usual rifle-shell, carry an explosive chamber that ignites in flight and inflames the substance against which it is shot. As aëroplane wings are oil-coated, they are highly combustible, and several disasters overtook German fliers in this way" (Swope 259). Lufbery was likely killed after his plane was struck with an incendiary bullet (see below). Notes historian Paul Cornish, "both sides accused each other of employing illegal small arms ammunition—either expanding or explosive bullets. The Hague Conventions of 1899 and 1907 outlawed projectiles of these types but, by 1914, advances in ammunition design had made defining them a very subjective process." Sometimes tracer bullets, with their spectacular sparks and colored smoke-lines, were mistaken by pilots on both sides as incendiary bullets.

8 Gibson is writing about the American war in Vietnam in his appendix, "The Warrior's Knowledge: Social Stratification and the Book Corpus of Vietnam." See also James Campbell's discussion of "combat Gnosticism," by which he means "a construction that gives us war experience as a kind of gnosis, a secret knowledge which only an initiated elite knows. Only men ... who have actively engaged in combat have access to certain experiences that are productive of, perhaps even constitutive of, an arcane knowledge" (204). Campbell argues that combat gnosticism is a "discursive construction," but that doesn't prevent it from pointing to something true in many soldiers' hellish experiences. Writes American infantry Lieutenant Hervey Allen (in one of the most powerful American books to come out of the First World War), "I was particularly impressed that night by Lieutenant Shenkel. A man who comes out of battle does not get over it for a long time afterward ..... He was a different man. Something had come to him which had not yet come to us. It was the trial of battle. No one who passes through that is ever quite the same again" (Allen 17, his ellipses).

3

Transfiguration: Chapman, Guynemer, Lufbery

The sky
Warms me and yet I cannot break
My marble bonds.

—Faulkner, "The Marble Faun" (1924)

where to-day a white stone colonnade of peaceful beauty commemorates, and
contrasts with, the bloodiest battle-hell of 1916
—Captain B. H. Liddell Hart, *The Real War: 1914–1918*

"A citizen of the air betrothed to death, he called him"
—Premier Poincaré speaking of Guynemer, reported
in NYT, May 1, 1922

In the memoir that introduces *Victor Chapman's Letters from France* (New York: Macmillan, 1917), John Jay Chapman, Victor's father, commemorates Victor's mother, Minna Timmins, who died when Victor was eight years old: "she was so much the author of the heroic atmosphere, a sort of poetic aloofness that hung about him and suggested early death in some heroic form" (4). After she died in 1898, Victor and his father moved to France and Victor became a dual citizen. Victor returned to New England in his late teens to attend preparatory school and college. After graduating from Harvard University, he returned to France. When war was declared, he joined the French Foreign Legion and was deployed as an infantry soldier in the trenches. After seeing friends die, he transferred to the French flying service where he was certified as a pilot. With Norman Prince and Elliott Cowdin, he helped to found N. [Nieuport] 124, the Escadrille américaine, soon to be re-named the Lafayette Escadrille after the German Ambassador at Washington "called the attention of the American Government to the fact that Americans were fighting with the French" at a time when the United States was a neutral nation (Hall and Nordhoff vol. 1, 36).

Writes Victor's father, "Victor's entry into the American Aviation was, to him, like being made a Knight. It transformed,—one might almost say,—transfigured him" (25). It was as an American Knight that Chapman would achieve that French apotheosis that seemed the fulfillment of his mother's spirit.[1]

As John Jay Chapman reflects,

> The great fact behind all was this: the French people were living in a state of sacrificial enthusiasm from which history shows no parallel. Their gratitude to those who espoused their cause was such as to magnify and exalt heroism. The French press blazed with spontaneous paeans. The American Church became, as it were, the shrine of both nations at Victor's funeral on July 4th. (26)

In the story of Victor Chapman's "trip to his friend, of the little basket of oranges, of his headlong plunge to save his comrades, America has sent us this sublime youth," writes Mme. le Verrier in a letter of condolence to his father. Chapman senior then quotes from a letter sent by André Chevrillon:

> That word hero is now commonly used for all those who die on the battlefield,— but they are the obscure heroes, of whom the numbers only and nothing individual will be recorded by history. The death fight of Victor Chapman touches our imagination with fire. Be assured that his name will stand forever in France. He died whilst rescuing,—*en combat singulier,*—three Frenchmen ....
> In those last minutes of his life he rose to the front rank of what we call our Saints: he carved his own statue; it has the essential simplicity of the supremely beautiful. (36)

In such letters that came to John Chapman from France after Victor's death, one hears the prose music of that uniquely French mode of canonization that so fascinated Faulkner as in the case of Victor Chapman and Georges Guynemer. Jacques Mortane, who published the first book about Guynemer, describes his proposal to the famous pilot to write what was originally conceived as merely a newspaper article about him:

> He looked at me with those piercing eyes of his, as if he were taking counsel with himself, and after several seconds, said:
> "All right, but on condition that you do not mention my name!" [....] Such was his modesty. He would not let me publish a name which soon thereafter was to be pronounced with veneration by the entire world. (Mortane 3)

Guynemer, a young god of the war, was by this point well on his way to "carving his own statue" and to feeling himself entrapped in the form. It would soon be possible to read his legendary disappearance, as does Mortane, as the expression of Guynemer's desire to free himself "of the encumbrance of marble" (Mortane xviii). Indeed Guynemer would disappear and only the marble would remain.

The newspapers were obsessed with scorekeeping in the air war, but any given victory could be officially established only "by the verification of three or more eye-witnesses" (Driggs 83). In the case of Guynemer's fall, there was no witness testimony to describe what could therefore only be imagined: "the living Guynemer, now borne away in a great apotheosis, amid the acclamations of his companions in glory, sound judges as to the matter of heroism" (French Prime Minister Georges Clemenceau qtd. in Mortane xiii). Laurence La Tourette Driggs, in *Heroes of Aviation* (Boston: Little, Brown, and Company, 1919), captures the essence of the Guynemer myth:

> No one can say how the miracle operated on that occasion, the eleventh day of September, 1917, for no one has been found who witnessed it .... The mystery of Georges Guynemer's disappearance is truly so baffling that one wonders little at the superstitious belief held by the French peasants that he did not come down but on the contrary ascended straight to heaven—a last miracle! (Driggs 87, 97)

"The people need legends," Clemenceau observed on the occasion. On September 11, 1917, Guynemer "disappeared from the eyes of the world while in the full exercise of his duty. The heavens swallowed him up, and to this day no reliable clue to his disappearance has been discovered" (qtd. in Driggs 84). "His heroism outstrips the imagination." He is "a sentinel lost from earth, who will exact something most beautiful for Humanity" (Mortane x, xi) amid the endless sorrow of "all the children of France" who had "written to him daily" (Mortane x, xi, xvi).

Losing sight of Guynemer during his final battle, his companion, Lieutenant Bozon-Verduras, searched the skies for "two and one half hours of fruitless probing" (Driggs 98), compelled to fly back to camp when his fuel tank was nearly exhausted. So Bayard Sartoris searches through the clouds in vain for his brother's falling body, as if the "heavens had swallowed him up" too: "And so I never could pick him up when he came out of the cloud. I went down fast, until I knew I was below him, and looked again. But I couldn't find him and then I thought that maybe I hadn't gone far enough, so I dived again" (FL 754).

One discerns perhaps Faulkner's first allusion to the Guynemer myth in a letter to his mother from New Haven dated April 5, 1918: "I saw a French flyer with only one arm and a Croix de Guerre with two palms, which is about as high as a Frenchman can go and live" (TH 46). Several years later Faulkner made his trip to Europe and wrote to his mother from Paris on September 6, 1925:

> In almost every house there is a picture of Saint Genevieve, the patron saint of Paris, staring out over Paris at dusk. There is a beautiful one by Puvis de Chavannes in the Pantheon, where the unknown soldier's grave is. There is also in the Pantheon, on a blank panel of wall, a wreath to Guynemer, the aviator, beneath an inscription. There is also a street named for him. And near the cathedrals, in the religious stores, any number of inscriptions to dead soldiers, and always at the bottom: "Pray for him." (SL 18)

In Faulkner's screenplay, "War Birds/A Ghost Story" the link between the "blank panel of wall," the empty page of a diary, and Guynemer's sublime disappearance is explicit. Here Bayard has survived his career as a test pilot (or perhaps he has been resurrected) in a filmic reparation of the tragic themes and revenge motifs of *Flags in the Dust* (Kawin, "*War Birds* and the Politics of Refusal"). As in the story "Ad Astra," a German prisoner of war is befriended by a group of Allied pilots on the evening of the Armistice. Sentiments of peace and brotherhood are expressed as alcoholic spirits are shared. "'But soon it will clear away,'" [the subadar] said. "'The effluvium of hatred and of words'" (Faulkner, "Ad Astra" 407).

Faulkner's screenplay is an adaptation of John MacGavock Grider's *War Birds: Diary of an Unknown Aviator* (New York: Grosset & Dunlop, 1926), freely woven with Faulkner's own Sartoris material in *Flags in the Dust* and "Ad Astra" (see Kawin's introduction to the script in *Faulkner's MGM Screenplays*, Solomon 45–51, and Fantini).[2] A major source for Faulkner's conception of the twin Sartoris brothers, in turn, is James Warner Bellah's *Gods of Yesterday* (New York: D. Appleton and Company, 1928), especially the story therein entitled "Blood" about twin German pilots (see Dillon): "They were blond men, the brothers Von Beulen, and tall …. So they had lived—one spirit in two bodies—" (Bellah 171). One of the twins, John, is killed in combat, and the story invites a deep identification with the surviving brother, Paul, through whom the narrative is focalized. Faulkner was deeply affected by the story, and one can discern the presence of its anti-militaristic and patricidal ethos in a number of his war fictions, including *Flags in the Dust*, "Ad Astra," "Victory," "Turnabout" (see the following chapter), and *A Fable*:

> "I'm cut in half! I'll never wear boots again! Wrong—all wrong!" And the breathing ripped out of him and stopped ….
>
> "I am sorry, but what shall one do? It is war."
>
> "War?" said Paul hoarsely. "War? Curse it! Curse the generals that make it!" (Bellah, *Gods of Yesterday*, 184–5)[3]

There is a resounding echo of *The Way of the Eagle* by Charles J. Biddle in Faulkner's vision of war and peace in those same fictions. Biddle, after shooting down a German Albatross two-seater aeroplane, describes a kind of day-dream in which former combatants share food and drink, after which the German enemy is invited by his American combatant to visit him at his home in America after the war. In a letter to his parents, Biddle describes meeting the German pilot who survived Biddle's attack. But first he describes the German observer who did not:

> He was a fine big strapping fellow, twenty-one years old, and looked like a gentleman. It gave me a queer feeling to stand there and look at that dead boy whom I had never seen before, stretched out with two or three of my bullets through this stomach, his fast-glazing eyes staring wide open and that nasty yellow look just coming over his face …. As I was standing there a gendarme went through the dead observer's pockets but did not find much except a pair of eye-glasses and a half-empty flask of whiskey. The former he gave to me and I have them. Inside the case was the man's name, "Lt. Groschel." The pilot's name was Johann Eichner and I enclose his card. Please keep it as a souvenir. The long word under his name is not an address but is the German for "Air pilot." (Biddle 243)

The following day Biddle went to see the German pilot now a prisoner of war.

> He seemed thankful to have escaped with his life and was anxious to answer my questions, for I think he realized that after I had knocked out his observer I could have killed him if I had wanted to …. The circumstances under which we questioned him were very unfavorable for getting the most out of him. He was in a small room with four American and three French officers, being continually plied with questions by them. If we could have taken him somewhere, given him a good dinner and a few drinks, and then gotten to swapping yarns in a friendly way about the war instead of firing a lot of direct questions at him, I think he would have told us everything he knew about Germany. He seemed more worried about not having anything to shave or brush his hair with than anything else. Also he had, the night before he was brought down, given his observer a hundred marks to buy him a flask of whiskey, which had only cost four marks. He wanted to know if the change had been found on the observer's body, for he did not have much cash with him to see him through till the end of the war. I felt like giving him some, but thought the guard would probably take it from him, and then also a Hun is not entitled to many favors, so I gave him a pack of cigarettes and called it square at that. He seemed pleased, said he thought the captain (being me) seemed like a pretty nice sort of a fellow, and wanted to know my name, so we exchanged cards and I have already sent you his. The one I gave him had "Andalusia, Pa.," on it so if he calls on you after the war do not be surprised. (Biddle 247, 250–1)

In "War Birds," the German pilot, Dorn, "suddenly appears" in the film's first shot, a scene set in Bayard and Johnny Sartoris's Mississippi hometown. A little boy, Johnny Sartoris's son, establishes the basis of the film's plot in addressing the German pilot officer:

> You are a German. You came back from the war with Uncle Bayard, and you knew my father. You were a soldier too. And dad and Uncle Bayard were aviators, and so you were an aviator too. (He looks at Dorn; he is about to learn something which he wishes to flee from. His gaze is wide, still; before him Dorn gradually becomes stiff at attention). They won't tell me, but I know. You were a German aviator. It was you that killed my father. (Kawin, *MGM* 278)

Bayard, by the end of this exceedingly sentimental film (never produced), declines to kill his brother's killer with the pistol Dorn proffers him. Bayard "flings pistol through window. The fractured glass is in the shape of a star." The scene dissolves and re-focuses on Johnny Sartoris's wife Caroline and their son Johnny who hover over the pages of the dead pilot's war diary:

> As DISSOLVE begins, the star shaped fracture in the glass begins to glow faintly as daylight begins behind it. It is brightest at the instant of complete dissolve, then it begins to a fade.

298. A PAGE OF THE DIARY [the final entry in Johnny Sartoris's]
Caroline's hand holding it open, one of Johnny's [his son's] hands beside it:
July 4th [The date of Victor Chapman's funeral] [....] Someday I will just get
beyond all loving and hating, and I will just fly on away somewhere and vanish,
like Guynemer did. Well, I have got beyond the loving and the hating. And so
who knows? Maybe the next time I go up will be the time when I will fly on away
into some sky without either air or gravity, where I will cruise on forever at about
fourteen fifty, watching my shadow on the clouds and not even remembering
how I got there.
Caroline's hand turns the page. The next page is blank [....]
DISSOLVE THROUGH BLANK PAGE [....]
300. THE BLANK PAGE, CAROLINE'S and JOHNNY'S Hand upon it. (409,
411)

The white page is Johnny's "blank panel of wall" in the Pantheon and the endless sky
through which he continues to fly as the screenplay ends:

323 IN DISSOLVE there passes behind Bayard the ghost of John's ship. John
looking down at them, his face bright, peaceful. The ship goes on in dissolve;
sound of an engine dies away.
     THE END. (420)[4]

Reporting Guynemer's Apotheosis and His Disappearance in the Mud

Stories about Guynemer—racking up scores, breaking records, being shot down and
escaping miraculously unhurt—appear with rhythmic fascination in the newspaper
chronicles of the era. Yet if they help to project him as something of a marvelous,
godlike figure, they also give us a realistic report of who he was as a combat pilot,
how he probably died, and why his body was never recovered. The stories also help
forge the deep mental links by which Guynemer, in the spectacular singularity of his
disappearance, becomes associated with "The Unknown Soldier" who stands in for
the unrepresentable masses of "conscripted populations slaughtering one another" all
along the Western Front (Sassoon, *Sherston's Progress* 16). "The truth of the new warfare
of peoples was beginning to come home to the civilian population," writes Liddell Hart
in *The Real War* (69), "man himself," in the words of historian Lynn Montross, "now ...
regarded as matèrial of war—a living projectile to be employed without stint because
of its very cheapness" (Montross, *War* 639). If the mass of the people had watched, as
if "from seats in the amphitheatre, the efforts of their champions" (Hart, *The Real War*
36), the death of Guynemer was a sign that the "'gladitorial' wars of the past" were
fully giving way to "the national war to which they were committed" (Hart, *The Real
War* 69).

When the newspapers in America first begin to notice Guynemer, he is marked out as a resolutely modern figure, a prodigy in a war of inexorable technological innovation:

FRENCH AVIATOR BAGS HIS FIFTH ADVERSARY. Guynemer Only 21 Years Old—One of His Victims Was a Fokker (NYT, February 8, 1916)

Sergeant Guynemer flies alone, as did Garros and Pegoud, but instead of a monoplane he uses a great biplane, on which he makes ninety miles an hour .... It is armed with a weapon which it is not permitted to describe. He handles it with remarkable facility and deadly precision, at the same time manoeuvring his aeroplane with great skill.

This secret weapon is a new type of machine, "nothing but a flying gun," as Guynemer had described it to Jacques Mortane (Driggs 100). As such it marks a formidable advance upon Boelcke's Fokker monoplane and its revolutionary synchronization of bullets and propeller blades. Guynemer's machine is a paradigm shift in fusing aeroplane and cannon. Moreover, the machine, so it is claimed, can fly at faster speeds and reach higher altitudes than anything else in the sky up to that point. The new aeroplane is a "Spad" (Société pour l'aviation et ses dérivés)

in which was mounted a 200-horse-power Hispano-Suiza motor which drove a propeller from the end of a hollow shaft. And through this hollow propeller shaft a light one-pounder gun fired straight ahead, without the risk and danger attending any attempt to synchronize its shells between the blades of his propeller.

It was his own idea! .... And now he had a weapon that would send ahead of his meteor-like craft explosive shells of an inch and a half diameter instead of the trifling little machine-gun bullets of one sixth that diameter. (Driggs 95)

Fighting another "spectacular duel," Guynemer in his flying weapon fires a shell through its 37-millimeter gun and hits the target at two hundred yards (the usual "recommended" distance from which to shoot down an aeroplane with machine-gun bullets was 50–100 feet). "His antagonist went to earth in flames after a short combat" (NYT, February 8, 1916).

In a letter to his parents, Charles Biddle provides a detailed gloss on the same "special type" of machine that he had also learned to deploy in the aftermath of Guynemer's death:

I now have a new machine of a special type mounting a most murderous weapon of a gun. I cannot tell you just what this gun is, but if I ever hit a Boche with it he should come down in small pieces. The trouble is to hit them, for the gun only shoots once and then must be reloaded by hand .... They gave it to me when Putnam was killed. Guynemer had one and Fonck and Deullin each have one and have used them with fair success. This special gun is difficult to use, but if a shot ever hits a Hun he might just as well say his prayers and give up, if he has time to think about anything at all. (Biddle 265)

In the book based on these letters that he published after the war, Biddle further explains in a footnote:

> The gun mentioned was a 37 mm. cannon, which shot through the hub of the propeller. It fired two kinds of ammunition, one like a huge shotgun cartridge loaded with a lot of slugs, and the other a combination incendiary and high-explosive shell, which would explode upon contact with any part of an aeroplane. If, therefore, a hit was scored even on the wing of an enemy machine, the resulting explosion would blow the wing off. It would consequently not be necessary with this gun, as it is with a machine gun, to hit that small area of a machine, which is ordinarily its only vital spot, in order to bring it down. (266n)

Guynemer's virtuosity and skill in command of such formidable firepower led to a mesmerizing series of performances.

GUYNEMER TWICE VICTOR. French Aviator Brings Down Two Foemen Within Three Days. (NYT, August 20, 1916)

FELLS 3 GERMAN FLIERS WITHIN 2½ MINUTES. Guynemer Is Timed by a Stop Watch in a Surpassing Exploit. (NYT, September 30, 1916)

"Hard pressed by five German machines," the article continues, "The King of Aces" fell 10,000 feet and crashed, but Guynemer escaped unhurt. Plunging "giddily earthward," he recounts to the reporters on the ground,

> I gave myself up for lost but after falling 5,000 feet I thought I would struggle all the same. The wind blew me over our lines and like a flash I had a picture of my funeral and all my good friends following the coffin. I continued to fall and the levers wouldn't budge. In vain I pushed and pulled to right and left. I made a last desperate effort all to no purpose, and then I saw the field toward which I was dashing down. Suddenly something happened and my speed diminished. Then there was a resounding crash and a violent shock. When I recovered my wits I was in the midst of the fragments of my machine and practically uninjured. How am I still alive? I asked myself. I believe it was the straps which held me to my seat which saved me.

The straps might have saved him but the physics of the escape seem supernatural, as does the experience of being a witness at one's own funeral. Guynemer continues to fly in the knowledge (his and the newspapers' both) that each "surpassing exploit" brings him a step closer to the final cessation of all speed and to the funeral he had foreseen while falling to earth in his disabled aeroplane.

GUYNEMER DESTROYS HIS 28TH AIRPLANE. French Aviator Wins Three Combats in Three Days—British Bag Five Machines. (NYT, January 27, 1917)

FELLED TWO AIR FOES IN FIGHT OF A MINUTE. Guynemer, Most Famous of French Aviators, Has Destroyed Forty-Three Machines. (NYT, June 2, 1917)

50TH VICTIM OF GUYNEMER. French Flier Brings Down Two Airplanes When Half Ill. (NYT, August 2, 1917)

GUYNEMER, AIRMAN, IS GIVEN UP AS DEAD. Victor in Fifty Combats Has Been Missing Since Flight Two Weeks Ago. (NYT, September 26, 1917)

He met his death, it is supposed, in a reconnaissance flight over Flanders on which he left Dunkirk Sept. 11.

SAW 40 AIR FOES AFTER GUYNEMER. Comrade Tells How French Aviator Assailed 5 Enemies and Others Swooped Down on Him. (NYT, September 27, 1917)

Guynemer sighted five machines of the Albatross type D-3. Without hesitation he bore down on them. At that moment enemy patrolling machines, soaring at a great height, appeared suddenly and fell upon Guynemer.

There were forty enemy machines in the air at this time, including Count von Richthofen and his circus division of machines, painted in diagonal blue and white stripes.

"Guynemer must have been hit. His machine dropped gently toward the earth, and I lost track of it. All that I can say is that the machine was not on fire."

The failure of the German military to confirm Guynemer's death—for the aeroplane had fallen within its lines—intensified the mood of suspended mourning, anguish, and uncertainty.

It has always been the German custom to announce promptly the fall of an enemy aviator. If the pilot has fallen from his machine and his identity lost, the number and name of his aeroplane is published and sent abroad. In the case of a German victory over a Guynemer, whose name and exploits were frequently published in the German press, the news would certainly flood the entire world. But for ten days after September 11th not a word came from Germany concerning Georges Guynemer. (Driggs 98)

A number of theories flowed into this silence, including that Guynemer was somehow still alive or that he had been given a military funeral by the Germans and was buried in a cemetery at Poelcapelle in Flanders. A few days later, however, Poelcappelle was captured by the British. "A diligent search was made for the grave of Guynemer, but none was found" (Driggs 99).

Meanwhile,

a London newspaper on September 17th printed the story of his disappearance. The enemy must now know of his loss.

Four days later, about the time required for a London paper to reach Germany through Holland, the *Cologne Gazette* printed the causal information that a Cologne fighting pilot, one Wissemann [or Weisemann in some spellings] heretofore unheard of, had written to his mother in Cologne informing her that he had shot down Guynemer, the French Ace of Aces .... (Driggs 98–9)

"Lieutenant Weisemann," continues Mortane, had written in his letter home: "Have no fears about me, I have brought down Guynemer, and I can never again meet so dangerous an adversary" (174–5). Weisemann, "who had committed the sacrilege of defeating this divinity of space survived his success but a few days" (Mortane 174). He was killed by René Fonck who would succeed Guynemer and survive the war as the French Ace of Aces.

Mortane then describes Guynemer's wounded corpse in reporting the testimony of two soldiers who "had been present at the place of catastrophe. One wing of the Spad had been broken. The pilot lay there, killed, with a bullet in his head, and one leg broken. On him was found his commission, which made it possible to identify the body" (173–4). It would be left to the brutal, boldface newspaper headline to render the corpse and the terminus that legend would also occlude behind the blank wall of marble.

GUYNEMER WAS SHOT IN THE HEAD. (NYT, October 5, 1917)

The death of Captain Georges Guynemer, the famous French aviator, has now been definitely confirmed. Information received by the Red Cross says Guynemer was shot through the head north of Poelcapelle, on the Ypres front. His body was identified by a photograph on his pilot's license found in his pocket. The aviator was buried with military honors in the Poelcappele cemetery.

That he had been so honored by the German military, however, was exposed as a wishful fantasy several months later in a letter to the editor published one day before Richthofen was killed and given the kind of funeral by his killers that many had dreamed of for Guynemer.

GERMAN COURTESY A MYTH. A Report Concerning Aviator's Funeral Denied. (NYT, April 20, 1918)

A few days ago I was present in a company where an American newspaper man gave an extremely interesting talk on aviation at the front, and he related the following story:

"Courtesy among aviators at the front is so great that when Guynemer was killed the German 'aces' invited their French colleagues to be present at the burial behind the German front. The invitation was accepted; the French came in their airplanes, were present at the funeral service, exchanged salutes with the Germans, and when about to turn back were surprised to see that the German aviators, with gracious hospitality, had had their tanks filled with gasoline." The story is a delightful one—so delightful that certain doubts arose in my mind as to its veracity. I therefore cabled my Government asking them to make inquires …. "You can absolutely and formally deny the story that French aviators were present at Guynemer's burial inside the German lines." [I therefore] request our American friends never to give any credence to stories of German courtesy or German generosity, even when related in perfect good faith. German generosity and German courtesy, we know by this time, are pure myths.

—Stephane Lauzanne, New York, April 13, 1918

Fifteen years later, now six months into Hitler's Thousand-Year Reich (1933–45), the newspapers publish a brief follow-up story about the corpse of Guynemer and the courtesy shown his memory by the head of Lufthansa, the state-funded civil airline now rapidly and openly weaponizing itself for another invasion of its European neighbors.[5]

GERMANY RETURNS FRENCH FLIER'S CARD. Document Identifying Famous Ace, Georges Guynemer, Has Been Put in Museum. (NYT, August 6, 1933)

German aviation has just accomplished an act of cordiality in returning to France the identity card which was found on the body of the famous French "ace of aces" in the World War, Georges Guynemer. The card recently came into the possession of Dr. Knauss, head of the German Lufthansa …. he was shot down in combat with a German reconnaissance plane September 11, 1917. Two German soldiers made their way to the plane and found the pilot was dead, shot through the head, and took his papers from the body. Later there was an unsuccessful attempt to find the grave, and it is presumed that burial never took place.

Driggs in 1918 already knew the likely truth of what happened: "Guynemer's body could not be removed and buried owing to the violent artillery fire that was directed against the spot by the British, which fire eventually obliterated and destroyed every trace of both aeroplane and pilot!" (99–100). It was as Clemenceau had said: "The heavens," or rather, we should say, the mud, "swallowed him up, and to this day no reliable clue to his disappearance has been discovered" (qtd. in Mortane 84). There was no grave and no funeral and that is why Guynemer can also return as a symbol of the Unknown Soldier whose tomb, as Faulkner understands it in *A Fable*, in fact lies empty, symbolizing all the missing soldiers who were vaporized in the war's artillery barrages.[6]

The dedication of Guynemer's tablet in the Pantheon was noticed in the American newspapers in 1922:

FRENCH SPIRIT SHOWN AT GUYNEMAR TRIBUTE. Poincare's Speech Cheered by Audience of Military Men and Their Families. (NYT, May 1, 1922)

Premier Poincaré seized the occasion of the unveiling today of a tablet in the Pantheon to the memory of Captain Guynemer, the most famous and most chivalrous of all French airmen, to preach to an audience almost entirely composed of famous soldiers and women whose sons and husbands had perished in the war that the victory which such men as Guynemer had won must not be lost by those who lived .... All the survivors of the famous Cigognes Squadron, of which Guynemer was the most famous member, were present and it was to men and women intensely moved by the memory of the attractive personality and gallantry of the dead airman that the Premier spoke.

"A citizen of the air betrothed to death, he called him."

Raoul Lufbery and the Winged Tank

What immortal spark did Raoul Lufbery fan into life during his combats in foreign lands to make his name a household word? .... Let us look at the details of Raoul Lufbery's life and see where this extraordinary claim on human appreciation begins.
—Driggs (101)

Lufbery was present at a service held for Guynemer on November 13, 1917, at the Headquarters of the Lafayette Escadrille "somewhere on the western front" ("Decorate 4 of Our Airmen," NYT, November 16, 1917). Decorated by "the commandant of all the French aeronautical forces," Lufbery was known by this time in the international mass media as "the American Ace of Aces" who could be mentioned in the same breath as Guynemer and whose every combat, decoration, and honor added to the luster of the national prestige. "Luf" was a classic American type. Where the French pilot was dauntless yet "mercurial" and the German "formidable as the automaton of a military machine," the American was distinguished by "his precision as a marksman and resourcefulness as an individual fighter" (Montross 634). Yet Lufbery, whose "precocious American childhood" helped to shape his powers as a "hero of aviation" (Driggs 102), was also a genuinely cosmopolitan figure.

AMERICAN AIRMAN HONORED. Sergeant Major Lufbery Gets Cross of Legion of Honor. (NYT, March 14, 1917)

The Cross of the Legion of Honor is only conferred on men in the ranks for exceptionally distinguished service .... Sergeant Lufbery spent his early years in New Haven, Conn. His parents died when he was very young and he was adopted by a family at Bourges, France. At 13 he ran away and wandered all over the world, turning his hand to many trades. In Asia he met the aviator Marc Pourpe, who trained him as his assistant.

Driggs straightens out some of the details of this brief biographical account. After "running away" from his father's home in Wallingford, Connecticut, Lufbery "spent three years wandering over the cities of France, the home of his maternal ancestors, working at any job he could find just long enough to give him funds with which to carry him to the next haven of his desires" (Driggs 102). His travels took him through Marseilles, Algiers, Tunis, Egypt, the Balkans, Germany, South America, and New Orleans, where he enlisted in the American army. He then served in the Philippines for two years. "And here we find the first item that helps to explain Raoul Lufbery's ultimate position as the American Ace of Aces. In the Philippines he won all the prizes for shooting. He was the best marksman in his regiment" (Driggs 102).

After completing his military service Lufbery traveled to Japan, China, India, and Cochin China where, in Saigon, he met Marc Pourpe, "the famous trick flier [who] was giving an exhibition in the Far East" (Driggs 103). Lufbery convinced him to take him on as a mechanic, and within a short time Lufbery came to know more about aeromotors, in Pourpe's words, "than most of the so-called mechanics of Paris" (Driggs 103). When war broke out in August 1914, Lufbery and Pourpe were in France and Pourpe enlisted at once, flying reconnaissance missions "to observe and report upon the movements of the inpouring German troops through the valleys of Luxemburg. Lufbery wished to enlist with his friend, but was declared to be an American, and found he must first join the Foreign Legion. This accomplished he was eventually permitted to accompany Pourpe to the front as a mechanic" (Driggs 105). Pourpe was killed on December 2, 1914, and Lufbery, "burning with desire to avenge his friend," joined the Air Service of France as a member of the Escadrille of Bombardment, transferring six months later to the Escadrille Lafayette (Driggs 111).

Now as a thirty-four-year-old pilot, considerably older than most of the American Ivy Leaguers flying in the Escadrille, Lufbery, in Eddie Rickenbacker's words, was "the most revered American aviator in France" (Rickenbacker 93), and his every move was followed by a floodlight of publicity.

The newspapers continued to write about him with a premonition (inherent, perhaps, in the very genre of air-war reportage itself) that the tally of his mounting successes was also a likely countdown to his inevitable annihilation.

MANY BATTLES IN THE AIR. Five German Aeroplanes Destroyed, One by an American Aviator. (NYT, December 30, 1916)

Adjutant Lufbery, an American from New Haven, Conn., adding the sixth to his string.

U.S. FLIERS BUSY ON WEST FRONT. Fight Twelve Separate Duels Friday— Lufbery is Victorious. (*Globe and Mail*, August 21, 1917)

When he landed Lufbery had twelve bullet holes in his plane .... A daring virage enabled him to disengage and withdraw unscathed.

HONORS FOR 4 AMERICANS. They Are Cited for Gallantry in Lafayette Squadron Work. (NYT October 20, 1917)

Lieutenant Raoul Lufbery of Wallingford, Conn., cited for "sixteen flights in a fortnight in which he brought down or disabled six enemies, scoring his eleventh victory on Sept. 4. His own machine was damaged five times during these flights."

Figure 3.1 Raoul Lufbery with the Lafayette Escadrille's mascots, the lion cubs Whiskey and Soda.

AMERICAN AVIATOR WINS GREAT DUEL. Lieut. Lufbery Brings Down His Thirteenth German Machine. (*Globe and Mail*, October 20, 1917)

LUFBERY GETS ANOTHER. American Aviator Brings Down His Fifteenth German Airplane. (NYT, November 4, 1917)

LUFBERY BAGS HIS 18TH PLANE; BAER OF MOBILE NOW AN ACE. (NYT, April 26, 1918)

LUFBERY IS LEADER OF AMERICAN AIRMEN. (NYT, April 28, 1918)

Faulkner arrived in New Haven on April 4th (TH 44) and reported Lufbery's death to his mother in a letter of May 19th: "The evening papers are full of the death of Major Raoul Lufbery, the New Haven aviator in the Lafayette Escadrille" (TH 56). Lufbery's final combat marked the death of an era—that of the solo pilot in his canvas and wire machine—and the birth of a sinister new development in the air war:

FLYING TANK DEFEATS ACE. His Machine in Flames, American Leaps Out to His Death. Charges on Enemy Twice. New German Giant of the Air Proves Impervious to Fire of Machine Guns. Bears Pilot and 2 Gunners. Lufbery's Companions, in Revenge for Him, Bring Down Another German Plane. (NYT, May 21, 1918)

Major Raoul Lufbery, the foremost American air fighter, was killed today in a sensational combat with a German armored biplane back of the American sector north of Toul.

Lufbery lost his life after six of our airmen had tried in vain to down the boche flying tank. The American ace leaped from his machine in mid-air after a German bullet had set his petrol tank on fire.

By this time other Americans were in the air, trying to bring down the German who loafed along not seeming to mind bullets at all. The scene, in full view for may miles, looked like a lot of swallows pecking at a giant bird of prey.

In this contest with the German flying tank, Lufbery became the last of a certain type, the singular fighting hero vanquished by the up-armoring of machines and the industrial massification of aerial warfare:

Fearless but of the coolest judgment, skilled in all the accomplishments, ruses, and dexterities of his perilous art, he won victory after victory .... He was a national, a European figure. He has fallen in no combat with more skillful or heroic men. He was conquered by a new giant of the ether, a new monstrous terror created by the Germans, against which there was no defense, which was invulnerable to bullets. As the flame rushed from his petrol tank he jumped, and that life that had been a flame of generous valor died out. He was the seventh of our airmen to struggle vainly against the impenetrable flying tank. ("Lufbery and the Winged Tank," *NYT*, May 21, 1918)

This gigantic German airplane was said to have a wingspread of sixty feet, two armored engines, a pilot, and two gunners. "The gunners wore armor and occupied protected positions, each manning a heavy machine gun." The pilot sat protected in a "steel house." With the arrival of this ironclad flying monster, as with "the triumph of the tank" at Cambrai on June 7, 1917, "at last the iron cavalry had come into its own, and the most conservative staff officers had to concede that a new era of warfare had dawned" (Montross 738). The mystique of dueling aristocratic professionals, facing off in "fair fight" on winged wooden horses, became antiquated and obsolete overnight even as it "thundered on ... wrapped still in the fury and the pride of the charge, not knowing that it was dead" (Faulkner, "Carcassonne" 896).[7]

> Meanwhile our air boys are hot to go up, volunteering copiously, and hope by a multitude of little machines to bring down Goliath by "a chance shot." By chance shots or not, the thing will be done. But is there to be, must there be, a revolution in airships? ...Each military invention is equaled or overcome by the other side. ("Lufbery and the Winged Tank," NYT, May 21, 1918)

The German "Goliath" demanded a psychological and strategic re-understanding of the main function of the single-seater fighting machine. The fighter pilot would not only face or "pursue" an enemy attacking over the lines but seek him out and destroy him behind his own lines or even before he managed to leave the ground. The business of aristocratic dueling was resolutely finished. As the allied air forces searched "opportunities for destroying matériel or personnel" (Montross 722), the fighter-plane's main function would be to protect the bombing convoys (the Allies' Goliath) that multiplied their assaults in the summer and fall of 1918 upon Germany's aerodromes, chemical and munitions factories, oil refineries, and transportation centers (Ledwidge, Overy). In American General William "Billy" Mitchell's conception, the air force was to become "an airborne artillery arm" (Montross 763).

Inherent in this strategic necessity was a vision of the complete metallization of flying machines, "these winged tanks, these battleships of the air" ("Lufbery and the Winged Tank"). In accordance with enduring metaphors and imperishable mystifications, some continued to imagine aeroplane metal, along with the tank and the infantry man's steel helmet, as the first major "revival of armor since the Thirty Years' War" (Montross 720). The commander of the Cambrai tank assault, Brevet-Colonel J. F. C. Fuller, D.S.O., dedicates his book, *Tanks in the Great War, 1914–18*, "to the modern knights in armour, the fighting crews of the Tank Corps; those Officers, Non-commissioned Officers and Men, who, through their own high courage and noble determination on the battlefield, maintained Liberty and accomplished Victory" (Fuller). In this conception of "the iron cavalry" and "the modern knights of armor" one understands how "the afterlives of romance .... continue to 'flash up' at moments of emergency" (Murphet 6, 3).

The emergency was becoming clearer: "great contests for control of the air will be the rule in the future" (Douhet 9). William ("Billy") Mitchell recalls a key moment in the planning for this air war of the future: "In 1919 we devised a super-bomber, capable of going 1300 miles without landing, to carry two four thousand pound bombs, and to be able to land or hit the ground at a speed of one hundred miles an hour without smashing up" (Mitchell 185). In this vision of armored speed, power, and endurance might be glimpsed the first outlines of the B-17 Flying Fortress (in which Joseph Blotner, Faulkner's biographer, was shot down [Blotner, *Unexpected* 175]), the B-29 Super Fortress, the AC-47 ("Puff the Magic Dragon"), and the A-10 Warthog.[8] Lufbery's airplane in flames and his solitary body in fall (perhaps like "the falling man" of DeLillo's 9/11 vision) would cast a shadow on the future of the total war in the air.

To his fellow pilots Lufbery's death was also a particularly haunting tragedy. "No form of death is so dreaded by the pilot as falling to the earth in flames," wrote Eddie Rickenbacker in his memoir, *Fighting the Flying Circus* (1919), and so "our most noted member leaped overboard to his death to avoid the slower torture of being burnt alive" (Rickenbacker 51).[9]

Leaps Out in Midair. (NYT, May 21, 1918)

[Lufbery] was seen to turn and start up at the enemy again, when suddenly he swerved and a thin line of flame shot from his machine, which seemed to hang still for a moment and then dart down. This took place at an altitude of 2,500 meters. When his machine was at an altitude of about 1,500 meters the American ace was seen to arise and leap into midair. From long experience he knew what awaited him, and that to stay in his seat meant to be burned to death horribly. His body fell like a plummet, landing in the midst of a flower garden back of a residence in the village of Maron. His machine fell in flames half a kilometer away and was burned to ashes.

His fellows rushed from the Aviation Field to the spot where their comrade had fallen. When they reached there some French people had straightened out the body in their garden and almost covered it with the flowers in the midst of which he fell.

There was no wound on Lufbery's body except a bullet hole through his right hand, which showed the incendiary bullet which had set his petrol tank on fire had passed through the hand which held the control lever a few inches from the tank.

He was 34 years old. He had been officially credited with bringing down sixteen boche machines, and his friends claimed many more for him. He wore the Legion of Honor, the Croix de Guerre, Ten Palms, and the Medal Militaire, in addition to four English medals, and the Montenegrin War Medal.

At the beginning of the war he enlisted as a second-class private in the French Army. He got to be a mechanic for airman, and rose to the position of First Lieutenant, which he held while in the Lafayette Escadrille.

Several accounts of Lufbery's death focus on this detail: "There was no wound on Lufbery's body except a bullet hole through his right hand, which showed the incendiary bullet which had set his petrol tank on fire had passed through the hand which held the control lever a few inches from the tank." "His machine had received a flaming bullet in the fuel tank. The same bullet evidently cut away the thumb of his right hand as it clasped the joystick" (Rickenbacker 97). The image of the wounded hand seems to pass into the figure of Donald Mahon in Faulkner's first novel, *Soldiers' Pay*, where the name of Lufbery is sounded upon his first appearance:

"Look at his wings," Lowe answered. "British. Royal Air Force. Pretty good boys."
"Hell," said Gilligan, "he aint no foreigner."

"You dont have to be a foreigner to be with the British or French. Look at Lufbery. He was with the French until we come in."
The girl looked at him and Gilligan who had never heard of Lufbery said: "Whatever he is, he's all right. With us, any way. Let him be whatever he wants." (SP 24)

Mahon returns from the war "sick" (oft repeated), a living corpse with "a dreadful scar across his brow" (SP 17) and a "right hand [that] was drawn and withered" (SP 19).[10] After a long process of working through, the scene of the wounding flashes up from Mahon's unconscious memory in the moments just before he dies (as if for a second time):

> he watched holes pitting into the fabric near him like a miraculous small-pox and as he hung poised firing into the sky a dial on his instrument board exploded with a small sound. Then he felt his hand, saw his glove burst, saw his bared bones. (SP 235)

Guynemer had also suffered a hand injury widely noted in descriptions of his corpse: "a sergeant of the German 413th Regiment certified that he had seen the Spad crash and identified the body, noting that Guynemer had died of a head wound, although one of his fingers had also been shot off and a leg was broken" (Mahieu). The wounds visible on the corpses of Guynemer, Lufbery, and Mahon enable us, perhaps, to imagine those suffered by Johnny Sartoris in the primal scene of *Flags in the Dust* when Bayard Sartoris watches the plane of his twin brother catching fire. Bayard relives the scene in the presence of his wife Narcissa, "she sitting with her arm taut in his grasp and her other hand pressed against her mouth, watching him with terrified fascination" (FL 754):

> "Then he quit zigzagging. Soon as I saw him sideslip I knew it was all over. Then I saw the fire streaking out along his wing, and he was looking back. He wasn't looking at the hun at all; he was looking at me. The hun stopped shooting then, and all of us sort of just sat there for a while. I couldn't tell what John was up to until I saw him swing his feet out. Then he thumbed his nose at me like was always doing and flipped his hand at the hun and kicked his machine out of the way and jumped. He jumped feet first. You cant fall far feet first, you know, and pretty soon he sprawled out flat. There was a bunch of cloud right under us and he smacked on it right on his belly like what we used to call gut- busters in swimming. But I never could pick him up below the cloud [....] I went down fast, until I knew I was below him, and looked again. But I couldn't find him and then I thought that maybe I hadn't gone far enough, so I dived again" [....] and suddenly she swayed forward in her chair and her head dropped between her prisoned arms and she wept with hopeless and dreadful hysteria [....] He lifted his hand and saw the bruised discolorations where he had gripped her wrists. (754–755)

Multiple articles with elaborate descriptions of Lufbery's funeral were published in the newspapers.

LUFBERY'S FUNERAL A TOUCHING TRIBUTE. French Join Americans at Military Rites, While Planes Soar Above, Dropping Red Roses. (NYT, May 22, 1918)

Eddie Rickenbacker was one of the memorial flyers:

I flew my formation twice across the mass of uncovered heads below, then glided with closed engine down to fifty feet above the open grave. As his body was being slowly lowered I dropped my flowers, every pilot behind me following in my wake one by one. Returning then to our vacant aerodrome we sorrowfully faced the realization that America's greatest aviator and Ace of Aces had been laid away for his last rest. (99–100)[11]

Within a month of Lufbery's death William Faulkner had joined the Royal Air Force and within two he had begun his training as a cadet-for-pilot in Toronto, Ontario, Canada.

Notes

1   See Poem XIV of Faulkner's *The Marble Faun*:
His mother said: I'll make him
A lad has never been
(And rocked him closely, stroking
His soft hair's yellow sheen)
His bright youth will be metal
No alchemist has seen.

His mother said: I'll give him
A brave and high desire
'Till all the dross of living
Burns clean within his fire. (34)
2   "*War Birds* was written in Oxford between late November 1932 and early January 1933" (Kawin, *MGM* 257).
3   See Robert Jackson's "The Anatomy of Thrift" for Faulkner's further rewriting of Bellah.
4   The legend of Guynemer suffuses one of the most vivid scenes in Faulkner's lifelong aviation passion play, his professed desire for invisibility as Malcolm Cowley was producing the one book that would do more to make Faulkner famous than any other, *The Portable Faulkner* of 1946. I take up this matter in Chapter 6.
5   "Military planners in interwar Germany regarded Lufthansa as an opportunity to train pilots for the bombers they were forbidden to have, but very much planned to develop" (Ledwidge 51).
6   See Hervey Allen, *Toward the Flame: A War Diary* (1926) and James Norman Hall, *Kitchener's Mob: The Adventures of an American in the British Army* (1916) for ghastly battlefield accounts of such barrages.

7   The phrase "in fair fight" and variations recurs as a kind of nervous spasm in the discourse of air-war coverage in this period. *The New York Times* announced Richthofen's death on April 23, 1918, thus: "**ARMIES FIGHT IN THE DARK. Foe's Greatest Ace Killed. Baron von Richthofen Shot Down After 80th Victory Had Been Claimed For Him. Buried With All Honors. Met His Death in Wild Melee of 50 Airplanes Over the British Lines. Philip Gibb's Story of the Great Battle.** [T]he German champion … had killed so many gallant fellows in fair fight, but with the most determined and ruthless desire to increase the number of his victims."

8   See also Faulkner's screen treatment "The Life and Death of a Bomber" and my essay, "'An Entirely New Way.'"

9   Mick Mannock was renowned for carrying a pistol on his missions and for educating all the younger pilots who would listen to him that he would use the gun on himself to avoid being burned alive should his machine ever catch fire: "Tell me, what do you imagine would be your first conscious thought in the event of your aeroplane catching fire in the air?" [asked Mick Mannock of Captain Cairns, "C" Flight commander]. Cairns was struck by Mick's thoughtful expression. "Good Lord! Well, I think my thought would be confused between whether I could put the fire out and what my fate would be." Mick digested the information, and then said: "My reply would be a bullet in the head" (Mannock 185). "The other fellows all laugh at me carrying a revolver. They think I'm doing a bit of play acting and going to shoot down a machine with it, but they're wrong. The reason I bought it was to finish myself as soon as I see the first sign of flames" (Mannock 166). Everyone knew (at some level) that the chances of escaping alive from a burning airplane—"fragile canvas, wood, and wire 'kites' powered by rasping engines and fueled with highly flammable gas and oil" (B 209)— were virtually zero. "When a pilot's benzine tank has been perforated, and when the infernal liquid is squirting around his legs, the danger of fire is very great. In front is an explosion engine of more than 150 h.p. which is red hot. If a single drop of benzine would fall on it the whole machine would be in flames" (Richthofen 63). Like Lufbery, Mannock didn't have any time to finish himself off before he hit the ground. Against all his principles, and in a manner that shocked all his companions, he had followed a wounded enemy machine as it descended, was struck by ground fire, and crashed immediately in flames.

10   See Jay Watson's discussion of the novel in *William Faulkner and the Faces of Modernity* and Chapter 6 in this book.

11   In *Pylon* racing pilot Roger Shumann steers his disintegrating airplane out over the lake to avoid crashing into the crowded grandstand. He falls free of the machine into the water, his body never to be found. The reporter who must write the article about Shumann's death is ridden with anger, grief, and guilt, and he can find only sardonic tones with which to describe the desolate scene: "At midnight last night the search for the body of Roger Shumann, racing pilot who plunged into the lake Saturday p.m. was finally abandoned by a threeplace biplane of about eighty horsepower which managed to fly out over the water and return without falling to pieces and dropping a wreath of flowers into the water approximately three quarters of a mile away from where Shumann's body is generally supposed to be since they were precision pilots and so did not miss the entire lake" (PY 991). One hears, perhaps, a dark parody of the First World War's funeral rites in Faulkner's fictional analysis of modernist irony here.

4

Faulkner and the Royal Air Force

There came to London yesterday the nearest vision of modern warfare that it has yet known.
      —"German Airmen Kill 97, Hurt 437 in London Raid," NYT, June 17, 1917

The Royal Air Force was a little over three months old when Faulkner arrived at the Recruits' Depot in Toronto on July 9, 1918. He was given a cadet's uniform and assigned to Class "A," Cadet-for-Pilot, at the rank of Private II. Basic training began immediately with military drill and exercise.[1]

RAF facilities and training operations were distributed across the city of Toronto and the province of Ontario. The Recruits' Depot at the Jesse Ketchum School was just north of the heart of the city. The flying camp at Long Branch, the original home of the Curtiss Aviation School, was west of Toronto by several kilometers along the shore of Lake Ontario. Long Branch was the main training facility for the cadets and Faulkner spent the majority of his time there. RAF flight training also took place at the Armour Heights aerodrome just northwest of Toronto's central area. Primary ground school for the cadets took place on the campus of the University of Toronto where Faulkner lived in the dormitory at Wycliffe College. The Leaside Camp on Toronto's east side had a flying field, nine hangars large enough for three flying squadrons, a "wing headquarters building, officers' and cadets' mess and quarters, a garage capable of housing 20 large motor vehicles, airplane and engine repair shop, and numerous smaller buildings" (Ellis 121). The engine-testing sheds, where Faulkner cranked an aero-motor, were at Leaside. The School of Aerial Fighting was at Beamsville on the Niagara Peninsula, about seventy miles from Toronto along the southern shore of Lake Ontario. RAF Camps Mohawk and Rathbun were 140 miles east of Toronto in Deseronto, Ontario. The School of Aerial Gunnery was at Camp Borden, west of Barrie, Ontario, about seventy miles north of Toronto. Borden was the home of the first military aerodrome of the Royal Flying Corps Canada and the site of Faulkner's apocryphal Armistice Day joyride and hangar crash (to be discussed in the following chapter). Camp Borden held special symbolic value for Faulkner. He signed the flyleaf of a copy of Swinburne he gave to Estelle in September 1919 thus: "W. Faulkner/Royal Air Force/Cadet Wing/S of A/Borden" (qtd. in Sensibar, *Faulkner and Love* 360).

On April 1, 1918—April Fool's Day and Easter Monday both—"the Royal Flying Corps and the Royal Naval Air Service in England were amalgamated and became the

Royal Air Force, operating under one command" (Ellis 126). Replacing these defunct aerial arms of the Imperial Army and the Royal Navy, the RAF became "the world's first independent air force" (O ix), capable of striking deep into Germany. Political and public pressures had demanded a response to the German terror bombing attacks on London that had reached a climax on June 17, 1917.[2] With the war's first August in 1914, German zeppelins bombed the residential areas of Antwerp and Liège, Belgium, killing hundreds of civilians indiscriminately.[3] Zeppelins bombed London and English coastal towns throughout the war, but by 1917 zeppelins yielded to Gotha bombers flying in diamond formation in broad daylight, the planes visible, if at all, merely as "silver specks" against the blue, well above the range of British fighter planes and antiaircraft guns.

> From every office and warehouse and tea shop men and women strangely stood still, gazing up into the air .... It was not easy to believe that those little silver specks far up in the heavens had the power to bring death and destruction and unendurable suffering to men, and women, and little children living at peace. ("German Airmen Kill 97, Hurt 437 in London Raid," NYT, June 17, 1917)

Figure 4.1 Gotha bomber being loaded with bombs.

On June 17, 1917, the dead included schoolchildren at their desks. As one eyewitness reported,

> There came to London yesterday the nearest vision of modern warfare that it has yet known. Many of the little ones were lying across their desks, apparently dead, and with terrible wounds on heads and limbs, and scores of others were writhing with pain and moaning piteously in their terror and suffering .... Many bodies were mutilated, but our first thought was to get at the injured and have them cared for. We took them gently in our arms and laid them out against a wall under a shed .... Some mothers were almost insane with grief, and when they couldn't find their own children would rush through the bodies looking for them, and when you remember that there was a hole in the roof four feet deep and covering the whole area of the classroom it will be understood what that meant.
>
> The worst part of our task was the last—that of picking up the mutilated fragments of humanity .... "The first lesson in kultur, gentlemen, the killing of women and children," called out a man in one crowd we passed through. ("German Airmen Kill 97, Hurt 437 in London Raid," NYT, June 17, 1917)

As Richard Overy explains, this raid was the catalyst for the formation of the RAF:

> The establishment of an entirely new branch of the armed forces was a political decision, prompted by the German air attacks on London in 1917, not a decision dictated by military necessity. The politicians wanted a force to defend the home front against the novel menace of bombing .... The Zeppelin raids encouraged the public to call for reprisals and the development of a dedicated bombing force, but the army and navy resisted the idea of attacks carried out simply for revenge .... One bomb hit a school in Poplar and exploded in an infant class, killing all the small children inside. It was the deadliest raid of the war, unexpected and without warning. A total of 145 people were killed, 382 injured, most of them in a handful of East End boroughs, but nothing matched the horror expressed across the capital at the slaughter of the eighteen infants in Poplar. Their funeral a week later sparked a deep emotional response and fueled an outburst of popular anti-German sentiment and calls for reprisals in kind .... Not until July 7, 1917 was London attacked again, but this raid has generally been taken as the point at which the government, alarmed by the growing public protest, began a search for a solution that ended with the creation of an air ministry and the RAF. (O xi, 15, 21–2)

"The air defence of Great Britain" included not only a network of searchlights, anti-aircraft guns, alarms (including "'sound rockets' or 'sound bombs' fired from police and fire stations or by policemen with whistles and rattles") (O 22), and fighter-plane squadrons spread around the city of London, but a strong offensive capacity to bomb military, industrial, and "moral" targets well behind the enemy's front lines.

Faulkner's poem "The Lilacs," first published in *The Double Dealer* in 1925, includes a scene from one of these RAF bombing operations:

We had been
Raiding over Mannheim. You've seen
The place? Then you know
How one hangs just beneath the stars and sees
The quiet darkness burst and shatter against them
And, rent by spears of light, rise in shuddering waves
Crested with restless futile flickerings.
The black earth drew us down, that night
Out of the bullet-tortured air;
A great black bowl of fireflies ....
There is an end to this, somewhere:
One should not die like this—(*A Green Bough* 9–11)

As a center for the production of steel, chemical weapons, and explosive munitions, Mannheim and the surrounding industrial region was a primary target. Its relative proximity to the Western Front also put it in range of the RAF's Handley Page bombers, though their fighter-plane escorts could not accompany them so far. The bombers could fly for eight hours and carry 2,000 pounds of bombs each. If the RAF commanders knew that "more damage was caused to Germany industry by air raid alarms driving workers from factories than the bombs themselves" (Ledwidge 48), they also knew that workers and civilians were being killed in large numbers as the bombing raids escalated in tonnage and frequency. Eddie Rickenbacker recalls the exclamation of his flying mate, Jimmy Meissner, upon hearing of the latest Allied bombing raid: "Gee Whiz! I hope they didn't kill my aunt! She lives in Cologne!" (Rickenbacker 292).

On May 30, 1918, eighteen women and children were trampled to death following an air-raid alarm in Mannheim: "The streets were crowded when the alarm was given and a wild rush for shelter ensued. It developed later that the warning signals were caused by the sighting of a squadron of German aviators returning to their base near Mannheim" ("18 Die in German Panic," NYT, May 31, 1918). An article on July 2, 1918 (just as Faulkner's RAF service was beginning), reported on the mass exodus from the Rhine towns being bombed by the RAF:

German families arriving at Basle and Kreuzlingin make no attempt to conceal their indignation against the German Government for not trying to prevent aerial reprisals, which seem to strike the German people harder than any other military, naval, or diplomatic weapon. An aged Hungarian diplomat living in retirement here publicly stated recently that the enemy was striking at the heart of Germany on the Rhine, and that 10,000 bombing airplanes would end the war sooner than a million extra American troops. ("Mannheim Terrified by One of the Worst Raids; Many Killed; Germans Fleeing Rhine Towns," NYT, July 2, 1918)

Newspaper articles on the Mannheim bombing raids ran throughout the war, becoming more frequent during Faulkner's time in the RAF (July-December 1918).

"Turnabout"

In Faulkner's story "Turnabout," published in *The Saturday Evening Post* on March 5, 1932, American Air Service pilots, Captain Bogard and bombardier Lieutenant McGinnis, fly a Handley Page bomber deep into Germany ("'Flying all night. That must have been to Berlin'" ["Turnabout" 499]), drop their bombs, and fight their way back to the French channel base with a young British sailor aboard as a passenger, observer, and gunner in the forward cockpit. The story opens with a description of Bogard's uniform, whose various elements—breeches, tunic, puttees, shoes, and ordnance belt

> did not match either of them, and the pilot's wings on his breast were just wings. But the ribbon beneath them was a good ribbon, and the insigne on his shoulders were the twin bars of a captain. He was not tall. His face was thin, a little aquiline; the eyes intelligent and a little tired. He was past twenty-five; looking at him, one thought, not Phi Beta Kappa exactly, but Skull and Bones perhaps, or possibly a Rhodes scholarship. ("Turnabout" 475)

He was not tall. His face was thin, a little aquiline; the eyes intelligent and a little tired. Michel Gresset would gloss the passage thus: "This 'objective correlative' of the ideal self, especially if it is related to the problem of Faulkner's small stature, is no doubt what Roland Barthes would have called a 'biographeme'—a private inscription (not a 'reflection') hidden within the fabric of the work" (Gresset, *Fascination* 4). In this story, an "instant" ("Turnabout" 495) is sufficient for hyperalert, status-conscious men to size each other up on the basis of their respective "insigne" of military rank and personal style, in keeping with the First World War tradition in which pilot-officer uniforms in all the major national services were always individually stylized and never in fact *uniform*.[4]

Ronnie, the young torpedo boat Captain, "glanced briefly at Bogard and then away. But in that instant Bogard caught something in the look, something strange—a flicker, a kind of covert and curious respect, something like a boy of fifteen looking at a circus trapezist" ("Turnabout" 495). Bogard, in turn, cannot help but admire Claude Hope's "blond head" and "that unmistakable and rakish swagger which no other people can ever approach or imitate, the cap of a Royal Naval Officer" ("Turnabout" 475). Later he notices Claude's "Soiled silk muffler, embroidered with a club insignia which Bogard recognized to have come from a famous preparatory school" ("Turnabout" 481). Their magnetic bond, as psychoanalysis would say, is "highly cathected," their mutual regard reinforced by overdetermined and pre-existing charges of social value and military prestige.

Much of the key airplane and battle imagery of Faulkner's story seems inspired by a fictional bombing raid on Mannheim that appears in Bellah's *Gods of*

Yesterday (1928), a book of linked stories based on Bellah's wartime experience as an RAF pilot. Bellah's story "Blood," as we noted in the previous chapter, about twin brothers—German fighter pilots one of whom dies in combat—was a template for Faulkner's conception of the RAF Sartoris twins in *Flags in the Dust*. Here is Bellah's impression of the Handley Page bombers warming up in the pitch darkness **"AT 2:42 A.M."** (the story's title) before their mission to "bomb Mannheim" (Bellah 61):

> Twelve feet over his head, a four-bladed propeller grinned ghoulishly as the light glinted upon the boltheads of its boss. Complacent monster, biding its time, waiting quietly while the frozen pygmies around its colossal wheels pumped a petrol soul into it, pounded its metallic body into trim …. Five huge moths, with wings still folded in their cocoons, waiting to go out and lay their eggs …. until presently the darkness trembled before one's eyes and light flashes from the exhaust pipes winked like tiny yellow pennants, frayed at the ends …. The noise from the simmering engines blasted all thought of speech …. (Bellah, *Gods* 67)

The bombers take off and fly to their objective as automatons, "pygmy" pilots and crew "dragged along," as Adorno might put it, as mere "appendages" (Adorno, *Minima* 15) of the gigantic apparatus in this new warfare of moral abstraction and disorienting remoteness:

> The engines whined quickly on a rising note until they reached their full pitch—a tremendous screaming monotone that thrust once fiercely into ear drums and stayed with such insistence that presently it was as if there was no sound …. Cavalry charging in a treadmill …. From take-off to landing—nothing to see but the instruments or perhaps a river glint in the darkness below …. Fighting? Humph! It was all worked out beforehand. Six little glass dials did the whole thing. Stupid. (Bellah, *Gods* 81)

Faulkner's story approaches the dwarfing magnitude and intimidating power of the Handley Page bombers through the focalized innocence of Claude Hope, "possibly eighteen" ("Turnabout" 475), who will be ascending in an airplane for the first time. The machines are heard before they are seen. Then, in the early-morning darkness, they are grasped only in profile, alien things never fully apprehended:

> When they emerged from the mess, the sound of the engines was quite loud— an idling thunder. In alignment along the invisible tarmac was a vague rank of short banks of flickering blue-green fire suspended apparently in mid-air …. They recrossed the aerodrome, approaching the muttering banks of flame. When they drew near, the guest began to discern the shape, the outlines, of the Handley-Page. It looked like a Pullman coach run upslanted aground into the skeleton of the first floor of an incomplete skyscraper. The guest looked at it quietly. ("Turnabout" 485–7)[5]

The guest looked at it quietly. In an exchange of position, the first "turnabout" of the story, Bogard experiences Hope's uncanny torpedo boat—"the long, narrow, still, vicious shape" of it, with "a machine gun swiveled at the stern" and "its single empty forward-staring eye" ("Turnabout" 493), in the same way:

> and he thought quietly: "It's steel. It's made of steel." And his face was quite sober, quite thoughtful, and he drew his trench coat about him and buttoned it, as though he were getting cold. ("Turnabout" 493)

Thus the chilling effect of these loud, futuristic machines of modern war whose bombs and torpedoes are loosed at the signal of a "right hand lifted, waiting to drop" just at the moment when the target "swings into the sights" ("Turnabout" 489):

> He dropped his hand; above the noise of the engines he seemed to hear the click and whistle of the released bombs as the machine, freed of the weight, shot zooming in a long upward bounce that carried it for an instant out of the [search] light. ("Turnabout" 489)

The critical event in the first aerial raid of the story is the release of a bomb that becomes entangled in the airplane's undercarriage. Only the boy in the forward observer's seat, from which the lower wing of the gigantic biplane is visible, can see what has happened. The scene has all the fascination and overdetermined portent of a dream:

> And even when the searchlights found them and Bogard signaled to the other machines and dived, the two engines snarling full speed into and through the bursting shells, he could see the boy's face in the searchlight's glare, leaned far overside, coming sharply out as a spotlighted face on a stage, with an expression upon it of child-like interest and delight [....] the English boy leaning far over the side, looking back and down past the right wing [....] where the searchlights probed and sabered. ("Turnabout" 489–90)

When Hope crawls through the channel of the fuselage to the pilots' cockpit in order to tell them about the stranded bomb, McGinnis, the bombardier, confronts him:

> "Get back!" he shouted. The other was almost out; they squatted so, face to face like two dogs, shouting at one another above the noise of the still-unthrottled engines on either side of the fabric walls. The English boy's voice was thin and high.
> "Bomb!" he shrieked. ("Turnabout" 490)

Hope misunderstands McGinnis's explanation, "Yes! Yes! All right. Back to your gun, damn you!," so he returns to his position, "looking backward and downward past the right wing ..... his face rapt, with utter and childlike interest" ("Turnabout" 491–2). The plane eventually lands without incident in a case of freakish good luck misrecognized by Hope as the pilots' "Skill. Marvelous. Oh, I say, I shan't forget it" ("Turnabout" 492): "The bomb, suspended by its tail, hung straight down like a plumb bob beside the right wheel, its tip just touching the sand. And parallel with the wheel track was the long delicate line in the sand where its ultimate tip had dragged" ("Turnabout" 492).

This episode of the "unreleased" bomb seems a direct revision of an event recounted in a book from which Faulkner also learned a great deal, Carroll Dana Winslow's *With the French Flying Corps* (London: Constable & Company Ltd., 1917):

> Another case of desperate courage that attracted widespread comment occurred about the same time. This also related to a bomber who had been over the German trenches. The pilot was about to spiral down for the landing, when his passenger looked out to see if everything was in good order. To his horror, he noticed that two of the bombs were still unreleased, having become caught on the chassis or running-gear of the machine. If they landed in this condition, there was every likelihood that there would be nothing to mark their landing-place but a deep crater in the ground. The two men were desperate. To climb down and unhook the bombs seemed impossible. No one had ever been known to do it. It was like clambering up to the main truck of a sailing vessel in the teeth of a hurricane. It was the only alternative left to them. The passenger mustered up his courage and climbed out on the wing and then down on the running-gear. Holding on with only one hand, he leaned down and carefully loosed the bombs with the other. It was a splendid exhibition of nerve and courage, and it saved the lives of both men. (Winslow 164–6)[6]

Faulkner's "Death Drag" and "Honor" feature intrepid ex-military pilots and wing walkers in the Winslow mold, but in "Turnabout"'s story of bombs released and unreleased, of bombs exploded and unexploded, of right hands that drop and that seem "would never drop" (182) upon their targets in the gunsights, "it is as if," in Donald Kartiganer's memorable formulation, "Faulkner were holding back the war, holding back history, holding back the murder" (Kartiganer, "'So I'" 642)—trying, and failing, to hold it all back.

When Claude Hope and his torpedo boat crew are later killed in action, Bogard's Handley Page conducts a bombing raid in rage and reprisal, as much against the German enemy as (symbolically) against Hope's and Ronnie's superior officers who had ordered their suicidal mission. An official bulletin gives the account:

> For extraordinary valor over and beyond the routine of duty, Captain H. S. Bogard, with his crew, composed of Second Lieutenant Darrel McGinnis and Aviation Gunners Watts and Harper, on a daylight raid and without scout protection, destroyed with bombs an ammunition depot several miles behind the enemy's lines. From here, beset by enemy aircraft in superior numbers, these men proceeded with what bombs remained to the enemy's corps headquarters at Blank and partially demolished this château, and then returned safely without loss of a man.

And regarding which exploit, it might have added, had it failed and had Captain Bogard come out of it alive, he would have been immediately and thoroughly court-martialed. ("Turnabout" 509)

This last formulation bears the unmistakable signature of Eddie Rickenbacker's tribute to legendary ace Frank Luke (May 19, 1897–September 29, 1918) of the United States Army Air Service (for whom Bogard also flies), the apotheosis of reckless valor in the American mode: "if Luke ever did come back we would court-martial him first and then recommend him for the legion of Honor! In a word, Luke mingled with his disdain for bullets a very similar distaste for the orders of his superior officers" (Rickenbacker 280).[7]

Hostility to superior officers and military war managers for the waste of their soldiers' lives is one of Faulkner's major themes (above all in *A Fable*), as is no more clear than in the story's conclusion:

Carrying his remaining two bombs, he had dived the Handley-Page at the château where the generals sat at lunch, until McGinnis, at the toggles below him, began to shout at him, before he ever signaled. He didn't signal until he could discern separately the slate tiles of the roof. Then his hand dropped and he zoomed, and he held the aeroplane so, in its wild snarl, his lips parted, his breath hissing,

Figure 4.2 Lt. Frank Luke standing by downed aircraft.

thinking: "God! God! If they were all there—all the generals, the admirals, the presidents and the kings—theirs, ours—all of them." ("Turnabout" 488)[8]

Here Captain Bogard shares a thought-crime with Claude Hope, who fires a "brief staccato burst" to test the Lewis machine gun he is asked to man in the Handley Page's forward cockpit:

> "It's quite all right," the English boy's voice said. "I pointed it west before I let it off. Nothing back there but Marine office and your brigade headquarters." ("Turnabout" 488)

In speaking of "Faulkner's staunch antimilitarist position" (152) in *A Fable*, George Mariani asks, "is Faulkner inciting soldiers to threaten their commanders with cannons, tanks, and grenades? .... Faulkner's address to soldiers could be read as a call to fight against the military from within and therefore by holding fast to the courage and determination we usually associate with the figure of the soldier" (153). Within the fuller history and genealogy of Faulkner's "address to soldiers" lies a pattern of extreme fratricidal and parricidal violence, the ultimate meaning, perhaps, of the "turnabout" announced in the story's title. In *Soldiers' Pay* (1926) Lieutenant Richard Powers is killed by a young soldier, Dewey Burney, who believes he has seen a cloud of poison gas forming itself in the dawn mist. Someone "screams Gas" and panic spreads throughout the disintegrating platoon as the officers attempt to restore discipline and order. "'You got us killed,' he shrieked, shooting the officer in the face at point-blank range" (SP 142). (I discuss this scene and the novel in Chapter 6.) In Faulkner's short story, "Victory" (1931), Private Gray, having been insulted by his senior officer, now encounters him alone in the trenches:

> Gray's bayonet goes into his throat. The sergeant-major is a big man. He falls backward, holding the rifle barrel with both hands against his throat, this teeth glaring, pulling Gray with him. Gray clings to the rifle. He tries to shake the speared body on the bayonet as he would shake a rat on an umbrella rib. He frees the bayonet. The sergeant-major falls. Gray reverses the rifle and hammers its butt into the sergeant-major's face, but the trench floor is too soft to supply any resistance. He glares about. (446)

A Fable ends with a gesture (via Humphrey Cobb's *Paths of Glory* [1935] and Sigfried Sassoon's George Sherston memoirs [1930, 1936]) of resolute insubordination and rage, one that anticipates the protests to be mounted by the Vietnam Veterans Against the War in April 1971: "'Listen to me too, Marshal! This is yours: take it!' and snatched, ripped from his filthy jacket the medal which was the talisman of his sanctuary and swung his arm up and back to throw it'" (FA 1071).

A premonition of this Vietnam protest might be felt in Faulkner's address to the Vietnam-bound cadets at West Point in April, 1962, one of whom asked Faulkner about the ending of the story they were reading in Captain James R. Kintz's class on

"The Evolution of American Ideals as Reflected in American Literature." Clearly the cadets seemed troubled by it. Faulkner answered them thus:

> I think that when he dove his bomber down on the roofs of that chateau, it was a gesture of revolt against all the brassbound stupidity of the generals and admirals that sit safe in the dugouts and tell the young men to go there and do that. That that was something that probably every soldier in war has felt. They have cursed the whole lot of them—that my brother is the man I am trying to kill. But you people safe at home—curse all of them. I am sure every soldier has felt that. (Fant 102)

This is also a remarkable thing to say when you are the personal guest of Major General William C. Westmoreland, whose "brassbound stupidity" in Vietnam would soon become notorious.[9]

The Bombing Air Force

Stories about British and, by the fall of 1918, American bombing raids on German munitions factories appeared regularly in the newspapers. The American raids, coordinated with the RAF and the French air force, were designed and led by General William "Billy" Mitchell, commander of the American squadrons.

> On October 10, to cover American crossings of the Meuse, two formations of 322 and 338 planes dropped a total of 81 tons of bombs on enemy munition dumps and troop concentrations in a single day. No such terrific blow had ever been dealt from the air before, and American forces not only crossed the river but also passed the barrier of the Argonne Forest. (Montross 752)

On the Western Front the RAF's "ground support for the other services" (O x–xi) also included aerial observation, photography, artillery registration, strafing, and trench bombing. During the Allied 100 Days Offensive, RAF and American airplanes bombed roads, railways, and retreating German troop columns. One of the most vivid descriptions of these operations as conducted by an RAF Camel squadron in the spring and summer of 1918 appears in the novel by V. M. Yeates that Faulkner admired so much, *Winged Victory*. The Sopwith Camel was a formidable fighter plane, but it was also a devastating strafing and bombing machine. On such missions it carried four 20-lb high-explosive Cooper Bombs.

As an "airborne artillery arm" (Montross 752) and long-range strategic bombing service, the RAF was hardly what Faulkner had in mind as a boyish dreamer about the legendary pilots of the RFC and

> the days of individual combat. The great fliers would roam over the lines like knights of old, flinging their gauntlets in the face of some specific enemy ace,

daring him to do battle to the death. The newspapers made much of these duels in the air. They made heady reading for adolescent boys, stirring many of us to dream of seeking glory in the cockpits of fighting planes. (Smith 13)

From 1914 to 1917, as we recall, William Faulkner was among these adolescent boys, "waiting, biding," as he remembered in 1954, "until I would be old enough or free enough or anyway could get to France and become glorious and beribboned too" (Faulkner, Foreword x).

The Royal Flying Corps was founded in May 1912 as the army's air wing in preparation for a future European war. The "kill-or-be-killed imperative" of the "total war" that broke out in August 1914 "vastly accelerated the development of aircraft technology, tactics, and operational thinking. Aircraft were a relatively rare sight over the battlefields of 1914. By 1918, aircraft were organized by major powers into vast air forces" (Ledwidge 23). The Royal Air Force that Faulkner joined in June 1918 had "a strength by the end of the war of 290,000 (including reserves) men and women, and 22,000 aircraft" (Ledwidge 39)—in England, France, and Canada. In the gigantic struggle of masses and matèriel, the air services were part of a modern war machine of vast scale. Even if you might think of yourself as part of a small air-force elite (Fernando Esposito notes that Italy "ended the war with 2,000 airmen and a ground army of 3,500,000") (Esposito 178), you were valuable to the military not so much as an individual personality but as an "integer," to use a term to which Faulkner would give a strong political charge in the 1950s.[10] As an anonymous American pilot put in a letter from Avord to his parents back home, "I'm where individuality does n't count much—I'm just an atom in this great war, but working for a cause we '_' die for" (Hall and Nordhoff vol. 1, 50).

Faulkner's first sense of the war's scale came to him in New Haven when he arrived there in the spring of 1918. Working as an accountant at the Winchester Repeating Arms plant, he knew that the war would soon demand much more of him. On May 27 he writes to his mother, "the bill has gone through drafting me when I become of age [i.e., 21 years old] and ... I had much rather beat them to it and enlist" (TH 58).[11] But not with the Americans: "there is no thing to be had in the U.S. Army now," he writes on June 7, "except a good job stopping boche bullets as a private" (TH 63). The English Army is the better alternative as its officers are more experienced while "the chances of advancement ... are very good; I'll perhaps be a major at the end of a year's service. I've thought about it constantly .... At the rate I am living now, I'll never be able to make anything of myself, but with this business I will be fixed up after the war is over" (TH 63–4). British Lieutenant Todd, "who was wounded at Vimy Ridge last year" (TH 56), has explained the situation to him over dinner:

> The English are trying to get officers now—they have two million unofficial reserve troops in house now, which they cant use at all. I can enlist as a second year Yale man, he will recommend me for a commission at once. It's the chance I've been waiting for. Every thing will be my way, I can almost have my pick of anything, I'll be in at the wind up of the show .... I shall probably

have to enlist in the line and take my chances of promotion, which I'd rather do than get in the U.S. Army and be sent into action under an inexperienced officer. The English officers are the best yet, take better care of their men and weigh all chances for them. So I shall learn war in the best of schools, where the elimination of risk is taught above every thing. So I think I shall enlist to-morrow. (TH 63)

One might be impressed by the lucid manner in which the twenty-year-old weighs the prospect of an officer's commission in the British Army, even as his excitement at making the leap from clerk to gentleman-officer ("I'll perhaps be a major at the end of a year's service") is more than a little breathless. "That move," writes Samuel Hynes of the military-age male civilian longing for transcendence in this period, "will be more than a change in the work he does; it will be a change of class" (H 13).[12]

But Faulkner's letter also bears the nervous trace of a deeper intimation than he would express to his worried mother of just what he may be signing himself up for. This was late in the war, he had seen the enormous scale of industrial war production first-hand at the Winchester munitions factory, had encountered wounded soldiers on the streets of New York and New Haven, and had met many veterans of the Western Front (TH 45–6, 48, 51, 54, 56). He knew, as the war of attrition continued to "grind on like a great iron machine, toward its necessary end" (H 246), that British officers had good jobs stopping boche bullets, or being obliterated by H.E. shells, too. As Robert Graves recalls in *Good-bye to All That* (1929):

At least one in three of my generation at school was killed. This was because they all took commissions as soon as they could, most of them in the infantry and flying corps. The average life of the infantry subaltern on the western front was, at some stages of the war, only about three months; that is to say that at the end of three months he was either wounded or killed. The proportions worked out at about four wounded to every one killed. Of the four one was wounded seriously and the remaining three more or less lightly. The three lightly wounded returned to the front after a few weeks or months of absence and were again subject to the same odds. The flying casualties were even higher. Since the war lasted for four and a half years, it is easy to see why the mortality was so high among my contemporaries, and why most of the survivors, if not permanently disabled, were wounded at least two or three times .... The few old hands who went through the last fight infect the new men with pessimism; they don't believe in the war, they don't believe in the staff. (Graves 61–2, 107)[13]

Within a few days, however, the plan to join the British Army evolved quickly when Faulkner met some Canadian RAF pilots at Yale who urged him and Phil Stone (who was also contemplating military enlistment) (Snell 102–9), "to pose as Canadians" (B 205–206). With "letters of reference from the British officers in New Haven," and one, fictionally forged, from "the Reverend Mr. Edward Twimberly-Thorndyke" whom Faulkner and Stone had made up (B 206), Faulkner joined the RAF at its New

York recruitment office in June, 1918, as a cadet pilot in training (Millgate, "William Faulkner: Cadet" 120).

The story, still in circulation, that Faulkner had already been rejected by the Aviation Section of the American Army's Signal Corps because he was too short, is false (Blotner, *Faulkner* one vol. ed. 60, Williamson 176): "Army Air Service records contain no evidence that Faulkner ever tried to enlist, nor do they specify any height and weight requirements" (Kartiganer 629). Besides, it should be clear from Blotner's account that the story Faulkner told of his "too-short" rejection was yet another of his "tall" tales for "impressing some woman" (*Mosquitoes* 460):

> He had heard about a desperate expedient for situations such as his and he tried it. He stuffed himself with all the bananas he could hold and drank all the water he could swallow, he said, and presented himself at the recruiting station. He was rejected as under regulation weight and height .... he talked about it in Clarksdale to Eula Dorothy Wilcox, a girl he had met there at a house party. (B 196)

In Oxford, just before leaving for the north, he was making an obviously comical, though nervous and typically deadpan, excuse for not being in the military already.[14]

On the Yale campus and around the town of New Haven, Faulkner felt that he could get away with just about anything if he could continue to keep a straight face. When the critical moment arrived, he was confident he could present himself to the RAF as a Canadian national and "second year Yale man" (TH 63) eager for combat. He would continue to pass as a Yale man in the RAF. One of Faulkner's contemporaries at the School of Military Aeronautics in Toronto, interviewed by Michael Millgate in 1966, recalls, "I always had the idea that he had been a student at Yale" (Millgate, "Faulkner in Toronto" 199).

Faulkner's confidence that he could "pass" into the RAF as an Ivy Leaguer also reflected the fluid and receptive atmosphere of the moment. Stone recalled in 1963,

> "If you wanted to volunteer they promised to get you to the front in thirty days and no questions asked. All you had to do was to say you were Canadian." Stone and Faulkner practiced Canadian English for "more than a month," but because they never mastered "rolling their 'r'"s, their accent was "too much even for a Canadian recruiting officer who was all too ready to believe anything you told him—so [they] decided to be Englishmen." (Snell 105)[15]

Canadian versus British identity was not a clear or especially meaningful distinction for the RAF. "The term 'Canadian National' had no legal status until legislation of 1921 and prior to that date persons living in Canada and exercising the rights of citizenship were, in law, British subjects, whether native-born or naturalized" (Wise xiv). Besides, "the enlistment of American citizens in the Canadian and imperial forces had been going on since the beginning of the war" (Wise 88), and once the RAF opened an office on Fifth Avenue in New York City (rent-free, in space owned by the Benson and Hedges Tobacco Company) (Hunt 105), the recruitment of Americans took place in plain sight, though cautiously: "Ostensibly seeking British subjects, [Brigadier-General] Hoare [who was in charge of the operation] was in fact recruiting American citizens under cover of the British Mission, and with the connivance of American and British authorities" (Wise 90).

Samuel Hynes explains why the RAF was so attractive to American volunteers:

Even after the United States became a belligerent, American volunteers continued to head for the British and French flying services rather than their own (all the eager young men... joined either the British or the French flying service *after the* American declaration of war). If you were eager to fly in combat, those forces were already doing it and had been for more than two years. Their flight schools were well established and were turning out pilots in substantial numbers ... the belated U.S. Air Service had little to offer applicants .... there was not yet an actual working system turning out pilots. Belatedness would always be part of the American story of the war .... Even if you wanted to join the Air Service, it wasn't at all clear, in those early months, how you did it. What were the rules and qualifications? To the candidates, they seemed to vary from place to place and day to day. (H 38–40)

This culture of free-for-all and impersonation, in which "cheating in the cause of flying were in itself heroic" (H 41), was well established when Faulkner, with Stone's and the Reverend Mr. Edward Twimberly-Thorndyke's help, jumped into it with full-body commitment. Hynes mentions the case of James Norman Hall, who "lied his way into the British army at the war's beginning, presenting himself as a Canadian citizen when in fact he was an American" (H 41–2); of John Grider (Faulkner lionizes him in "Mac Grider's Son"), who "claimed a college education he didn't have, and nobody noticed" (H 42); and Quentin Roosevelt who, with "his weak eyes and bad back (bad enough that he couldn't take part in athletics at Harvard") ... seemed an unlikely candidate for any fighting role, yet he, too, was commissioned—as a first lieutenant in the U.S. Air Service" (H 42) before he volunteered to fly with the French. Dead at twenty years old, like Quentin Compson.

In presenting himself at the RAF offices in New York, Faulkner must have seemed nearly an ideal recruit, as S. F. Wise, drawing on contemporary advertisements, describes him in the official history of the Royal Air Force Canada. He should be "between eighteen and twenty-five years of age, have matriculated from high school, and have spent a couple of years at university. He should be well grounded in algebra and geometry, be able to 'speak the King's English,' and bear the 'ear-marks of a gentleman.' Above all, he should be 'very keen to join the Royal Flying Corps'" (Wise 87). "The escalating demands of the war" (Hunt 101), though, combined with declining enlistments, helped to lower admission standards in 1918: "cadets did not need a university education, but merely 'a fair education.' Later press releases changed this to 'ordinary intelligence and education'" (Hunt 103). "The gigantic struggle that went on overseas" was a "heavy drain" on the RAF's pilot reservoir and the demand for pilots in 1918 "was cruelly urgent" (Ellis 130, 123).

Once the recruits were accepted by the RAF, however, the "weeding process" was "relentless" (Hynes 48). Washing out meant you would "immediately thereupon become liable to military service with the Canadian Expeditionary Force" (qtd. in Wise 109). The cadet's, or even the commissioned pilot's, fear that he could be sent to the Western Front as an infantry soldier, there to be shelled and machine-gunned in muddy, rat-infested trenches, is reflected in the literature of the period, as in, for example, Yeates' *Winged Victory*, in which Camel pilot Tom Cundall, survivor of many careless accidents, is also accused by his commander, the Major, of failing to demonstrate a sufficiently bloodthirsty determination to kill the enemy: "Could he send him back to the infantry in disgrace?" (Y 405).

He should "be able to 'speak the King's English,' and bear the 'ear-marks of a gentleman'." The role Faulkner needed to perform was already a kind of parody, as the institution itself well knew. He was especially ready to throw himself into it, for performing as an officer-pilot in embryo would serve not only the Allied cause but his purpose in becoming the man he wanted to be, respected and admired (especially by Estelle and her father and by his own father, mother, and brothers), a man capable, as he would put it in "Carcassonne," of doing "*something bold and tragical and austere*" (899) in the public eye. All he needed were the right chances to earn the pilot officer's wings and uniform. The RAF Canada was not the French Foreign Legion which had "always welcomed *les étrangers*, no questions asked; criminals, fugitives, and vagabonds could submerge their old selves in the anonymity of the Legion—all you had to do was remember the alias you made up" (H 10).[16] The flying corps, rather, was "an occupation for a gentleman .... the brightest, nerviest, most efficient of our youth—what might be called the flower of our chivalry" (H 19), like those "dashing" Americans who, in *Flying for France* (McConnell), and dying for France, became legendary founders of the air war myth: Raoul Lufbery, Victor Chapman, Norman Prince, Kiffin Rockwell, James McConnell, Quentin Roosevelt, Ivy League men, knights of the air. By the spring of 1918 Faulkner had been hearing the siren call of this "cavalry of the clouds" (flyers and angels both) for months and years, and he was stepping into the line now to join them. Just in time: the Governor General of Canada closed down the RAF recruiting office at the end of July (Hunt 107).[17]

After a brief trip home to Oxford, Faulkner arrived in Toronto for training on July 9th. "This place is about twice as big as Memphis" (TH 80) is the first thing he notes about this Canadian city of close to 500,000 people. Wycliffe College, where he lodges, and the University of Toronto campus generally, remind him of Yale University. Quentin's and Shreve's Harvard and the Cambridge surround in *The Sound and the Fury* are thus also a layered imaginary geography shaped by Faulkner's memory of New Haven and Toronto (with strong traces of Ole Miss too) in this period.

Daily routine in the RAF included physical conditioning, military drill, and menial work in the barracks. But the main "work here is very interesting," Faulkner writes on September 28. "I wish they allowed us to go into detail about it. We have all sorts of engines, map reading, wireless, artillery observation" (TH 109). Ground school's "comprehensive curriculum" also covered "the theory of flight, meteorology, astronomy ... rigging ... instruments, bombs, and machine guns" (Hunt 112).

They Whirled Me by Machinery

Faulkner is given a test on his first day in the service, as he tells his "Mother and Dad" on July 9, in a letter forthright in describing a scene of corporeal humiliation in which he also manages to discover in himself a filament of compensatory pride and integrity:

> I passed my examination today and I would not go through with what I have today for all the democracy that could be produced. It was about ten times as bad as the one in New York .... I got the chair. My being a pilot or a gunner-observer depended on this, for Col. Wellesley had recommended me for a commission.
>
> They put me in the chair and had me focus my eyes on a bulls eye about 15 yards off, I closed my eyes and they whirled me by machinery. Then I had to focus on the bulls-eye again, which had failed to stop when I did, and they timed me to see how long it took me to re-focus. Then they whirled me the other way. Same thing. Next they whirled me so fast that I had to hold in, stopped me and put my finger—eyes still closed—on a mark, made me move it and replace it. Of course, I felt as though I were still whirling. Then I had to lean forward with my head touching my knees. This gave the sensation of the chair revolving at a 45 degree angle. Stopped me, then the other directions.
>
> They kept this up for about 30 minutes and I was beginning to fear that I wouldn't faint, being terribly sick, when the doctor said—all right. You can dress now. (TH 74)

My being a pilot or a gunner-observer depended on this. Faulkner claims to have passed the test (the purpose of which will be explained in the following chapter), but his account comes across as somewhat "groggy" in itself: "There were three poor devils who failed on the chair test, so I was the only pilot to qualify. Three observers did, however. They are not given the chair test. I am still groggy from it, but the next time I get to see you I shall be a lieutenant-pilot" (TH 74). What has actually happened and what is he saying?

The term "observer" can mean being a pilot of an observation aircraft or being the passenger—gunner, photographer, bomb thrower/dropper, wireless operator—in the two-seat biplane, typically the Royal Aircraft Factory B.E.2 or R.E.8.

In the culture of all the major flying services—in England, France, Germany, Italy, the United States—"the highest rating was pursuit, followed by bomber, observation, and finally Corps d'Arme—the aerial direction of artillery fire, reconnaissance, and liaison flying under the control of ground forces. Almost without exception cadets aspired to a pursuit rating" (Smith 62). In effect, however, "there were two classes of military pilots: the *chasse* pilots, and all the rest, who flew the observation, bombing, and artillery-spotting planes" (H 101). To the Americans especially, the French resonance of the word *chasse* was an important element of the mystique. As American volunteer Carroll Dana Winslow recalls of getting his wings in the French Flying Service, "I was a *pilote aviateur*, a full-fledged member of the aerial light cavalry of France" (Winslow 74).

Figure 4.3 A Royal Aircraft Factory B.E. 2. Aircraft.

For Faulkner's Julian Lowe, eternal cadet, or what "the French so beautifully call an aspiring aviator" (SP 3) ("un aviateur en herbe"), failure to become an aerial cavalier is a "smoldering" humiliation: "they had stopped the war on him" before he could get his wings. "So he sat in a smoldering of disgusted sorrow ... spinning on his thumb his hat with its accursed white band," the cadet's conspicuous mark of shame (SP 3).

Cadets are the lowest of the low in the RAF, "the mulattoes of the army" in John McGavock Grider's (or more likely his ghost writer Elliott White Spring's) nasty phrase in *War Birds: Diary of an Unknown Aviator*. "They get the privileges of neither enlisted men nor officers and get all the trouble coming to both" (35). At the base of the photo below, Faulkner's penning of "Royal Flying Corps" is a compensation, an early sign that, in mirroring himself to the civilian world, he is choosing history, myth, and metaphor over reality.

Faulkner may or may not have passed the test to train as a pilot. Either way, very likely, he would have been assigned to the "observer" rather than the "pursuit" class of training. Such an assignment would have reflected not so much the RAF's valuation of Faulkner's potential as a pilot as its need "to replace the heavy losses suffered during the Battle of the Somme and to keep pace with the rapid development of aerial operations on the Western Front as a whole" (Millgate, "William Faulkner, Cadet" 117). As Faulkner noted on his first day in the service, "They are sending bunches of flyers over seas constantly from here" (July 9, 1918, TH 81), flyers (whether pilots or passenger/observers) to be deployed in bombing, escort, reconnaissance, photography, artillery registration, and strafing operations.[18]

Figure 4.4 William Faulkner, Cadet.

Naturally, the distinction between the singular pursuit pilot, in the romantic tradition of the RFC and the Lafayette Escadrille, and all the rest, continued to be meaningful and, in historical retrospect, imperishable, as in Faulkner's letter to his mother on August 22, 1918, in which he notes, "My squadron commander is an observer, the wing commander, however, is a pilot, an ace who has nine Huns officially, Major Samson" (TH 94). For someone who has had RFC glory on his mind, being assigned to the "observer" class would have been a humiliation, as it was, and remains, for Faulkner's "Lowe, Julian number——, late a Flying Cadet, Umptieth Squadron, Air Service, known as 'One Wing' by the other embryonic aces of his flight, [who] regarded the world with a yellow and disgruntled eye" (SP 3). "Umptieth" and the indifferent term "Air Service" signify the institution's mass and the bland, functional anonymity to which Lowe has been consigned at the lower reaches of the hierarchy.

Samuel Hynes clarifies the "One Wing" reference further. "If being an observation pilot wasn't considered adventurous, being an observer was even less so" (H 181). He recounts an episode in which an observer, seeking to impress some young women on a date, is asked

> to be taken up in his airplane. Then he opens his coat, and one of the girls sees that the flying insignia on his chest has only one wing on it, not the two wings that a pilot would wear. "Wild eyed and with marked disdain, she exclaimed sneeringly to the others, 'Oh, he's only an observer! A half aviator!'" Half an aviator, half a man. (H 181–2)

As Captain Alan Bott remembers too in his memoir, *Cavalry of the Clouds* (1918), the pursuit pilots get the glory and the girls, "whereas I am but an observer—that is to say, an R.F.C. doormat" (230).

"All the Dead Pilots"

In Faulkner's "All the Dead Pilots," however, even the observer can win the erotic competition with a Camel pilot if the latter is named Johnny Sartoris. Captain Spoomer, Johnny Sartoris's rival in both the short story and the screenplay based upon it (along with Elliot Spring's/John Grider's *War Birds: Diary of an Unknown Aviator*), is a "one-wing" aviator despite his Mons Star, "two ribbons," and D.S.O. In bed with Antoinette, the woman Sartoris loves, Spoomer had left his uniform, as Sartoris discovers it, on a chair outside the bedroom. "Upon it lay a pair of slacks, neatly folded, a tunic with an observer's wing and two ribbons, an ordnance belt" ("All the Dead Pilots" 524). After a turbulent and absurd series of plot turns, in which Sartoris steals Spoomer's clothes and dresses an unconscious ambulance driver in Spoomer's uniform, Spoomer is forced to wear Antoinette's clothes to return to the RAF base. "An ox cart turned onto the aerodrome and stopped, with, sitting on a wire cage containing chickens, Spoomer in a woman's skirt and a knitted shawl. The next day Spoomer returned to England. We learned that he was to be a temporary colonel at ground school" ("All the Dead Pilots" 527). Thus is Spoomer's humiliation transformed, with a little help from nepotism, into a ridiculous promotion to a rear area in this complex and overdetermined story about military ranks and roles.[19]

Sartoris' ostensible victory in the battle for pure RAF prestige, if not rank and medals, is reflected in his assignment to a Camel squadron in France. To him, however, this transfer is nothing but an extension of the bitter "joke" that his entire deployment has been from the outset ("Because the RFC had ceased to exist on April Fool's day," recalls Levine bitterly in *A Fable*, 747). So he understands his comical condition in conversation with the teller of the story:

> "The joke is," [Sartoris] said, "it's another Camel squadron. I have to laugh."
> "Laugh?" I said.
> "Oh, I can ride them. I can sit there with the gun out and keep the wings level now and then. But I can't fly Camels. You have to land a Camel by setting the air valve and flying it into the ground. Then you count ten, and if you have not crashed, you level off. And if you can get up and walk away, you have made a good landing. And if they can use the crate again, you are an ace. But that's not the joke."
> "What's not?"
> "The Camels. The joke is, this is a night-flying squadron …. That's why I have to laugh, see. I cant fly Camels in the daytime, even. And they don't know it." ("All the Dead Pilots" 528)

The comedy of "With Caution and Dispatch," the succeeding story in which Sartoris tries to fly across the Channel in the rain to his new squadron, only to crash blindly into the stacks and wires of a passing ship, is a continuation of the dark oneiric joke that leads inexorably to his death in France, as his brother Bayard remembers and mourns it in *Flags in the Dust* and "Ad Astra." "Johnny Sartoris, Camel pilot," represents, then (among many additional things), Faulkner's vexed attempt to work through and displace the taint of "cadet" and "observer status" in his aviation memory and consciousness, along with the fear that he would have been nothing but "cold meat" in any contest with Richthofen's Jagdgeschwader, "the Flying Circus." One might also discern "the return of the repressed," and the attempt to negate the shameful affect it continues to generate, in some of the biographical sketches of Faulkner that his publishers ceaselessly demanded of him, especially after the publication of *Sanctuary* in 1931 and for years afterwards. Such biographical notices are major sites of what Thomas McHaney has termed the "impersonations, imitations, fabrications, fictional personas, role-playing, and legends about himself that Faulkner employed in both life and art" (McHaney, "Faulkner and Autobiography" 163; see also James Watson, *William Faulkner: Self-Presentation and Performance*). Faulkner's "series of impersonations" includes, as Donald Kartiganer has noted,

> the English Dandy, the bohemian poet, the town bum, the Southern aristocrat, the ex-bootlegger and gun-runner, the romantic suitor, the cynical father of illegitimate children, and eventually the hard-working farmer who happened to do some writing on the side. But his greatest role, the one he played the longest and most insistently, and which represents his deepest personal involvement in the clash of Old South and modernist forces, is that of the World War I aviator. (Kartiganer, "'So I'" 627–8)

But this "World War I aviator" was, essentially, an "observer," as Faulkner was confessing.

One of the most vivid and telling of such miniature biographies appears in *Twentieth Century Authors: A Biographical Dictionary of Modern Literature*, edited by Stanley J. Kunitz and Howard Haycraft (New York: H. W. Wilson, 1942), in which the editors note, "Every living author in this volume who could be reached was invited to write his own sketch" (vi). The entry for FAULKNER, WILLIAM, includes the following:

> Biographers who say he got no nearer France than Toronto are mistaken. He was sent to France as an observer, had two planes shot down under him, was wounded in the second shooting, and did not return to Oxford until after the Armistice. (439)

In "William Faulkner: That Writin' Man of Oxford" (*Saturday Review of Literature*, 18, May 21, 1938), Anthony Buttitta tells another version of the story that may also reflect the career of James Gatz/Jay Gatsby:

> Two years later, he dropped out [of high school] to join the Canadian Flying Corps and was transferred to Oxford, England, where he was in training as a non-commissioned officer for more than a year. He spent his spare time taking courses at Oxford and reading in the University library …. He became a lieutenant in the British Royal Air Force, was sent to France as an observer, crashed twice and was once injured, and remained abroad until after the Armistice. Following his return from France, he enrolled officially in the University of Mississippi, and remained there from 1919 to 1921. (10–11)

These accounts of Faulkner's service history as an observer, including his crashes and injuries, possess a quality of realism and plausibility that weighs against the core disappointment (his own and the public's and possibly his publishers' too) that he was not a brave pursuit pilot in the war, let alone an "Ace" holding in his hand a "bag" of individual combat victories.

The atmosphere of deflation and disappointment associated with being an RAF observer is also evident in the story of David Levine in *A Fable* who finds himself immured in a

> squadron itself reduced to a handful of tyros who barely knew in which direction the front lay, under command of a man who had never been anything but a poor bloody observer to begin with and had even given that up now for a chessboard; they still sat there; he, and the other new men who had—must have—brought out from England with them the same gratitude and pride and thirst and hope. (FA 751)

The image of his "smoldering" sidcott is the novel's central emblem of a dream, and a life, consuming itself in fatal disappointment, and a direct link between Levine and the aptly named Lowe of *Soldiers' Pay*.

As Hynes has written, "Pilots who flew observation planes don't figure in the myth of the war much" (H 174), but it is also important to realize, as Bott, Winslow, and many others show in their richly detailed accounts, that "aerial observation [was] the main *raison d'etre* of flying at the front" (Major-General W. S. Brancker, Deputy Director-General of Military Aëronautics in the Royal Air Force, in the introduction to Bott vii). Nevertheless, observation crews got little public credit for their dangerous and valuable work, and their names seldom appear in the newspapers of the period except in long funereal lists.

New York Times, December 29, 1918:

AMERICAN FLIERS KILLED IN ACTION: War Department Gives Out List of 150 Who Met Death in 1918. TEN FROM NEW YORK CITY Quentin Roosevelt and Major Lufbery on the Roll of Those Who Gave Lives for Country. The List in Full.

As Tom Cundall bitterly reflects in Yeates' *Winged Victory,* "Bravery was nothing without publicity and popularity" (Y 175), rank, and medals.

In the most popular memoirs of the period, by such famous and decorated chasers as Billy Bishop, James McCudden, Mick Mannock, Eddie Rickenbacker, and Manfred von Richthofen, observation pilots and crew members play a central role in being the hunters' plentiful prey (prey that can bite back, too).[20] They are hunted, machine-gunned, and consumed in explosions of flaming gasoline with sickening regularity, as even their pursuers sometimes acknowledge. The observers' charred, smashed, and shot-up bodies and machines fill up the legendary aces' kill "bags" to the bursting.

Richthofen's memoir, along with his after-action reports discovered in the German archive by his first biographer, American Floyd Gibbons, offers a clear view of the slaughter of the observers over the Western Front, the gigantic primal scene in this aerial war of so-called "individual combat," "courage," and "sportsmanship" (Gibbons 4) into which "there came a refreshing gleam of the chivalry of old, when the pick of the flower of youth on both sides carried the conflict into the skies …. that Knighthood of the Blue" (Gibbons 5).[21] In one of his first kills, Richthofen came across "a Vickers two-seater" (more commonly called the F.E.2b)

which peacefully photographed the German artillery position. My friend, the photographer, had not the time to defend himself. He had to make haste to get down upon firm ground for his machine began to give suspicious indications of fire. When we airmen notice that phenomenon in an enemy plane, we say: "He stinks!" As it turned out it was really so. When the machine was coming to earth it burst into flames.

I felt some human pity for my opponent and had resolved not to cause him to fall down but merely to compel him to land. I did so particularly because I had the impression that my opponent was wounded for he did not fire a single shot. (Richthofen 59)

This expression of pity stands virtually alone in Richthofen's relentless chronicle of victories in which "single combat" means, essentially, being singled out by the Red Baron for slaughter from behind, typically because, as a novice, you were flying at the back of the squadron to follow, and cover, the leader's rear. Richthofen, it should also be noted, never claims that he was "flying alone" except in a very special sense. The Flying Circus was an "aggregation of gaily decorated Fokker triplanes and Albatross scouts, numbering anywhere from twenty to fifty planes, and flying in various formations under a central command. Richthofen had developed mass manoeuvres for the air, and the British had been forced once more to follow his lead" (Jonathan Reeves qtd. in Richthofen 130). As Richthofen's 49th "victory witness," Second Lieutenant W. N. Hamilton, recalls of the attack he survived, "I looked up and saw that Richthofen in his all-red plane had been cruising about two thousand feet above his circus, which incidentally was his usual position" (qtd. in Richthofen 185). One can read the Red Baron's combat reports in "Appendix 1: The Red Baron's Combat Reports and Interviews with Some of His Victims," published in Richthofen's *The Red Baron* (149–212). This first "kill" set the pattern for scores more to come: "(1st Victory, September 17, 1916): I singled out the last machine and fired several times at close range (ten meters). Suddenly the enemy propeller stood stock till. The machine went down gliding and I followed until I had killed the observer who had not stopped shooting until the last moment" (149).

Poor bloody observers indeed. Second Lieutenant Albert Woodbridge, observer in a plane piloted by Captain Donald Cunnell, recalled of their missions,

> It was all makeshift, but it was the best we had, and we had to "carry on." We were "cold meat," and most of us knew it.
>
> And our job was offensive patrolling—in other words, we were supposed to go out and light into any enemy planes we could find. We knew the Albatrosses and Halberstadts could fly rings around us and shoot hell out of us from that blind spot under our tails. Right you are, we were like butterflies sent out to insult eagles. (qtd. in Richthofen 191–2)[22]

As Allied aerial hunters with massive scores, Bishop, Mannock, McCudden, Guynemer, and Rickenbacker were certainly not outclassed by the Red Baron. Yeates gives an illuminating account of McCudden's tactics in *Winged Victory* when his protagonist, Tom Cundall, finds himself seated beside the great man during one of his "tours of encouragement before returning to England" (Y 52).

> McCudden was quiet and not disposed to riotousness. Tom found him a fount of information, about two-seaters particularly. He knew all their habits and weaknesses and liked to tackle them single-handed. He would sit about high up alone on a favourable day and wait for a two-seater to appear. He did not attract much attention high up alone, and was often able to drop out of the sun or a cloud and shoot the Hun unawares. Or if the Hun had warning and made off, he got into position under its tale and waited till he couldn't miss. If you sat properly under its

tail-plane, the Hun couldn't touch you. Of course, you had to keep there; that was a matter of flying, and a scout ought always to outfly a two-seater. Then, when the Hun flew straight for a quarter of a second, you put in a burst. One burst should always be enough. Good gunnery was the key to Hun-getting. The finest pilot on earth was little use unless he had the nerve to shoot from point blank range. McCudden flew an SE5. (Yeates 52–3)

McCudden in his own words, however, does not always seem encouraged by the service he renders to the Royal Air Force and his King: "one has to do one's job of killing and going on killing" (McCudden 214). Here is his description of his "first Hun in flames":

As soon as I saw it I thought "poor devil," and really felt sick. It was at that time very revolting to see any machine go down in flames, especially when it was done by my own hands. One seems to feel it more than sending a Hun to Hell out of control or crashed or in pieces. However, I had to live down my better feelings. (McCudden 176)

His memoir is a relentless record of such "remorseless" yet soul-destroying victories:

And I watched him the whole way until he crashed in our lines near St. Julien. I never have seen anything so funny for a long time as that old Hun going round and round for over two minutes. I bet the pilot and observer had a sick headache after that. (180)

While the Hun was turning to the left I could see the unfortunate observer standing up in an attitude of abject dejection. (209)

[he] went down in a dive and then broke to pieces. (209)

I think that this was one of the best stalks that I have ever had. (214)

the observer was just standing in his cockpit looking at me, but not firing at all. (243)

One encounter with a "dud" observation crew fills McCudden with especial disgust for the enemy he has killed so easily, for they have helped to destroy his self-respect as a fighter pilot:

This D.F.W. [German reconnaissance biplane] crew deserved to die, because they had no notion whatever of how to defend themselves, which showed that during their training they must have been slack, and lazy, and probably liked going to Berlin too often instead of sticking to their training and learning as much as they could while they had the opportunity.

I had no sympathy for those fellows, and that is the mental estimate which I formed of them while flying back to my aerodrome to report the destruction of my 43rd aerial victim. (McCudden 254)

And so "I realise," he concludes, "that war is the most fiendish and cruel slaughter that it is possible to conceive" (McCudden 24). At one point this revelation splashes upon the "screen" of his consciousness in what he calls "a queer experience":

> It seems all very strange to me, but whilst fighting Germans I have always looked upon a German aeroplane as a machine that has got to be destroyed, and at times when I have passed quite close to a Hun machine and have had a good look at the occupant, the thought has often struck me: "By Jove! There is a man in it." (McCudden 179)

> Then as I zoomed away I saw that my wind-screen was covered with blood. At first I thought my nose was bleeding but soon assured myself that it was not. Then I saw that the blood was on the outside of my screen. Not having much more petrol I flew back to the aerodrome and landed, after which I walked around my machine and found it covered with blood from the Hun two-seater. This is absolutely true, for I have a dozen different people who will vouch for it. (McCudden 236)

McCudden was twenty-three years old when, probably exhausted, he died in a crash, possibly as a result of engine failure and excessive airplane weight, on July 9, 1918 (the day Faulkner arrived in Toronto to begin his RAF training).[23]

The memoirs of Mannock, Bishop, and Rickenbacker tell similar stories. For Rickenbacker, the American Ace of Aces now that Lufbery was dead, "the pleasure of shooting down another man was no more attractive to me than the chance of being shot down myself. The whole business of war was ugly to me. But the thought of pitting my experience and confidence against that of German aviators and beating them at their own boasted prowess in air combats had fascinated me" (Rickenbacker 7). The trouble was that many of the German aviators he killed were little more than poor, inexperienced novices as the Allies, having killed many of the most experienced German pilots, continued to win the air war over the Western Front in 1918:

> He had stalled just at the moment he was upright on his tail, and in this position he was now hanging. And more extraordinary still, his engine had stalled and his propeller was standing absolutely still. I could see the color and laminations of the wood, so close had I approached to my helpless victim.
> On March 10th, 1918, there is the following entry in my flight diary: "Resolved to-day that hereafter I will never shoot at a Hun who is at a disadvantage, regardless of what he would do if he were in my position." (Rickenbacker 338–9)

After a terrible succession of victories Bishop too confesses, "For the only time in my life it entered my thoughts that I might lose my senses in a moment, and go insane" (Bishop 161). All the pilots take "convalescent leaves" at some point while, as Courtwright notes, "half of all pilots developed serious neuroses during their tours" (43).[24]

Figure 4.5 Lt. James McCudden, V.C.

Notes

1   The Royal Flying Corps was established in Canada in January 1917 and "swelled towards its final training strength of well over 10,000 men" (Ellis 122). The RAF took over its facilities. "Ranks in the new service were army ranks" (O 50). See Millgate, "William Faulkner, Cadet;" Millgate, "Faulkner in Toronto;" Blotner, Harrison, Weber, Price-Stephens, and Bostwick for pioneering research on Faulkner in the RAF Canada. See also Sullivan (1919), Ellis (1954), Hunt (1980), and Wise (2009) for official histories of the RAF and the RFC in Canada.

2   The word "terror" appears throughout news reports on aerial bombing in this period.

3   See Tuchman (403) for an account. The newspapers covered the story in scores of articles. See, as one example, "Saw Zeppelin Drop Bombs in Antwerp. Mrs. George Sparrow of New York Describes Night of Terror in Belgian City," NYT, August 28, 1914.

4   "A glance at almost any photograph of a group of RFC fliers will show a great variety
    of dress, and the confusion increased after April 1, 1918" (Price-Stephens 124n).

5   I think there are some visual links here with the uncanny Pegasus pony of Faulkner's
    "Carcassonne"—"And me on a buckskin pony *with eyes like blue electricity and a
    mane like tangled fire*" (Faulkner, "Carcassonne" 895, his ellipses)—and Jewel's horse
    in *As I Lay Dying*: "It is as though the dark were resolving him out of his integrity,
    into an unrelated scattering of components," "an *is* different from my *is*" (56). I
    develop the matter later in this book.

6   Accidents and near misses are recalled throughout the aviation war literature of the
    period. Jimmy McCudden witnessed an accidental explosion early in his training as
    an RAF pilot. "Two bombs had exploded during the loading process. I ran over to
    render assistance and found about a dozen men lying around the Morane, all badly
    mutilated …. I do not think that the cause of the mishap was every really discovered.
    It was surmised that during the loading of the bombs a safety wire was accidentally
    pulled" (McCudden 64).

7   Here reads Luke's Medal of Honor citation (he was the first to receive it): "After having
    previously destroyed a number of enemy aircraft within 17 days he voluntarily started
    on a patrol after German observation balloons. Though pursued by 8 German planes
    which were protecting the enemy balloon line, he unhesitatingly attacked and shot
    down in flames 3 German balloons, being himself under heavy fire from ground
    batteries and the hostile planes. Severely wounded, he descended to within 50 meters
    of the ground and flying at this low altitude near the town of Murvaux opened fire
    upon enemy troops, killing 6 and wounding as many more. Forced to make a landing
    and surrounded on all sides by the enemy, who called upon him to surrender, he drew
    his automatic pistol and defended himself gallantly until he fell dead from a wound in
    the chest." https://web.archive.org/web/20121017112625/http://www.militarytimes.
    com/citations-medals-awards/recipient.php?recipientid=896

8   "To throw good money after bad is foolish. But to throw away men's lives where there
    is no reasonable chance of advantage is criminal. In the heat of battle, mistakes in the
    command are inevitable and amply excusable. But the real indictment of leadership
    arises when attacks that are inherently vain are ordered merely because if they could
    succeed they would be useful. For such 'manslaughter,' whether it springs from
    ignorance, a false conception of war, or a want of moral courage, commanders should
    be held accountable to the nation" (Hart, *The Real War* 185).

9   See Neil Sheehan's damning portrait in *A Bright Shining Lie: John Paul Vann and
    America in Vietnam* (New York: Random House, 1989): "I asked the general if he
    was worried about the large number of civilian casualties from the air strikes and
    the shelling. He looked at me carefully. 'Yes, Neil, it is a problem,' he said, 'but it does
    deprive the enemy of the population, doesn't it?'" (621).

10 "It was late spring of 1916 when the runner joined the battalion …. to be an integer
    in what would be known afterward as the First Battle of the Somme" (FA 795). In his
    essay "On Privacy (The American Dream: What Happened to It?)" (first published
    in *Harper's*, July 1955), Faulkner wrote of the individual reduced "at last to one more
    identityless integer in that identityless anonymous unprivacied mass which seems to
    be our goal" (71).

11 "Onward, conscript soldiers, marching as to war,/You would not be conscripts, had
    you gone before" (qtd. in Grider 10).

12 In Oxford, Mississippi, in the years before he first came north in 1918, Faulkner had shown no inclination to advance himself in any professional manner (other than as a poet) or to attend the university, Ole Miss, whose "graduates were expected to become lawyers or doctors or politicians—professions that did not appeal to Faulkner .... His grandfather put him to work as a bookkeeper in the First National Bank of Oxford" (Rollyson 45, 47). With a pilot-officer's commission he could leap beyond them all.

13 Captain B. H. Liddell Hart, in a book Faulkner sent to his brother Murry in 1936 (SL 97), describes the lethal stupidity of advancement upon entrenched machine-gun positions: "It was difficult to adjust ... to conditions where one man with a machine-gun might count for more than a score, or a hundred, or sometimes even a thousand, who were advancing upon him with the bayonet. As the capacity to make such an adjustment proved to be lacking, the formula of victory became merely a formula of futility—and death. The more ranks of attackers, the more swathes of dead: that was all" (Hart, *World War I* 71). This vision of hell is central to Faulkner's screenplay with Joel Sayre, *The Road to Glory* (1936) (see Gleeson-White 43–9) and to *A Fable*.

14 See Michel Gresset on Faulkner's primary impulse to "'elongate' or magnify" himself and his "'great small characters,' for example, Popeye, Flem or Mink Snopes, Ratliff and the old general in *A Fable*"—"by riding horses, flying aeroplanes, or having tall statues or monuments erected on their tombstones" (*Fascination* 270). The claim that Faulkner was "rejected for pilot training in the U.S. Army" continues to appear in prominent places, like the *Biographical Note* to *Selected Stories of William Faulkner* (Modern Library, 2012).

15 "[Faulkner] fakes the British accent—not as difficult for a white Mississippian of the planter class as you might think, a southern accent transformed from stigma to enablement in a different cultural environment" (Hagood 51).

16 See Hall and Nordhoff (vol. 2, 7) for the original anecdote.

17 The phrase "cavalry of the clouds" was used by Alan Bott as the title of his 1917 memoir. Perhaps its most famous deployment was in the speech by British Prime Minister, David Lloyd George, in November, 1917, "The Thanks of the Nation": "The heavens are their battlefield; they are the cavalry of the clouds. High above the squalor and the mud, so high in the firmament that they are not visible from earth, they fight out the eternal issues of right and wrong. They are struggling there day, yea, and by night, in that titanic conflict between the great forces of light and of darkness. They fight the foe high up and they fight him low down; they skim like armed swallows along the front, taking men, in their flights, armed with rifle and with machine gun. They scatter infantry on the mark; they destroy convoys; they scatter dismay. Every flight is a romance; every record is an epic. They are the knighthood of this war, without fear and without reproach. They recall the old legends of chivalry, not merely by daring individually, but by the nobility of their spirit, and, amongst the multitudes of heroes, let us think of the chivalry of the air."

18 Ellis gives the figure of 2,539 as the number of cadets trained in the RAF, Canada, who went overseas (128).

19 Yeates' Tom Cundall reflects on "the progressive foulness of nearly everyone as they rose in rank and removed further from contact with the enemy" (242). *Winged Victory* also describes a courageous Major who goes in the opposite direction, giving up his Army rank to become a Lieutenant Pilot in the RAF on the Western Front.

20 Biddle confesses that he never felt confident in his tactics when attacking the German observation aeroplanes. "I think the most difficult attack of all to make is upon a two-seater that sees you, for with a fixed gun ahead for the pilot and the machine gunner in the rear with a movable gun they possess an enormous field of fire, and can shoot you almost anywhere except under their tails" (87).

21 Gibbons, who with the American Marines at Belleau Wood lost an eye as a war correspondent for the *Chicago Tribune* (see his account, "Wounded—How It Feels to Be Shot"), knew better, but he wanted to sell his book (who doesn't?). He sold a great many.

22 On July 6, 1917, Richthofen sustained a serious head wound in combat with this Woodbridge and Cunnell airplane, an F.E. 2d. They shot the Red Baron down (in official language he was "forced to land"). He survived, wrote his memoir while convalescing, and returned to service in October. He died the following April.

23 "[H]e was killed in a trivial accident of the kind which had cost us so many of our best pilots. On leaving the aerodrome his engine stopped, and in trying to turn in order to get back into the aerodrome he side-slipped into the ground" (McCudden 279).

24 Yeates' *Winged Victory* gives one of the deepest analyses on record of "war neurosis" in the soul of a Camel pilot.

5

The Embryo Pilot

"I got the chair …. I closed my eyes and they whirled me by machinery."
(Faulkner, July 9, 1918)

In *Aviation in Canada 1917–1918* (Toronto: Rous & Mann Limited, 1919), Alan Sullivan, official historian of the Canadian Royal Air Force, clarifies the purpose of the rotation test Faulkner claimed he passed on his first day in the service. As he had written to his mother, he would not go through that test again "for all the democracy that could be produced. It was about ten times as bad as the one in New York" (TH 74). The cadets experience "the chair" as a hazing ritual. The RAF justifies it as a way to assess the "personality and characteristics" (SU 112) of the trainees, for "an exhaustive study of the ideal pilot established the fact that he should have an acute and correct sense of equilibrium …. Above all there is demanded a sound physical condition, by which alone all bodily functions will respond normally" (SU 112–13). The medical thesis here might strike us as counter-intuitive: "The more sensitive, theoretically, a man is, as shown by 'turning tests,' the more likely he is to be a good pilot" (SU 117). A "sensitive" internal gyroscope is necessary when the ground and horizon end up in the "wrong places" or when they disappear altogether in rainstorms and gigantic cloud formations.[1]

Sullivan expounds on ear canals "filled with a clear fluid and lined with a membrane intimately connected by delicate nervous elements with the brain" (SU 113) in claiming that "intense nausea and emesis" can be inverse signs of a robust health that "nervous" types should be incapable of dissembling.

> The psychological side of medical service takes on new proportions in a flying camp. The personality and characteristics of the patient in question must be always kept in mind so that when investigating air sickness the medical officer may determine whether it is real or assumed. The question of fear, i.e., "aerophobia," in its actuality, and any loss of nervous control, must be established if existing—and obversely. Any excitement or tension must be carefully distinguished from natural recklessness or other characteristics of what is termed a "thrusting disposition."
> (SU 112)

Acknowledging, perhaps, an aggressive if not irrational tendency in the institution's confidence that it can distinguish between "assumed" and "real" symptoms, Sullivan reassures his readers that manifestations of "air sickness," "excitement or tension," vertigo, nausea, "loss of nervous control," and "fear, i.e. 'aerophobia'" are *treated sanely and sympathetically,* till the individual with all his personal variations becomes as it were a human barometer, which infallibly records the actions and reactions of the flying man's life" (SU 121, emphasis added).

The chair test begins the RAF's long surveillance of the cadet's "personal variations" during the training regime. Any "psycho-mental problems" are identified and a "history compiled for every would-be pilot and observer, an intimate history unapproached in detail and interest by any other tabulation of personal phenomena" (SU 122). This "complete history of each cadet from the time he first made application until the time he proceeded overseas, through every stage of training and every movement, has been kept in minute detail" (SU 151–2).

Alas, the full barometric report ("unapproached in detail and interest") on William Faulkner ("with all his personal variations" as an RAF pilot in training) has not been found, or perhaps it never existed at all in any such narrative form. All that remains in the archive with the demobilization order dated January 4, 1919, is a file of rubber-stamped official forms, as Blotner discovered:

> Page 3 of the four-page form was headed "Character and Trade Proficiency." In the place for the former, there was another blue stamp: ASSESSMENT OF CHARACTER DISCONTINUED. Under the legend "Degree of Proficiency," following the trade classification "Cadet for Pilot," the clerk had on January 4 written, "Groundwork 70%." The meticulous notes and precise drawings had somehow in the end merited no more than this. (Perhaps Cadet Faulkner had not been so meticulous and precise on examinations). On page 4, the "Special Qualifications and Courses of Instruction" column listed only Cadet Wing and School of Aeronautics. "Time Forfeited" was blue-stamped—NIL—and under "Casualties, Wounds, Campaigns, Medals, Clasps, Decorations, Mentions, etc." appeared again only that dead and empty word:—NIL [....] "Discharged in consequence of being Surplus to R.A.F. requirements. (Not having suffered impairment since entry into the Service)." (B 228)

No matter. Faulkner's aviation fiction itself is no doubt the richer and deeper "intimate history," a powerful self-analysis, in fact, of the "personality and characteristics" Faulkner wished he possessed, or lamented that he actually did possess, as an "incipient aviator" (as he described himself in a letter to his mother on July 9, 1918, TH 72) and "embryo pilot" in the Royal Air Force Canada.[2]

Faulkner's aviation fiction harbors the memory of his realistic fear that he might be killed or wounded in a training accident in Toronto or in combat in France or Germany if the war lasted into the winter and spring of 1919. He mentions the latter prospect several times in his letters home to his mother while also trying to soften her fears, or disguise his own, about what he is essentially being trained for, namely "gunnery for boches" (TH 104). On September 5, he writes: "I am looking forward to the furlough I'll get before I go overseas" (TH 98). On September 17: "We have six weeks at the

S of A [School of Aeronautics], and if we are sent overseas then, we get leave to go home. It is something like a girls finishing school, teaches us not to eat with our knives, and trifles like that; lest we disgrace the King's Commission that we hope to receive" (TH 103). Sick of menial work in the barracks and the entire "hardening process" (July 22, TH 82) of the Long Branch experience, he looks forward to a substantial change of routine, while acknowledging that the schooling for war is now becoming more deadly serious and practical. On September 19 he writes, "Golly, but I'm glad to go! Good food, good quarters, no drills, just lecturing, acquiring knowledge in the gentle art of gunnery for boches. The S of A is the University of Toronto, in town instead of being in the woods like the Cadet Wing" (TH 104). In a letter of October 21, he is fully expecting to be deployed: "I am saving up, for it is customary, before a cadet is sent overseas, to give him indefinite leave" (TH 117).

There was much to be afraid of now. In his foreword to John MacGavock Grider's *War Birds: Diary of an Unknown Aviator* (1926), Elliott White Springs gives us a realistic sense of it: "Of the two hundred and ten men [U.S. Army flyers] who landed in England and trained with the Royal Flying Corps, fifty-one were killed, thirty were wounded, fourteen were prisoners of war and twenty became mentally unfit for flying before they finished their training" (vii).[3] Perhaps, in the soul of the aspiring aeronautical cavalier, the fear of being found "mentally unfit for flying" is even deeper than the fear of being wounded or killed. On the basis of his experience in 1916 "with the French flying corps" (so he titles his memoir), Dana Carroll Winslow declares: "Some men cannot fly: their temperaments prevent it, and try as they will they cannot improve. This is generally due to sheer stupidity or to lack of nerve. One thing is certain, and that is that these men will kill themselves sooner or later if they persist in their efforts to fly" (Winslow 86).

Faulkner explores this fear along with a complex of others in his fictional analysis of "nervous," sick, or wounded pilots and demobilized war veterans, including Cadet Thompson of "Landing in Luck" (see below), Bob Jeyfus of the story "Love" (see Chapter 7), Donald Mahon of *Soldiers' Pay* (see Chapter 6), Johnny and Bayard Sartoris of *Flags in the Dust* and "All the Dead Pilots" (discussed in Chapter 4), and David Levine of *A Fable* (see Chapter 8). At the base of this series (like the dreaming figure of Pierrot in Faulkner's early symbolist play, *The Marionettes*, discussed in Chapter 6) lies the RAF veteran William Faulkner who, feeling himself under a kind of social surveillance after the war, responded by walking with a limp, drinking too much, and claiming that he had a silver plate in his skull. Like Bayard Sartoris (FL 753) he also suffered war nightmares and flashbacks ("whether real or assumed") in company of some of the women he loved, as in this account given by Meta Carpenter Wilde with whom Faulkner had a long Hollywood affair beginning in 1935:

The bag of groceries I had bought on the way dropped out of my hands as I saw Bill huddled on one corner of the bed, hands stretched out, palms foremost, as if to ward off something menacing. His head was bent, eyes mercifully turned away from whatever it was that threatened him, and he moved as I observed him into a crouched position—knees up, shoulders sagging .... He looked up, no recognition whatever in his face, and screamed, "They're going to get me! Oh, Lordy, oh, Jesus!" He covered his head with hands that alternately flailed and supplicated, shouting over and over in a litany of dread, "They're coming down at me! Help me! Don't let them! They're coming at me! No! No!"

He was a man I no longer knew, and when I tried to touch him, he recoiled from me convulsively.

"Who?" I asked him. "Who's trying to hurt you?"

"They're diving down at me. Swooping. Oh, Lordy!"

"Faulkner, what are you talking about? Who's after you?"

He turned a face as white as library paste toward me. "The Jerries! Can't you see them?" Suddenly he was doubled over, trying to crawl into himself. "Here they come again! They're after me! They're trying to shoot me out of the sky. The goddam Jerries, they're out to kill me. Oh, merciful Jesus!" (Wilde 142–4)[4]

With the help of a medical expert Wilde's diagnosis was delirium tremens, "the d.t.'s," "a hallucinatory state" (144). The general lesson of Faulkner's chair test as it emerges from this scene is that extreme sickness, vertigo, and fear are signs of mind and humanity under siege.

"Do Not Do It, One Thousand Times"

Faulkner's letter to his mother dated October 25, 1918, suggests that he had an early, "cosmopolitan" ear for war's fundamental insanity:

[October 25, 1918] [Toronto] I heard a funny story today—It was in the medical examining room of a draft exemption board. There were three men at the doctor's desk—a little, undersized Jew, and two Americans. The doctor called up the Yid first—"Well, what exemption do you claim?"

"I dont claim notting's, doctor. I only want I should be sent right away to France tomorrow. I dont want the Government should spend no money on me training me und buying me a outfit, I only want to go to morrow to the trenches to fight."

The doctor clapped him on the back and told him what a fine patriot he was, and turned to the other two. One of them claimed a bad heart and the other flat feet. "You are a fine pair," he told them, "you, American-born, trying to evade the draft! Just look at this poor Jewish lad, foreign born, who has had none of the priviledges you two have abused all your lives! Look at him, willing to give his life for you two slackers!"

The Jew, in his corner, spoke, insinuatingly—

"But, Doctor, dondt you t'ink I'm a liddle crazy?"

We are going on a 25 mile route march to-morrow. Ye Gods! (TH 120)[5]

The subversive philosophy of this very serious joke extends into Faulkner's story "Death Drag" (1932) and the David Levine sections of *A Fable* and elsewhere. Here, for the moment, is that Jewish barnstorming daredevil otherwise known as Ginsfarb:

> "Were you a flyer in the war, Mister?" the boy said.
>
> The limping man turned upon the boy his long, misshapen, tragic face. "The war? Why should I fly in a war?"
>
> "I thought maybe because of your leg. Captain Warren limps, and he flew in the war. I reckon you just do it for fun?"
>
> "For fun? What for fun? Fly? Gruss Gott. I hate it, I wish the man what invented them was here; I would put him into that machine yonder and I would print on his back, Do not do it, one thousand times." ("Death Drag" 192)[6]

And yet so many did. Samuel Hynes quotes from a letter by George Clark Moseley, American volunteer in the Lafayette Escadrille in 1916, who explains one of his reasons why: "'I am going to take these tests ... because then I will be able to find out the truth about myself as far as flying is concerned.' The truth about myself, that's what they're all after: myself as a man" (H 45). Being a first-team All-American football player, as Moseley was at Yale, is not enough. In the age of military aviation, the truth about oneself as a man can only be discovered by risking death in war. Eddie Rickenbacker, as a professional race-car champion in America between 1912 and 1916, experienced nothing like the inner radiance he felt as a combat pilot returning from his first flight over enemy lines:

> I forgot entirely my recent fear and terror. Only a deep feeling of satisfaction and gratitude remained that warmed me and delighted me, for not until that moment had I dared to hope that I possessed all the requisite characteristics for a successful war pilot. Though I had feared no enemy, yet I had feared that I myself might be lacking .... This feeling of self-confidence that this first hour over the Suippe battery brought to me is perhaps the most precious memory of my life. (Rickenbacker 7)

In surmounting his fear and terror over enemy lines, the supreme American fighter pilot of the First World War was born:

> For with the sudden banishment of that first mortal fear that had so possessed me came a belief in my own powers that knew no bounds .... The pleasure of shooting down another man was no more attractive to me than the chance of being shot down myself. The whole business of war was ugly to me. But the thought of pitting my experience and confidence against that of German aviators and beating them at their own boasted prowess in air combats had fascinated me. (7)

Figure 5.1 Eddie Rickenbacker in his SPAD.

Faulkner admired Rickenbacker and wrote a poem about him during the Second World War, as Blotner explains:

> Captain Eddie Rickenbacker had survived three weeks in a life raft after a plane crash in the Pacific [in October 1942]. Here was a man who had been, in the other war, what Faulkner had hoped to be .... Faulkner composed a three-page poem entitled "Old Ace." In six emotional stanzas of free verse he flashed from Rickenbacker's ordeal to his past heroism. (B 1132)

If Faulkner had hoped to be a Rickenbacker at some point in his earlier life, he also knew, against the pressure of his own family's expectations, that he was never really cut out for Rickenbacker's kind of physical heroism and success as a warrior.[7]

Is there an "obverse reflection" of Edward V. [for Vernon] Rickenbacker in "Ernest V. Trueblood," Faulkner's comical and subversive alter-ego? Here Blotner recalls the "hanger-flying days" he shared with Faulkner and Frederick Gwynn at the University of Virginia in 1957–8:

> We collaborated on [a scroll] to commemorate what we called the 1st Balch Experimental Hangar-Flying Squadron. He sketched in the device, an adaptation

of the RAF winged insignia, with the motto "Ad Astra Per Jack Daniel's." All were signed by "Ernest V. Trueblood, Adjutant" .... His scroll, framed, would stand on the mantlepiece in the office at Rowan Oak. (B 1694)[8]

First Solo, Terror, and Mortal Fear

"Terror" and "mortal fear" (Rickenbacker 7) have always been part of the embryo pilot's experience. Manfred von Richthofen reports that when his teacher told him, "'Now go and fly by yourself' .... I must say I felt like replying 'I am afraid.' But this is a word which should never be used by a man who defends his country" (Richthofen 35). He remembers feeling shame and confesses that he failed his first solo twice before succeeding:

> I acted mechanically and the machine moved quite differently from what I had expected. I lost my balance, made some wrong movements, stood on my head and I succeeded in converting my aeroplane into a battered school bus. I was very sad, looked at the damage which I had done to the machine, which after all was not very great, and had to suffer from other people's jokes .... On Christmas Day, 1915, I passed my third examination. (Richthofen 35–6)

Billy Bishop had trouble on his first solo flight too. He took off without incident and flew around in circles as instructed. "For a time I felt very much pleased with myself," he recalls, until he realized that "somehow or other I had to get that machine down to the earth again." Nosing down too steeply, then pulling up too abruptly, he continued to move the stick back and forth while losing altitude in a series of awkward steps. "About forty feet from the ground, however, I did everything I had been told to do when two feet from the ground. So I made a perfect landing—only forty feet too high" (Bishop 32).

These solo-flight survivors and future aces give perspective to all the others who never got beyond their first solo tests and who are seldom seen or even named in the memoirs and histories of the period. In *Canadian Airmen and the First World War: The Official History of the Royal Canadian Air Force*, S. F. Wise reports that "[o]verall, RFC/RAF Canada lost 129 of its cadets in fatal flying accidents, one for every 1902 hours logged by the training scheme" (Wise 107). David Courtwright notes that "[a]n American pilot's chance of dying in a training accident was 40 percent higher than his chance of dying in combat" (C 44). American Army Signal Corps flyer Dean C. Smith, as I noted in Chapter 1, gives a close account of such training-accident carnage in *By the Seat of My Pants* (18).[9]

If the cadet emerged from his first solo flight with body unscathed and "all his fac—with all his f-a-c-u-1-t-i-e-s intact" (Salinger 114) the next step for most was deployment to the war front in France where nothing much could prepare you for the moment when "live ammunition approaches" (Tuchman 169).[10] Mick Mannock never got used to the recurrence of this moment and was always "held back by the waves of fear and nausea, which overtook him before, and sometimes during, action" (as his squadron mates recall in Mannock 155). Still, like McCudden and so many others, he continued to do the "job of killing and going on killing" (McCudden 214) until he himself was killed.

The prospect of Faulkner's first solo flight in the RAF vanished with the peace of November 11, but the event, long and deeply imagined, was given narrative form as his first substantial solo publication, a short story. The embryo pilot, William Faulkner, first flew, that is, as an aviation writer already richly fledged. "Landing in Luck" appeared in the University of Mississippi's student newspaper *The Mississippian* on November 26, 1919, as a surprisingly realistic confession of how his first solo had gone, and continued to go, in his own mind. The main lesson of the story is the same as that presented by Wilbur Wright before the Western Society of Engineers on June 24, 1903: "Before trying to rise to any dangerous height a man ought to know that in an emergency his mind and muscles will work by instinct rather than conscious effort. There is no time to think" ("Experiments and Observations in Soaring Flight," qtd. in M 92). In Faulkner's story, the thinking takes place afterwards, as a narrative account of the pilot's thoughts, instincts, and actions during the flight's critical moments, as he himself describes them to an audience of his fellow cadets and "hangar flyers." This in itself is a stunning conception at the dawning of the genre itself of what an "aviation narrative" essentially is. Like the ones to whom he attempts to justify himself, Cadet Thompson does not really know whether he is lying or telling the truth in his "re-vision" of the event because he has "no grip on what [he] had been through" (Saint-Exupéry, *Wind* 61). If there is some kind of line between truth and lies in his story, it is entangled in the thickets of his own language. Cadet Thompson's ego alone, in its hall-of-mirrors narcissism, can't be much help in finding or extracting this line. Rather, the narrative textuality and symbolism of the story, overall, know more than he himself does, and tell more than he himself can. Drawing on all he had observed at the Long Branch aerodrome and had read in memoirs like those of Bishop, Bott, and Winslow, Faulkner's story is also one of the earliest fictional descriptions of aeroplane-flying in American literary history. Its essential narrative logic and form are those of a dream.

"Landing in Luck"

The story is set at the RAF "aerodrome" in Canada (the mention of Camp "Borden" locates it there) where "wild and hardy amateurs took off, landed and crashed. A machine descended tail high, levelled off too soon and landed in a series of bumps like an inferior tennis ball" (43). Cadet Thompson, a fluent "barracks ace," thinks he has "just made a fairly creditable landing" (43) with his flying instructor, Mr. Bessing, in the front cockpit of the two-seat Jenny trainer. Mr. Bessing thinks otherwise:

> Swear I don't know what to do with you. Let you try it and break your neck, or recommend you for discharge. Get rid of you either way, and a devilish good thing, too.... you cut your gun and sit up there like a blind idiot and when you condescend to dive the bus, you try your best to break our necks, yours and mine too. (43)

Like a blind idiot. Far from "improvis[ing] new powers of alertness and seeing" (Duffy 5), Cadet Thompson is "paralyzed" (Faulkner's word, 48) by the experience of speed and flight. He goes through the motions of controlling the aeroplane only to render himself up to the new kinetic forces as a wholly passive object, just as Cadet Faulkner had done during the chair test he had taken on the first day of service: "I closed my eyes and they whirled me by machinery .... they whirled me so fast that I had to hold in" (TH 74).

Nothing has essentially changed for Cadet Thompson as he faces his first flight alone. Taking off might *seem* easy enough, a gentle tug on the stick as the accelerating aeroplane, "hooked by the propeller" (de Saint-Exupéry, *Southern Mail* 14), rises naturally into the wind. One of the fascinations of the story is that smooth and graceful flight such as this can't even be dreamed. Getting the plane back down safely again will also be a harrowing physical and psychic trial. "Here it may be pointed out," observes Frank Ellis in *Canada's Flying Heritage* (University of Toronto Press, 1954), "that the most critical event in a learner's life was not so much the first take-off and flight, but the first solo landing. It was indeed an achievement to bring your roaring Juggernaut back to mother Earth, without splitting it and her wide open" (123). To accomplish it the pilot needs confidence in himself and trust in his teachers, a good memory of what he has learned in training, an awareness of surrounding wind conditions, and a calm feel for the responses of the aeroplane to the controls he operates with hands and feet as the ground steadily approaches. All this in accordance with the system that Wilbur and Orville had imagined and realized, by which "the operator could vary *at will* the inclination of different parts of the wings, and thus obtain from the wind forces to restore the balance which the wind itself had disturbed" (Wilbur and Orville Wright, "The Wright Brothers's Aëroplane," *Century* Magazine, September 1908, in JY 26; emphasis added).

Perhaps the Wright brothers, in their preternaturally calm temperaments, had not considered very deeply the extent to which emotional and psychological turbulence in the soul of the pilot might put the whole system at risk. Cadet Thompson is in trouble before he begins:

> Thompson pulled down his goggles. He had been angry enough to kill his officer for the better part of a week, so added indignities rested but lightly upon him. He was a strange mixture of fear and pride as he opened the throttle wide and pushed the stick forward—fear that he would wreck the machine landing, and pride that he was on his own at last. He was no physical coward, his fear was that he would show himself up before his less fortunate friends to whom he had talked largely of spins and side slips and gliding angles.
>
> All-in-all, he was in no particularly safe frame of mind for his solo flight. (44)

Billy Bishop began his first solo in a similarly unsafe "frame of mind." As he climbed into the cockpit, he recalls, "all the other business of flying had suddenly ceased so that everybody could look at me" (32). Noticing an ambulance nearby with its engine running, he imagined the "doctors at the hospital expectantly fondling their knives. Everybody looked cold-blooded and heartless" (Bishop 32–3). Ellis notes that

> In the early summer at Camp Borden in 1918 ... 19 airmen lost their lives in flying accidents in 21 consecutive days. Whenever there were planes in the air, a high-powered Packard ambulance was kept standing by, ready to speed away the moment a crash was reported. The ambulances were nicknamed 'Hungry Lizzies,' and there was work enough from them at all the airdromes. (Ellis 128)

Sullivan adds some important details:

> A Packard machine, provided with a special type of shock absorbers and every possible requisite, not only for first aid but also for fire extinguishing, was stationed at each field, and remained on constant and watchful duty from the time the first aeroplane took the air till the skies were empty for the night. So close was the lookout, that "first aid" was often tearing full-powered to the rescue before the crash completed its descent .... Chemical extinguishers and asbestos blankets, the latter introduced for protection of the pilot in case the crash was in flames, were also carried as part of the equipment. (SU 111)

The ambulance and its "gaping" crew are also there in Faulkner's "Landing in Luck," and Cadet Thompson, looking down on them as he makes careful turns in the air, lets them know how he feels about their morbid expectation:

> Below at the edge of the aerodrome stood the ambulance, its crew gaping foolishly at him. "Like fish," he thought, "like poor fish." He leaned out of his cockpit and gestured pleasantly at them, a popular gesture known to all peoples of the civilized world. (45)

As if in response to this gesture, the field soon fills "with people running about and flapping their arms" (45). Another aeroplane passes nearby "in a long bank, its occupants shouting at him" (45) in alarm and consternation. In the ritual of Icarus that Cadet Thompson has set in motion, flying "as the expression of dream and desire" (Salaris 27), "an act of volition ... capable of generating libido" (Freud, *The Interpretation of Dreams* 452), is transgressive by definition. It affronts the countervailing forces of gravity and proscription that the pilot also internalizes as a fear of "rising too soon" or "daring" too much. In accordance with Freud's classical dream theory, this "phantasy" of flight in the soul of the dreamer is also "acted out" at the level of plot, the realm of motility and action where physical and mental impulses mobilize the reactions of an "external" world. The narrative work of "secondary revision" produces a plausible visual explanation for the aeroplane's struggle to ascend: "a cable" suddenly stretches across the path of the rising aeroplane.[11]

> His subconscious mind had registered a cable across the end of the field, and he had flown enough to know that it was touch and go as to whether he would clear it.

He was afraid of rising too soon again and he knew that he would not stop in time were he to close the throttle now. So, his eyes on the speed indicator, he pulled the stick back. The motion at once became easier and he climbed as much as he dared.

A shock; he closed his eyes, expecting to go over and down on his back in the road below. When nothing happened he ventured a frightened hurried glance. (44)

"Nothing happened." A violent impact and fall should have been expected, yet as Freud might observe, there is nothing in Faulkner's story "which responds to a belief in death. This may even be the secret of heroism .... 'Nothing can happen to *me*'" (86).[12]

This element of Faulkner's story—the aeroplane's striking of the telephone cable in a way that does no violent harm to the pilot—might also be read in light of a traumatic and highly publicized event in the history of the Lafayette Escadrille, the death of American Ace Norman Prince, winner "successively the Croix de Guerre, the Médaille Militaire, and the Croix de la Légion d'Honneur," veteran of "122 aerial engagements" and "officially credited with five Boches brought down in battle, not to mention four others not officially recorded" (Babbit 8). Returning from an escort mission over Oberndorf, Germany,

Norman's Nieuport machine struck an aerial cable while he was endeavoring to make a landing in the dark within the French lines near Luxeuil. In this collision his machine was overturned and wrecked and he was thrown violently to the ground. On being rescued by his comrades, it was found that both his legs were broken and, as was subsequently found, he had sustained a fracture of the skull .... [He] cheerfully requested the attending surgeons who were setting the bones of his broken legs to be careful not to make one shorter than the other! The skull fracture was not discovered until later, and it was as a result of this latter injury that Norman died from cerebral hemorrhage on the following Sunday morning, October 15, 1916. (Babbit 9–10)

Faulkner's story seems a kind of reparation or negation of such tragedy (as echoed in wounds to leg and head that Faulkner would act out upon his return to Oxford, Mississippi—as I discuss in the following chapter). In representing Cadet Thompson's unconscious belief in his own protection from violent death or injury by the halo of a "lucky" providence, Faulkner's story also accords with Freud's insight (after Lucretius) in "Thoughts for the Times on War and Death" (1915): "It is indeed impossible to imagine our own death; and whenever we attempt to do so we can perceive that we are in fact still present as spectators. Hence the psychoanalytic school could venture on the assertion that at bottom no one believes in his own death, or, to put the same thing another way, that in the unconscious every one of us is convinced of his own immortality" (77).

In this brilliant fusion of aviation realism and oneiric symbolism, Faulkner's story illuminates the essential "conflict of will" inherent in the operations of the psyche, such conflict helping to produce our typically "inhibited" dreams of flight and motion. Freud cites these typical examples: "*a young man carries his mistress upstairs in his*

Figure 5.2 Norman Prince.

arms; at first she is as light as a feather, but the higher he climbs the heavier grows her weight." Or, *"One tries to move forward but finds oneself glued to the spot, or one tries to reach something but is held up by a series of obstacles"* (Freud, *Interpretation of Dreams* 286, 238). "A volition is opposed by a counter-volition. Thus the sensation of the inhibition of movement represents a conflict of will" (Freud, *Interpretation of Dreams* 452). The expectations of this Freudian logic are certainly fulfilled in Faulkner's story. The rising aeroplane meets a "shock" that threatens to turn it on its back and onto the road below. The pilot closes his eyes but "nothing" happens. He realizes after "a frightened hurried glance" that the aeroplane had pushed through this first obstruction: "So the cable had broken! Must have, for here he was still going forward"

(45). Full of righteous self-approval, he feels like shouting: "Now he'd show 'em what flying was. Rotten, was he?" And so he flies on, but the people on the ground see something the pilot cannot, something damaged and dangerously exposed on the aeroplane's undercarriage (a motif that will recur in Faulkner's "Turnabout," as we have seen). There follows a display of cryptic hand signals, and indecipherable shouts drowned out by the sound of motors and wind. Suddenly the message becomes clear as in a "rebus" or "picture-puzzle" (Freud, *Dreams* 277–8) successfully decoded. An occupant of a passing aeroplane "carried something to which he gestured and pointed frantically .... he saw that the object was about the size and shape of a wheel? A wheel from the landing gear of a machine. What kind of a joke was this? .... Then Thompson remembered the cable. He had stripped a wheel on that cable, then" (46). Exhibited to all below, this partial gelding of the aeroplane, along with the pilot's professed desire to "kill his officer" (43) and then show him his "utter adoration" (49), places the story "in the constellation of the Oedipus dream" (Freud, *Interpretation of Dreams* 523n), one of whose star-groups includes "Embarrassing Dreams of Being Naked": "The people in whose presence one feels ashamed are almost always strangers, with their features left indeterminate," strangers who stare at the dreaming protagonist "in astonishment and derision or with indignation" (Freud, *Interpretation of Dreams* 341). The primary desire to exhibit one's nakedness before "'a lot of strangers' ... stands as the wishful contrary of 'secrecy'" (Freud, *Dreams* 344). "The unconscious purpose requires the exhibiting to proceed; the censorship demands that it shall be stopped" (Freud, *Interpretation of Dreams* 345).

Cadet Thompson continues to fly in circles with all eyes upon him until, "out of petrol at last," he is forced to land on one front wheel. Just at this point he is "paralyzed" with eyes at first closed and then wide shut, "all staring." "When conscious purposive ideas are abandoned," it seems, "concealed purposive ideas assume control ... " (Freud, *Interpretation of Dreams* 679):

> For Thompson's nerve was going as he neared the earth. The temptation was strong to kick his rudder over and close his eyes. The machine descended, barely retaining headway. He watched the approaching ground utterly unable to make any pretense of levelling off, paralyzed; his brain had ceased to function, he was all staring eyes watching the remorseless earth. He did not know his height, the ground rushed past too swiftly to judge, but he expected to crash any second. Thompson's fate was on the laps of the Gods. (48)

There follow the inevitable crash-landing and the resolution of the turbulent scene in a characteristic tableau, with pilot "[h]anging face downward from the cockpit" (49).[13]

> The tail touched, bounded, scraped again. The left wing was low and the wing tip crumpled like paper. A tearing of fabric, a strut snapped, and he regained dominion over his limbs, but too late to do anything—were there anything to be done. The machine struck again, solidly, slewed around and stood on its nose.
> Bessing was the first to reach him.

"Lord, Lord!" he was near weeping from nervous tension. "Are you all right? Never expected you'd come through, never expected it! Didn't think to see you alive! Don't ever let anyone else say you can't fly. Comin' out of that was a trick many an old flyer couldn't do! I say, are you all right?"

Hanging face downward from the cockpit, Cadet Thompson looked at Bessing, surprised at the words of this cold, short tempered officer. He forgot the days of tribulation and insult in this man's company, and his recent experience, and his eyes filled with utter adoration. Then he became violently ill. (48-9)

With Freud we should say that "the insistence with which this dream exhibits its absurdities could only be taken as indicating the presence in the dream-thoughts of a particularly embittered and passionate polemic" (Freud, *Interpretation of Dreams* 436).

Perhaps a reading of this kind can help bring out what remains latent in Faulkner's RAF letters: the cadet's rebellious anger and resentment at not being sufficiently seen or respected by the authorities whose approval he craves. "If the subject asks himself the question what kind of child he is, it isn't in terms of being more or less dependent, but as having been recognised or not" (Lacan, *Seminar* 42). They have placed him in a series of contradictory and untenable positions, or so it seems to the cadet under the stress of his turbulent emotions and anxieties. The authorities are both imperious and negligent. They don't really think he's good enough to fly. They don't really want him to learn to fly at all. They want him to learn to fly but don't especially care if he ends up dying in a crash or in combat. His role is to replace the dead flyers in France and to be replaced by new pilots in turn. "He had been angry enough to kill his officer for the better part of a week" (43-4). The antic and immoderate features of Faulkner's flying story seem to flow from the fundamental "absurdity" of the cadet's situation:

A dream is made absurd, then, if a judgement that something "is absurd" is among the elements included in the dream thoughts—that is to say, if any one of the dreamer's unconscious trains of thought has criticism or ridicule as its motive …. the *mood* of the dream-thoughts … combines derision or laughter with the contradiction. (Freud, *The Interpretation of Dreams* 564)

Faulkner's anti-militaristic attitude as it is most fully articulated in *A Fable* seems traceable to the criticism, ridicule, and derision he felt during his RAF experience.

Having somehow landed "in luck"—despite his utter passivity and nauseating terror and disorientation—Cadet Thompson tries to gather up his unraveled dignity by means of a retrospective narrative account:

—and so when the petrol gave out, I knew it was up to me. I had already thought of a plan—I thought of several, but this one seemed the best—which was to put my tail down first and then drop my left wing, so the old bus wouldn't turn over and lie down on me. Well, it worked just as I had doped it out, only a ditch those fool A. M.'s had dug right across the field, mind you, tripped her up and she stood on her nose. (49)[14]

In his memoir of the Vietnam War, Michael Herr captures the essence of the encounter Faulkner seems to be exploring here, the site at which the telling of "what happened" converges with a language inflected by the teller's ego and self-serving memory.

> Sometimes I didn't know if an action took a second or an hour or if I dreamed it or what. In war more than in other life you don't really know what you're doing most of the time, you're just behaving, and afterward you can make up any kind of bullshit you want about it, say you felt good or bad, loved it or hated it, did this or that, the right thing or the wrong thing; still, what happened happened. (Herr 20–1)

What happened happened. Sometimes what happened at the aerodrome can be read clearly enough in the wreckage of the aeroplane or in its survival partially intact. But that doesn't prevent "any kind of bullshit you want about it" from also existing in subsequent and possibly competing or inconsistent narrative accounts. As Cadet Thompson tells his story, his fellows "watch him with varying expressions" (50). They can't be absolutely sure that he is not a supremely talented natural pilot, and so they try to reassure themselves that they can see right through him: "That guy? That guy fly? He's so rotten they can't discharge him. Every time he goes up they have to get a gun and shoot him down. He's the 'f' out of flying. Biggest liar in the R.A.F." (50).[15]

As a "flyer/liar" Cadet Thompson is in the best possible company. McCullough notes that until they shocked the world with their public demonstrations in 1908 and 1909, the Wright brothers were also subjected to withering skepticism. "[T]the *Paris Herald*, an English language paper, mocked the brothers in an editorial titled 'Fliers or Liars' [March 1906]: 'The Wrights have flown or they have not flown. They possess a machine or they do not possess one. They are in fact either fliers or liars. It is difficult to fly …. It is easy to say, 'We have flown'" (M 132). (Wilbur's notoriously taciturn demeanor might be recalled at this point. "Well, if I talked a lot I should be like a parrot, which is the bird that speaks most and flies least" [qtd. in M 215].) Billy Bishop stands accused to his day of lying about the event for which he was awarded the Victoria Cross. After giving a dramatic account of his most recent victory, as Manfred von Richthofen recalls, a rude interlocutor at the base camp "was convinced that I was a fearful liar" (Richthofen 65). Richthofen enjoyed seeing the look on the skeptic's face later that evening when Richthofen walked into the dining room with the Blue Max on his uniform. Roy Brown, in turn, who may actually have killed the Red Baron (see Chapter 7 in this book),

> was known for the modesty of the reports he made concerning his combats in the air. He had both disbelief in and dislike for the flyers who made victory claims after every engagement. He knew how difficult it was to obtain corroboration. He knew that many flyers actually discredited their good work by telling tall stories. Some of his successful engagements only reached his credit list because they were reported by other observers. (Gibbons qtd. in Richthofen 129)

Cadet Thompson, however, shows his critics that the one whose credence he needs most is his commanding officer's. If he has Bessing's blessing, his own self-regard will surely follow, and all the rest of the sceptics can go hang. So the story ends, with a more subtle and sublimated version of that "popular gesture known to all peoples of the civilized world" (45) that Cadet Thompson had earlier shown the gaping groundlings from his aeroplane circling aloft:

> Thompson passed through again, with Bessing, and his arm was through the officer's. He was deep in discussion evidently, but he looked up in time to give them a cheerfully condescending:
> "Hello, you chaps." (50)

The medium itself of "Landing in Luck" as a work of literary art is its primary message. It is as if Faulkner is saying, I am more than what I pretend, and greater than you imagine, a flyer of a special kind, for whom writing is already a superior form of flight, an incandescent sublimation of that "allegory whose master narrative is the story of desire itself, as it struggles against a repressive reality, convulsively breaking through the grids that were designed to hold it in place" (Jameson, *Political Unconscious* 67). Just hang on, and watch.

"Landing in Luck": A Coda

After I had written the section above I was reading Major Charles J. Biddle's *The Way of the Eagle* (New York: C. Scribner's Sons, 1919) when I came across this passage:

> I had a thrill a couple weeks ago when I sent a new man up for his first ride in a Spad. In getting off the field, which is rather rough, he bumped a bit and bent an axle so that the wheel was at an angle of about 45 degrees, with the axle almost touching the ground. I knew that if he bounced at all when he landed the wheel would probably snap off or that the axle would at least catch in the ground and throw the machine over. As it was his first trip he would probably land fast so as to be sure not to lose his speed too soon, and I had visions of seeing him turn over at sixty miles an hour. I said good-by to that new machine and only hoped that the pilot would not be killed or seriously injured. There is almost nothing one can do to prevent such an accident once a machine gets up with a bad wheel, except stand on the side lines and hope for the best. While this man was flying around the field I sent a man out with a spare wheel to wave it at him in the hope that he would catch on to the fact that there was something wrong with his wheel and land as slowly as possible. Also sent for the doctor and the ambulance, got a stretcher ready and had men out on the field with fire extinguishers. A cold-blooded performance, perhaps, but I thought we might as well be ready for anything.

Luck was with us, however, and the pilot as he passed over the field saw the man waving the spare wheel and realized for the first time that something must be wrong. When flying your lower wings prevent you from seeing any part of the landing carriage. I held my breath when the plane came down to land but if the pilot had been flying for five years and had tried a thousand times he could not have made a softer landing. The bad axle held and the plane rolled along and stopped as though there was nothing at all the matter. (222–3)

It was fascinating to find myself following the path of Faulkner's reading here and the way he had imagined himself into the pilot's seat in this scene. It was fascinating too to imagine Faulkner talking through his experience with Major Biddle's arm around his shoulder.

Aero Motor

Before receiving actual flight training, including practice in gunnery and combat aerobatics, RAF cadets attended ground school whose "comprehensive curriculum" included lessons in "the theory of flight, meteorology, astronomy … rigging … instruments, bombs, and machine guns" (Hunt 112). "The work here is very interesting," Faulkner wrote to his mother on September 28, 1918. "I wish they allowed us to go into detail about it. We have all sorts of engines, map reading, wireless, artillery observation" (TH 109). Four days earlier, his class "went out to flying camp … and I learned how to crank an aero motor by swinging the propeller. I was rather surprised when I did it. It's rather scary though, the thing goes off with such a roar" (September 25, TH 107).

Faulkner's note is laconic yet the impression it describes was undoubtedly a deep one. At the Camp Leaside engine-running sheds, the gasoline-powered dynamos are bolted onto wooden frames set on concrete slabs. The engines, Curtiss OX5s, stand behind protective screens through which the cadets can "smell the reek of castor oil and feel the heat from the flames that leaped from their exhaust stacks" (Harrison 48). Unprotected by any screens, the cadets are exposed to the propellers at "the starting end" which is the entire point of the exercise. At full throttle the nine-foot propellers spin at 1,500 revolutions per minute, their "blade points cutting the air at the rate of eight miles a minute" (SU 48).[16] The object of this phase of the training is to "drill" the operations of the machines "into all pupils under conditions which simulated those on active service as nearly as possible" (SU 166).

A simulation, perhaps, but the fear and the danger of what the spinning blades would do to human flesh were real enough. The aeroplane-mounted versions of these model "instruments of war, new and strange and dangerous" (H 45) were capable, moreover, of shooting machine-gun bullets through their propellers in synchronized bursts. Facing the engines, the cadet might shrink at this prospect before remembering (in a reversal of perspective mandated by his overall course of study) that he was

ENGINES MOUNTED FOR TEST.

THE STARTING END.
(NOTE PROTECTIVE SCREEN).

253

Figure 5.3 Engines Mounted for Test. *"It's rather scary though, the thing goes off with such a roar."*

being prepared to sit in the cockpit or gunner's seat of the attacking aeroplane on the Western Front where, in the fall of 1918, the strafing of enemy troops "retreating along roads and rail lines" (H 221) was a primary mission for Allied combat planes. As Eddy Rickenbacker recalls, "The aeroplanes swoop down so swiftly and are so terrifying in the roar of their engines and the streams of bullets issuing forth from two rapid-fire guns that an ordinary soldier always looks for a hole rather than for any weapon of defense" (Rickenbacker 30).

At Camp Leaside, close exposure to the machines "under conditions which simulated those on active service as nearly as possible" (SU 166) was meant to inoculate the cadet against his natural impulse to cower before the machine. It was also meant to stimulate his imagination and readiness for war. The unarmed and underpowered Curtiss Jenny with "her lithe, intricate body" (Harrison 48) was being asked in this sense to stand in for the Sopwith Camels, Nieuports (flown by Billy Bishop, whom Faulkner reports having seen in the camp), S.E.5s (McCudden's plane), or SPADs (Rickenbacker's) of the news reports and cadets' conversations and fantasies, the combat aeroplane as endowed with quantum increments of horsepower and "armed with a machine gun that discharges bullets at the rate of 600 per minute through a four-bladed propeller revolving at the rate of 1,200 times a minute" (SU 170). At the Armament School to which the cadets would proceed after courses at the School of Aeronautics were completed, "the question of a method of sighting which would allow a deflected aim to be laid on a moving machine" would also receive "mathematical attention" (SU 173). Synchronization of engine, propellers, machine gun, and pilot's "line of aim" (Virilio, *War and Cinema*) was the linking principle in "the weapons system he was destined to use" (SU 170) on the Western Front.[17]

Speaking for the RAF throughout his treatise, Sullivan claims that "the embryonic pilot was keen for intimate knowledge of the guns on the efficiency of which his future victories depended" (SU 173). Perhaps some were keen. In the engine-testing sheds at the Leaside Aerodrome, Faulkner seems intimidated and mistrustful—certainly not especially passionate or expansive—as he stands before the clamorous aero engines and "the dizzying whirl of the scythe-like propellers" (Saint-Exupéry, *Wind* 47). The scene of Faulkner cranking the propeller of the aero-motor, then recoiling from the noise, power, and smoke (search Curtiss OX5 on YouTube for an additional sense of this), served, as I read it, as a kind of "point on the graph curve showing the evolution of the character of war" (Douhet 26) in the twentieth century, and thus as an opportunity, which I think Faulkner took, to look back at a point already far behind him. Any residual imagination of himself as a solo *chasse* pilot, engaged in "a series of duels in which the skill and courage of the individual aces were displayed in all their brilliance .... as knights-errant of the air" (Douhet 43), was already, by the late fall of 1918, antiquated, historical, obsolete. As Douhet was observing from Italy, "war is no longer fought in a series of scattered individual encounters, no matter how brave or skillful the individuals may be. War today is fought by masses of men and machines" (43–4), men and machines synchronized, as Faulkner was learning, into vast and complex systems linked by wireless networks. In this context of aerial warfare *en masse*, "there is a simple method of foretelling the future, simply asking of the present what it is preparing for the future" (Douhet 146). Let Antoine de Saint-Exupéry offer us a view of this future as he contemplates it in *Wind, Sand and Stars* (1939):

> Every week men sit comfortably at the cinema and look on at the bombardment of some Shanghai or other, some Guernica, and marvel without a trace of horror

at the long fringes of ash and soot that twist their slow way into the sky from those man-made volcanoes. Yet we all know that together with the grain in the granaries, with the heritage of generations of men, with the treasures of families, it is the burning flesh of children and their elders that, dissipated in smoke, is slowly fertilizing those black cumuli. (62)

In September 1918, Faulkner's response to the machine—to "the almost demonic technological element" (Zischler 16)—seems a prototypical event in the history of modernism. Kafka captures the essence of it in the first sentence of his diary of 1908. He has just seen the Lumière brothers' film, "The Arrival of a Train at the Station of La Ciotat" (1895) and notes, "The onlookers freeze when the train goes by" (qtd. in Zischler 9).[18] Hanns Zischler offers a brief reading of the scene Kafka is describing:

> The stupor and the shock ... that are recorded in this sentence are preserved more than once in early cinematic history .... Kafka's journal entry sounds like a distant echo, a protoliterary reminiscence of the first milliseconds of the cinematic big bang .... What can be experienced during the assault of the images? ... This is a problem for the increasingly shattered faculties of perception. (Zischler 9–10)[19]

To Henry Adams in "the great hall of dynamos" at the 1900 Paris World's Fair,

> the dynamo became a symbol of infinity. As he grew accustomed to the great gallery of machines, he began to feel the forty-foot dynamos as a moral force, much as the early Christians felt the Cross. The planet itself seemed less impressive, in its old-fashioned, deliberate, annual or daily revolution, than this huge wheel, revolving within arm's-length at some vertiginous speed, and barely murmuring— scarcely humming an audible warning to stand a hair's-breadth further for respect of power—while it would not wake the baby lying close against its frame. Before the end, one began to pray to it .... the break of continuity amounted to abysmal fracture .... and thus it happened that ... he found himself lying in the Gallery of Machines at the Great Exposition of 1900, his historical neck broken by the sudden irruption of forces totally new. (380–2)[20]

Listening to the hypnotic whisper of the electric dynamo that beckons worship, however, Adams also knows that it threatens violence just as "the automobile, which, since 1893, had become a nightmare at a hundred kilometers an hour, is almost as destructive as the electric tram which was only ten years older; and threatening to become as terrible as the locomotive steam-engine itself, which was almost exactly Adam's own age" (380). The aeroplane with its scythes rotating in the open air, along with its quantum increments of gasoline-driven sound and horsepower, can only represent a nightmarish extension of this awesome destructive power. Winslow describes a typical scene of terror at the French aerodrome when a novice pilot loses control of his aeroplane. "The ground was muddy and very slippery, which made escape almost impossible. In their hurry to get away several men lost their footing and fell down in the very path of the onrushing biplane. We thought that at least a dozen would be crushed or else decapitated by the rapidly revolving propeller" (Winslow 87).[21]

Recall that Adams is touring "the Gallery of Machines at the Great Exposition of 1900" with his friend Samuel Pierpont Langley whose "chief interest was in new motors to make his airship feasible" (Adams 380). Forerunner and principal rival of the Wright Brothers, Langley had engineered a few years before "a strange-looking, steam-powered, pilotless 'aerodrome,' as he called it, with V-shaped wings in front and back that gave it the look of a monstrous dragonfly. Launched by catapult from the roof of a houseboat on the Potomac River in 1896, the year of Lilienthal's death, it flew more than half a mile before plunging into the water" (M 33).[22] On December 8, 1903, a week before the Wright brothers first flew in their gasoline-powered machine, Langley would risk another attempt to launch his "aerodrome," this time with a human pilot aboard:

At exactly 4:45 he gave the signal to release the catapult. Instantly the machine roared down the track and leaped 60 feet straight up into the air, only to stop and with a grinding, whirring sound, hang suspended momentarily, nose up, then, its wings crumbling, flipped backward and plunged into the river no more than 20 feet from the houseboat. (M 100)

The pilot, Manly, survived, but Adams seems to hear the "roaring," "grinding," and "whirring" dynamo as a voice summoning numberless human sacrifices to come.

The loudness of the airplane is a disturbing factor that all the early flyers explicitly separate from the visual and bodily wonder of sailing aloft. For Wilbur Wright, flying produces a

sensation ... so keenly delightful as to be almost beyond description. Nobody who has not experienced it for himself can realize it. It is a realization of a dream so many persons have had of floating in the air. More than anything else the sensation is one of perfect peace, mingled with the excitement that strains every nerve to the utmost, if you can conceive of such a combination. (qtd. in M 126)

There are countless records of some version or another of this sensation in the aviation literature, but many pilots also make a point of noting the invasive power of the aero-engine's piercing sound. In the open cockpit of the typical First World War aeroplane, "the noise level, 125 decibels, exceeded that of pneumatic drills," and many pilots suffered permanent hearing loss from the "engine racket" (C 41). One of Wilbur Wright's earliest passengers, "Major Baden Fletcher Smyth Baden-Powell, brother of the founder of the Boy Scouts," was "astonished by the noise": "'All the time the engine is buzzing so loudly and the propellers humming so that after the trip one is almost deaf'" (qtd. in M 204). Sometimes, though, you pass through the wall of sound into a kind of deafening, hypnotic silence. "The engines whined quickly on a rising note until they reached their full pitch—a tremendous screaming monotone that thrust once fiercely into ear drums and stayed with such insistence that presently it was as if there was no sound" (Bellah, *Gods* 77–8). Orville Wright describes the experience of really hearing the sound of the engine only after it has ceased: "The motor close beside you kept up an almost deafening roar during the whole flight, yet in your excitement, you did not notice it till it stopped!" (qtd. in M 127). Plugging one's ears against the sound, however, was no option. "When flying, the pilot can usually tell by the sound of his motor whether it is running perfectly or not" (Winslow 29). The pilot must listen to his aero-motor, "the soul of my aeroplane" (Lufbery qtd. in Driggs 118), with a kind of prayerful concentration as sensitive and intent as Henry Adams's before the huge though "barely murmuring—scarcely humming" wheel, revolving "at some vertiginous speed."

The dynamo as a symbol of "an insolent, steely, polluting Machine Age" (Galassi 18) that, for Henry Adams, was bound to endure throughout the new century, was for F. T. Marinetti and the Italian Futurists a matter for feverish celebration. As Jonathan Galassi writes, "The Futurists were dedicated to motion … the revving of a Lamborghini, or better yet a Ducati motorcycle, relentlessly powering up, up, up and away, its engine knocking, spewing exhaust, mowing down everything in its path. The Futurists believed in the machine" (Galassi 18). Faulkner believed in flight, but his recoil from the clamorous aero-motor that makes heavier-than-air flight possible marks the beginning of his skeptical and "decaffeinated" response to the machine age.[23]

The Aerialization of Human Vision

Before actual flight training and, eventually, live bombing and strafing practice at the School of Aerial Gunnery at Camp Borden and the School of Aerial Fighting at Beamsville, cadets at the School of Aeronautics in Toronto (where Faulkner remained until the end of the war) were trained in "camera gunnery" under the sign of what Paul Virilio would call the "aerialization of human vision" (*War and Cinema* 46). Notes Sullivan, "The Air Force is the eye of the army, and the camera the recording eye of the airman" (SU 205). Hence

> embryo pilots and observers are required to attain a certain standard in camera gun work.… The camera used is designed to resemble, both in operation and in appearance, the Lewis machine gun, the difference being that upon the trigger being released the camera gun registers a photograph upon a film. Reloading is by pulling back the cocking handle, which brings another film into place. (SU 193)[24]

The cadet learns to "shoot" aerial photographs and, from an elevated tactical position, to "apply his map-reading knowledge to an immense reproduction of part of the actual theatre of war, showing whole battlefields in faithful outline .... He delved into air and weather conditions in northern France and learned what targets looked like when seen from the air." In this way "he was introduced to the science of bombing" (SU 80). Historian S. F. Wise adds further details:

> The school had two huge maps prepared from aerial photographs of sections of the Western Front, each studded with hundreds of light bulbs which could be flicked on singly or in combinations to represent shell bursts from one or more batteries. The cadets sat on elevated benches above the maps, noting shell bursts and passing information by "buzzer" to the instructor. (Wise 102)

Faulkner described the scene in a letter to his mother on November 5:

> It is a map built to represent the earth at a height of 5000 feet, every thing complete, with tiny electric bulbs to represent shell bursts. We pin point them and send the location— something like this—A 21 G 18 C 8-2—by wireless to the instructor, who replies by a series of white strips of cloth laid upon the floor. It is going to be very interesting, and if you find it interesting, you never have any trouble in passing it. (TH 125)

By means of this indoor simulation of the air war scene, in which "British and German trenches are shown on a scale of approximately five inches to one hundred yards" (SU 201), cadets were taught "the value of shadows in estimating heights" (SU 205), including shadows cast by 1,360 "electric globes" lit up randomly to "simulate the bursts" of an artillery barrage (SU 201) or the explosions of an aerial bombardment. The cadets were tested on their skill in "buzzing (telegraphic receiving and sending)" (SU 76), that is, on how quickly they could locate enemy targets and communicate their map coordinates to the communicating battery via the "wireless system" (SU 197). The pressures and the stakes in this setting were intense, as Faulkner noted to his mother on July 16: "I am quite proficient in telegraphy now. I shall pass that test, I think. If we pass 75% of our work, we are lieutenants, 50%, sergeant pilots, below that, mechanics" (TH 79).[25]

Sitting on elevated benches the cadets imagined themselves into the cockpit of the aeroplane in order to plot aerial courses from point to point and to calculate wind velocity, air speed, and petrol volumes. From the benches the cadets also "heard lectures on picture target work and artillery coöperation from experienced observers" (SU 198) and how to "adjust his bomb sights both for the speed and altitude of his machine" (SU 198).

Winslow describes the French air force's version of this preparatory "course in bomb dropping."

> This was a practical course, and our method of learning was as peculiar as it was ingenious. A complete bomb-dropping apparatus was mounted on stakes about twenty-five feet above the ground. Under this there was a miniature landscape

painted to scale on canvas. It was a regular piece of theatrical scenery mounted on rollers so that it could be revolved to represent the passage of the earth under your machine …. Through our range-finder we would gaze down at the "land," and as a town appeared we would make allowances through the system of mirrors arranged by the range-finder for our speed and height and for an imaginary wind. At the calculated moment the property bombs would be loosed. (Winslow 94)

He also reports that the habits of mind inculcated in this theatrical environment could not help but be carried over into his real combat experience. "The atmosphere was extraordinarily clear. Every detail in the landscape stood out boldly, and as we rose the dozens of camps in the immediate vicinity spread out below us like models set in a painted scenery" (Winslow 133). The battlefield "sets" that were constructed at the base, "with a skill once reserved for theatrical property making" (Montrose 719), were not necessarily designed to be aesthetically appreciated. The pilots were taught, rather, to think of the battle-ground as nothing but a grid-map of targets to be analyzed and tactically engaged. For Tom Cundall in *Winged Victory*, the conceptual fusion of map and ground constitutes the essential ontology of the pilot's point of view, but his resistance to the war can be read, perhaps, in his propensity to flash between "aesthetic" and "tactical" modes of perception.

He turned over on his longitudinal axis so that he was sitting at a right angle to the plane of the earth, and by turning his head to the left he was looking straight sideways on to the roofs of the town, which was as it were on a hanging map. By letting his joystick come back a little he made the world-map rotate about the hub of the town, which, slowly spinning, approached steadily. When it took up most of the visible map, he straightened things out, and went for a trip among the chimney pots. (Y 190)

Jorge Luis Borges represents the hegemony of cartographic logic in Western imperialism in "On Exactitude in Science":

In that Empire, the Art of Cartography attained such Perfection that the map of a single Province occupied the entirety of a City, and the map of the Empire, the entirety of a Province. In time, those Unconscionable Maps no longer satisfied, and the Cartographers Guilds struck a Map of the Empire whose size was that of the Empire, and which coincided point for point with it. (325)

When map and ground coincide point for point, the destruction of targets can begin in the planning room where lines and circles tend to proliferate in "an excess of spirits" (Wright, *Meditations in Green* 125). For Giulio Douhet, imagining the air war of the future in 1921,

it would be advisable to subdivide the area into zones of 50 targets each. If we get 10 zones when the subdivision is mapped out, it means that the Air Force has the potential capacity to destroy all enemy objectives in that area of land or sea in ten days of operation, after which its striking power can be transferred to other zones designated for destruction. (Douhet 50)[26]

Winslow recalls how, on one of his bombing missions, "the entire Verdun sector was spread out like a relief-map" below (Winslow 134), but there was no longer any correspondence between the map and the ground it purported to represent. On one of his reconnaissance missions, Biddle recalls:

This place appeared on my map and although I thought I had the spot exactly located and searched carefully from only five hundred metres above it, I could find no trace of it. I asked a Frenchman and he explained the mystery by saying that it had been entirely blown off the map. There is absolutely no trace of it left that can be distinguished from the surrounding country. Even several macadamized roads which ran through it, are blown out of existence. (52)

On patrol as an artillery spotter in the northern sector of the French front, Jimmy McCudden expresses a certain satisfaction in the knowledge that, as targets are destroyed by explosive ordnance, new maps will have to be drawn: "On January 3, 1916, I was up again for two hours with Major Hewitt, again ranging on Salomé, and this time we had the satisfaction of fairly blowing portions of it quite off the map, for a 9.2 high-explosive shell is not to be despised at all when it gets going" (McCudden 89). For Biddle and for many others, watching the slow-motion progress of ecological destruction was one of the primary horrors of the war:

You can trace the advance by the slow changing of green fields and woods into a blasted wilderness which shows a mud brown color from the air. Fields become a mass of shell holes filled with water and a wood turns from an expanse of green foliage into a few shattered and leafless trunks. For weeks I have watched in particular the destruction of a certain forest. (90)

James Norman Hall offers an infantry-man's view of this anguish in his memoir, *Kitchener's Mob*:

Rarely a night passed without its burial parties. "Digging in the garden" Tommy calls the grave-making. The bodies, wrapped in blankets or waterproof ground-sheets, are lifted over the parados, and carried back a convenient twenty yards or more. The desolation of that garden, choked with weeds and a wild growth of self-sown crops, is indescribable. It was wreckage-strewn, gaping with shell holes, billowing with innumerable graves, a waste land speechlessly pathetic. The poplar trees and willow hedges have been blasted and splintered by shell fire. Tommy calls these "Kaiser Bill's flowers." Coming from England, he feels more deeply than he would care to admit the crimes done to trees in the name of war. (52–3)

The pilots know at a certain level that violence marked out on a map of grid coordinates was anything but abstract to those occupying the places on the ground where the lines and bombs converge. Recalls American infantry lieutenant Hervey Allen of the Aisne-Marne offensive of July–August 1918, "In order to keep from drawing a shelling, the men had not moved anything in the yard. There was a child's bicycle by the station and a little wagon. To have moved these would have shown up in aerial photos and might have brought a bombardment on that part of the town. One learned quite a few wrinkles like that by bitter experience" (Allen 55). But the pilots also report that, when seen from the air, explosions and bursts of light seem the only real and dynamic things in a scene dominated by a kind of painterly stillness or cinematic silence, as though of an early black-and-white film.[27]

> It is a weird combination of stillness and havoc, the Verdun conflict viewed from the sky. (McConnell 55)

> For us the battle passes in silence, the noise of one's motor deadening all other sounds. (McConnell 55)

> Tiny flashes showed where the guns were concealed, but to us the battle was a silent one. (Winslow 135)

> The battle area, two miles below, dirty brown and foul yellow, gashed with tortuous lines of trenches, pencil-marked with the queer blue of wire entanglements, littered with ruins of town and villages, might have been a picture done by a mad painter, a map of desolation, rather than anything real, except that there were puffs of yellow-grey smoke and red flashes, and fires smouldered here and there. There was no movement. (Y 291)

> Columns of muddy smoke spurt up continually as high explosives tear deeper into this ulcered area. During heavy bombardment and attacks I have seen shells falling like rain. The countless towers of smoke remind one of Gustave Doré's picture of the fiery tombs of the arch-heretics in Dante's "Hell." A smoky pall covers the sector under fire, rising so high that at a height of 1,000 feet one is enveloped in its mist-like fumes. Now and then monster projectiles hurtling through the air close by leave one's plane rocking violently in their wake. Airplanes have been cut in two by them. (McConnell 54–5)

Bott reports that his assigned RAF bombing targets included "Forts, garrison towns, railway junctions and railheads, bivouac grounds, staff headquarters, factories, ammunition depots, aerodromes, Zeppelin sheds, and naval harbours" along with trains and troop columns (Bott 214). "But if the bombs fall on something that does not explode or catch fire, it is almost impossible to note exactly what has been hit" (Bott 214). It is "quite impossible to tell the extent of the damage" when "the raid is directed not against some definite object, but against an area containing troops, guns, and stores" (Bott 217). Hence the natural propensity to fetishize the bright explosion and the flowering burst of flames. Biddle reports that "there is a great advantage in setting a machine on fire, for there is then no possible doubt, and it can be seen to fall for miles, which makes confirmation much easier" (165). Whatever the bombs hit is a legitimate target and a visual index of success and accomplishment. The main thing is just to let the bombs go. As Richthofen reflects,

> Now comes the enjoyment of bombing. It is splendid to be able to fly in a straight line and to have a definite object and definite orders. After having thrown one's bombs one has the feeling that he has achieved something .... It gave me a good deal of pleasure to throw bombs. (Richthofen 44–5)

Armistice and Demobilization

In the letters to his mother and father, Faulkner sometimes implies or claims that he had flown in the service, but, as we know, he did not receive any flight training in the RAF and never flew at all in this period even as a passenger (Millgate, "Faulkner in Toronto" 197–8). But he received a rigorous education in modern war systems, technologies, and mentalities that included imaginary, simulated, and practical exercises in viewing the ground from the air. He also had ample opportunities to observe aeroplanes in flight, and his letters are rich with expressions of wonder and anticipation. "The next time I get to see you I shall be a lieutenant-pilot," he writes on July 9 (TH 74). In the letters to follow in the subsequent weeks and months, he gazes, longingly, at the planes flying "all the time" and "every where" around him:

> July 13: We can see planes from the aviation field in the air all the time. (TH 77)
> July 19: Every where I look I see planes from the flying schools. (TH 80)
> July 28: There are planes in the sky all the time. (TH 85)
> August 18: I have been out this morning watching Captain Leigh doing stunts in a brand new plane. (TH 93)
> September 25: Saw lots of flying, as yesterday was very clear, a great flying day. (TH 107)

In this ritual of Tantalus, the spectacle of flight was a wholly visual, vicarious, and imaginary phenomenon, even if, in the summer and fall of 1918, Faulkner did not yet know that he would remain forever trapped in this kind of endless "mirror stage" (Lacan), the image of his future aeronautical prowess and "coordination" as an officer-pilot aloft always shimmering before his eyes to remind him of his inadequacy and grounded condition.

Still weeks away from actual, though still elementary, flying instruction, let alone the School of Aerial Fighting at Beamsville, preparatory to being transferred to the war front in northern France, Faulkner hopes in the meantime to catch an unofficial recreational joyride with one of his more advanced colleagues. As the summer deepens, this poignant fallback possibility is perpetually deferred.

> July 16: I am hoping to be moved to Long Branch soon and I am going to try to get one of the cadets to let me make a flight with him out at Lake Side. (TH 79–80)
> July 24: Unless something happens I shall make a flight tomorrow morning. (TH 84)
> September 3: There was a 'plane from the aerobatics school at Beamsville over just now. Tomorrow is a holiday, and I am going out if I can and get one of the cadet-pilots I know to take me up. (TH 97)

But the climate is changing and the chances of taking flight as a passenger, let alone as a pilot, are beginning to fade with the deepening gloom of fall and the rumor of armistice.[28] Though not yet completely dispossessed of the hope of transcendence, Faulkner remains emphatically stuck in the mud as the longed-for aeroplane ride, never actually described, "takes place" in the blur of a temporal ellipsis:

> September 15: It rains now every day, very methodical and very damp, with a queer, impervious detachment, worthier of a far better cause than that of producing gelatinous mud in such quantities …. I am watching for better weather, so I can get my friend at the flying camp to take me up again. Lieutenant Todd will be in flying camp shortly, then I'll probably be able to make lots of flights with him. (TH 102)

By October 31, the dream of flight is pretty much over. "I didn't intend to give the impression of such abysmal depression as I think you got from my letter—I think you would have known it any way, even if I had not written, I have never been very successful at fooling you, have I?" (TH 123). A few days later, on November 3, however, he sees a new aeroplane (or, as we have noted, an illustration of one) at the air field and has the day-dream that he might fly such a plane in Billy Bishop's squadron, a final manic flaring up of his mood near the end (TH 124). On November 11 "they had stopped the war on him" (SP 3) and in December Faulkner's entire class was abruptly "discharged in consequence of being Surplus to R.A.F. requirements'" (qtd. in B 228).

War surplus. There it is. In his attempt to salvage something worthwhile from the overall wreckage of his aviation dream, he cannot even call the modern bureaucratic institution that has just "discharged" him by its proper name. "I am rather disappointed in the Royal Flying Corps," he writes to his mother on November 24, referring to the old legendary service that had been, and must also somehow continue to be, the source of enduring fantasy. As a thwarted aviator he is left with nothing but shreds of glory—counterfeit shreds at that. "I have got my four hours solo to show for it," he goes on to claim, a meager achievement, perhaps, by the scale of real pilots, but to someone in his circumstances, a quantum leap into actual doing and magnificence that could only be dreamed.

> I am rather disappointed in the Royal Flying Corps, that is, in the way they have treated us, however, I have got my four hours solo to show for it, but they wont give

us pilot's certificates even. Nothing but discharges as second airmen. It's a shame. Even the chaps who have their commissions and are almost through flying are being discharged the same way. I am too glad to be on my way home at last, to let things like that worry me. They might at least have let me have another hours solo flying, so I could have joined the Royal Aero Club and gotten a pilot's certificate. As it is, I have nothing to show for my six months except my 18 pounds I've gained. (TH 135)

Tradition, often supported by readings of Cadet Lowe of *Soldiers' Pay* and David Levine of *A Fable,* maintains that Faulkner was "bitterly disappointed at not seeing combat" (Price-Stephens 127). The record of the letters suggests a more complicated set of feelings. Faulkner's disappointment at not becoming a pilot is clear, but so is his frank admission of relief (how could there not be relief?) that the war has ended before his group could be sent to the slaughter-bench of the western front. Talk about landing in luck:

November 7: It looks like the whole thing is over. The whole wing has taken a holiday—took it, not received it—and have all marched down town with the band. It will be quite a while until the air clears enough for me to know exactly where I am as regards leave home. (TH 126)

November 13: I suppose you are not glad the whole show is over? We have gone more or less wild since things happened over there …. Of course we are all glad that the fighting is over, but I am certainly glad it lasted long enough for me to get a pilot's license which I can do quite easily now. (TH 129)

November 15: There will probably be no more flying in Canada this winter. Glad I've gotten in what I have. (TH 129–130)

In a post-script Faulkner mentions the possibility for the first time of coming home with "a regular pilot's brevet" (TH 130), a "gold pin like this," as he draws it in the letter, "a crowned eagle with wings spread," as James Watson reports. He will not return to Oxford without the miniature metallic wings themselves, conceived, originally, it seems, as a gift for his mother. He will wear them proudly too, as shown in the famous "photograph of Faulkner taken in Oxford following his return from Toronto" in which he wears "a similar pilot's brevet on the uniform of an R.A.F. officer" (Watson, TH 130n; see the Coda to this book).[29]

In the meantime, Faulkner's shock at being discharged without wings can be discerned in his late-November grousing to his mother and father. No longer would he "be called at some such hour as four o'clock A.M., made to stand shivering on an aerodrome, waiting for enough light to go up and freeze by. Flying is a great game, but I much prefer walking in the winter. Still, I wouldn't take anything for my little four hours" (*TOH* 132). Even Cadet Lowe of *Soldiers' Pay,* who occupies the lowest rung of the aviation ladder in Faulkner's fiction, had more than "my little four hours": "'Seven hours and nine minutes, sir'" (SP 42), in fact. Thus, Faulkner grants himself the barest quantum of honorable military experience in what has turned out to be both a personal and collective relief bought at the price of deep humiliation.

His first practical problem was what to put on as the Armistice celebrations unfolded. The second was what to wear on the journey home.

> Some time before this he had ordered a complete officer's uniform. As usual, where clothes were involved, he had ordered the best—a garrison cap made by William Scully, Ltd., Montreal, the smart, blue-gray belted tunic, trousers, and a trench coat complete with the flaps and equipment rings that made it combat-worthy as well as smart. He would make the trip home in style. (B 229–30)

In the meantime, "I borrowed some civilian clothes and wore them down town Monday. Had a great time, too. Every one thought I was a flying officer in mufti" (November 17, TH 130). This experience of mistaken identity gave Faulkner one of his early thrilling lessons in becoming what psychoanalysis calls "the object of the transference." Although, in Žižek's formulation, "the subject can never fully dominate and manipulate the way he provokes transference in others there is always something 'magic' about it. All of a sudden, one appears to possess an unspecified X, something that colors all one's actions, submits them to a kind of transubstantiation" (Žižek 77). Dean C. Smith describes what such a transubstantiation must have felt like when he finally got his commission as a Second Lieutenant:

> Forty years ago the gulf between enlisted ranks and officers was as wide and deep as the ocean. For seventeen-year-old Smith a lieutenant's gold bars were about as appropriate as the cap and gown of a university professor. The effect on my ego and self-esteem was incalculable—and insufferable. But I had no qualms about assuming the dignity and responsibilities of an officer. My uniform had long been ordered; it hung in all its glory in my quarters. My first act was to hurry outside to find a soldier to salute me. (Smith 62)

Faulkner would do the same back home in Oxford where he was also ready to amp up the stakes to the maximum degree in presenting himself to his family, friends, and general Oxford community as a pilot officer wounded in the war. Let's just keep in mind, as the scene unfolds, that Faulkner was also beginning the process of becoming a professional storyteller, one of the best the world has ever seen.

Notes

1   See Saint-Exupéry, in such works as *Southern Mail, Night Flight,* and *Wind, Sand and Stars,* for unsurpassed representations of the pilot's "battle with chaos" when "vertical, oblique, horizontal, all of plane geometry [is] awhirl" (*Wind* 53). See also Dean Smith: "Then, again without warning, the ground, which was nicely spread out on the horizontal, rapidly tilted sideways until it was standing on edge, and I was once more

pressed into the seat .... and earth mixed with sky in complete confusion" (24). "I was straining against my seat belt so hard it was nearly cutting me in two, oil and gasoline were pouring by, the engine had cut out, and the earth was overhead, a green and brown disk whirling like a phonograph turntable. Sky, earth, and directions were all in wrong places; whatever was going on was going on fast, and I was doing something I had never heard of before" (67). Courtwright describes some of the physical stresses First World War combat pilots typically experienced: "Climbing for altitude drove blood pressure from a normal 120 systolic to a hypertensive 200 by the time pilots reached 6,000 feet. The higher they flew, the worse they felt. Teeth throbbed. Brains swelled. Vision blurred. At 18,000 feet the volume of abdominal gas doubled, a problem not helped by the castor oil spewing from rotary engines" (C 41).

2   The phrase "embryo pilot" and variations is common in the period. One encounters it in McConnell's *Flying for France: With the American Escadrille at Verdun* (1917), Winslow's *With the French Flying Corps* (1917), James Norman Hall's *High Adventure* (1918), Sullivan's history of the RAF (1919), Frank H. Ellis's *Canada's Flying Heritage* (1954), and many other places. The metaphor implies, of course, the possibility of the cadet's washing out or being "aborted" before coming to term as a fledgling pilot.

3   Springs, a South Carolinian, flew with Billy Bishop's squadron in France and won the Distinguished Flying Cross. Grider's diary (substantially ghost-written by Springs), as we've mentioned, is the basis of Faulkner's screenplay *War Birds/A Ghost Story*. Faulkner lionizes Grider in the newspaper essay, "Mac Grider's Son." Speaking of the last months of the war, Sullivan adds: "The battle proceeded with unprecedented intensity, and with it a never-ending aerial warfare. Pilots were rushed from England with a few hours' solo work and absolutely no gunnery practice, to find themselves instantly in the thick of the combat. It is, therefore, not astonishing that the wastage of our fighting men ran up to twenty-five per cent. per month" (SU 15). "Had the war continued into 1919," Wise also observes, "RAF Canada would have met about a fifth of the estimated pilot and observer reinforcements needed for the Western and Italian fronts. A statistical summary and operational forecast prepared in the Air Ministry in November 1918 found that the average pilot casualties per month, during 1918, for all overseas operational units was 551, a wastage rate of 32 per cent a month" (Wise 118).

4   See also Reid's interview with Wilde, listed under "Broughton" in the Works Cited.

5   In a letter dated December 5, 1942, Faulkner told his stepson Malcolm Franklin, who was about to deploy as an Army medic in Europe during the Second World War, that "No sane man likes war." But he also made it clear that "when I can, I am going too," if they would only let him: "it's a strange thing how a man, no matter how intelligent, will cling to the public proof of his masculinity" (SL 166). Of the months before Faulkner died—a time of illness, alcoholic relapses, and chronic hospitalizations— Blotner reports that Faulkner spoke often "about the men and planes of the First World War." Near the end, Faulkner also intended to build a library for his daughter Jill's children and made a list of "the books he wanted to have around them as they grew up .... his usual favorites plus a few new ones" (B 1807–8), including Jaroslav Hašek's *The Good Soldier Schweik* (1921–3), one of the twentieth-century's great military satires. I thank Karel Foustka for alerting me to it.

6   See Lind on Ginsfarb and Faulkner's Jewish characters.

7   On military traditions and pressures in Faulkner's own family, see Kartiganer, Lowe, Hagood, Wells, Blotner, Williamson, Sensibar, James Watson.

8   Such scenes were always a little awkward. Blotner and Gwynn, young American
     literature professors at the University of Virginia and among the earliest of the
     great Faulkner worshippers in the academy, were both combat aviators during the
     Second World War. See Blotner's *An Unexpected Life* for his account of being a
     bombardier in the "First Division, Fortieth Combat Wing, of the eighth Air Force,
     368th Squadron of the 306th Heavy Bombardment Group." He was shot down on his
     sixth mission and held as a prisoner by the Germans until the end of the war. He was
     also decorated with the Air Medal: "For meritorious achievement while participating
     in sustained bomber combat operations over Germany and German occupied
     countries. The courage, coolness and skill displayed by these Officers and Enlisted
     Men upon these occasions reflect great credit upon themselves and the Armed
     Forces of the United States." Blotner comments: "I did not feel that I had displayed
     any exceptional coolness or skill in opening and closing bomb-bay doors and
     dropping bombs. As for courage, I had been moved along in the air corps pipeline,
     and it would have been unthinkable to do anything to get myself out of it" (Blotner,
     Unexpected 76).

9   See Richard Hillary's *The Last Enemy* (1942), a Spitfire pilot's memoir of aerial
     combat in the Second World War and London during the Blitz. Hillary recalls a
     training accident involving a South African RAF cadet named Edmonds. "He was
     the worst-burned pilot in the Air Force to live. Taking off for his first solo in a
     Hampden at night, he had swung a little at the end of his run and put a wing in. The
     machine had immediately turned over and burst into flames. He had been trapped
     inside and fried for several minutes before they dragged him out. When he had first
     been brought to McIndoe he had been unrecognizable and had lain for months in a
     bath of his own suppuration .... Never once had Edmonds complained .... It would
     take years to build him a new face .... Both his top lids and his lower lip were done
     together .... Sometimes he behaved as though he had been almost guilty not to have
     been shot down, as though he were in the hospital under false pretenses; but if ever a
     pilot deserved a medal it was he" (161–2). Hillary himself was shot down and badly
     burned. He describes his hospitalization and medical treatment in one of the most
     important war narratives of the twentieth century.

10   Dean Faulkner Wells tells us that as a high school student in the mid-1950s she gave
     Faulkner "J. D. Salinger's *Nine Stories*. His favorite was 'For Esmé—With Love and
     Squalor'" (Wells 220).

11   Secondary revision: "Rearrangement of a dream so as to present it in the form
     of a relatively consistent and comprehensible scenario" (Laplanche and Pontalis
     412). Phantasy (or fantasy): "Imaginary scene in which the subject is a protagonist,
     representing the fulfilment of a wish (in the last analysis, an unconscious wish) in a
     manner that is distorted to a greater or lesser extent by defensive processes .... In so
     far as desire is articulated in this way through phantasy, phantasy is also the locus of
     defensive operations .... Such defences are themselves inseparably bound up with the
     primary function of phantasy, namely the *mise-en-scène* of desire—a *mise-en-scène*
     in which what is *prohibited (l'interdit)* is always present in the actual formation of the
     wish" (Laplanche and Pontalis 314, 318).

12   "How strange that I, the I who had seemed undying, should hit the ground like all
     the rest!" (Clyde Balsley, to whom Victor Chapman had attempted to bring oranges,
     in his account of being shot down, in Hall and Nordhoff vol. 2, 60). Dean Smith, in
     describing the harrowing and absurd character of just-out-of-control flight as the U.S.

Signal Corps trainees "stagger into the air at the last second, miss[ing] the telephone wires by inches—telephone wires around a field were almost universal" (Smith 111)—helps us appreciate how much realistic aviation material, and fear, Faulkner was condensing, displacing, and working through in his first flying story.

13 Hanging upside down is the position Faulkner assumed for himself in numerous autobiographical retellings of what was for him the prototypical aviation event. I discuss this element in the following chapter.

14 A.M's: air mechanics or "ack emmas": a general term covering a general range of ground-crew roles.

15 Dean Smith offers an uncanny analogue of this scene in recalling his own miraculous escape from an "outside spin" he found himself in during his time as a U.S. Army Air Service flying instructor: "A group of officers had come out of the mess just in time to see me hurtling out of the sky.

'That was terrific,' one of them said. 'So that's what an outside spin looks like. I've heard of them, but I'd never seen one before. That's what you were doing, isn't it?'

'Why thanks,' I answered, thinking fast. 'Yes, that's an inverted spin. Pretty rough on the plane, though. I don't think we'd better try to teach it to cadets, do you?'" (68).

16 "The Canadian Aeroplanes Limited propeller is five-ply white oak, blued, compressed and formed up by machinery that is almost human—and took its origin from a lathe designed by Peter the Great to make gun stocks .... The successor of Peter's lathe carves them, four at a time, to one thirty-second of their finished form, and the final touches and balancing are hand work. To anyone who has seen a nine-foot propeller running at 1,500 revolutions per minute, its blade points cutting the air at the rate of eight miles a minute, it will be apparent how fine a workmanship and accurate a design is embodied here" (SU 48–49).

17 This synchronized "'line of aim' anticipated the automation of perception" (Virilio, *War and Cinema* 3) in the drone technologies of remote warfare. See Zeitlin, "'An Entirely New Way.'"

18 "Just back from an excursion on a new section of railroad, the editor of the *Cincinnati Enquirer* reports, in 1846, that he saw 'herds of cattle, sheep, and horses, stand for a few seconds and gaze at the passing train, then turn and run for a few rods with all possible speed, stop and look again with eyes distended, and head and ears erect, seemingly so frightened at the tramp of the iron horse as to have lost the power of locomotion'" (qtd. in Leo Marx, *The Machine in the Garden* 195).

19 I discuss Kafka's stunning encounter with the aviation spectacle in his report, "The Aeroplanes at Brescia," in this book's *Pylon* chapter.

20 See Jay Watson on the composition of *As I Lay Dying* and what he understands as Faulkner's more positive relation to the dynamo as he wrote to its music at the Ole Miss power plant in 1929. "Where a half-century earlier Henry Adams had recoiled from the dynamo's implications as an emblem of modernity, Faulkner embraced them—indeed, emulated them—drafting his manuscript with breakneck speed, on a writing schedule dictated by the machine. The result was audacious, visionary, unrelentingly experimental—dynamic in the most literal sense. The novel, Faulkner recognized right away, was a *tour de force*. And that force stemmed in no small part from the scene and circumstances of its composition: within the force field generated by industrial modernity" (Watson, "Under the Spell"). See Watson's *William Faulkner and the Faces of Modernity* for a rich and wide-ranging discussion of Faulkner, modernism, and modernity.

21　The literature is full of stories about the menace of the aeroplane to people and
animals. Members of Winslow's squadron used aeroplanes to hunt partridges: "Our
speed would enable us to overtake and hit them with the wires of the machine and
kill them. Running along the ground in this way is always attended with danger, but it
was real sport. One morning in twenty minutes we killed six partridges in this novel
manner" (58–9). Of his dog Moritz, Richthofen recalls, "He has a silly peculiarity.
He likes to accompany the flying machines at the start. Frequently the normal death
of a flying-man's dog is death from the propeller. One day he rushed in front of a
flying-machine which had been started. The aeroplane caught him up and a beautiful
propeller was smashed to bits. Moritz howled terribly and a measure which I had
hitherto omitted was taken. I had always refused to have his ears cut. One of his
ears was cut off by the propeller. A long ear and a short ear do not go well together"
(Richthofen 95).

22　Wrote the Wright brothers in *Century Magazine* (September 1908), "In the field
of aviation there were two schools. The first, represented by such men as Professor
Langley and Sir Hiram Maxim, gave chief attention to power flight; the second,
represented by Lilienthal, Mouillard, and Chanute, to soaring flight. Our sympathies
were with the latter school [and with] the extraordinary charm and enthusiasm
with which the apostles of soaring flight set forth the beauties of sailing through the
air on fixed wings, deriving the motive power from the wind itself" (JY 25). Both
Langley and Maxim failed spectacularly. On "Hiram Maxim, a self-made inventor,
made wealthy by his invention of the first machine gun in history" (A 3), Liddell Hart
comments: "His name is more deeply engraved on the real history of the World War
than that of any other man. Emperors, statesmen, and generals .... found themselves
puppets in the grip of Hiram Maxim, who, by his machine-gun, had paralyzed the
power of attack" (*The Real War* 250).

23　Marinetti liked to describe himself as "the caffeine of Europe" (Flint 6). I discuss
Pylon in relation to Italian Futurism in this book's *Pylon* chapter.

24　In Billy Mitchell's post-First World War vision of the proximate future, the camera
and the bomb are part of one fused apparatus: "These airplanes are equipped with
cameras that are snapped by the device that would drop the bomb. The photograph
indicates where the bomb would hit" (Mitchell 164). See Zeitlin, "'An Entirely New
Method.'"

25　By this reckoning, Faulkner's overall grade, "Groundwork 70%" (B 228), would have
placed him below the officer line, a crushing disappointment. Is this a slip of the
pen, another "confession through a parapraxis"?: "TO Mrs. M. C. Falkner, Friday,
November 22, 1918: Mother darling—[....] I passed my examinations, though it will
do me no good, still knowing the I was one of the 20% who ~~failed~~ passed and not one
of the 80% who failed, is some thing" (TH 133).

26　This conception of a kind of "Northwest Ordinance" of the bombing zone would
come to dominate bombing operations in the Second World War and the American
wars in Vietnam, Iraq, and Afghanistan. "The selection of objectives, the grouping
of zones, and determining the order in which they are to be destroyed is the most
difficult and delicate task in aerial warfare" (Douhet 51). Therefore, as Neil Sheehan
writes in *A Bright Shining Lie*, "Free-fire zones proliferated so rapidly with new red
lines on maps for laying waste that it was no longer possible to keep track of their
number and the total area they encompassed" (96). The brutality and the futility of

this logic in the American war in Vietnam are resolutely exposed in Stephen Wright's incomparable novel, *Meditations in Green* (1983), in which an intelligence officer named Griffin unwinds a spool of film. "He reached forward, turned the crank on his right, and the film, unrolling from a reel on the left, moved smoothly across a long rectangle of illuminated glass. The military name for this task was image interpreter. Griffin was required to translate pictures into letters and coordinates that were instantly telexed to such important addresses as III MAF, 1 AIRCAV, 25DIV, III MAG, MACV, CINCPAC, and most impressive, JCS. The data went round and round and where it came out he preferred not to hear. A camera fixed in the belly of a Mohawk OV-1A had collected today's images during a morning break in the weather above a sector of suspected hostile activity approximately fifty kilometers southwest of Griffin's stool. His job was to interpret the film, find the enemy in the negatives. He turned the crank. Trees, trees, trees, trees, rocks, rocks, cloud, trees, trees, road, road, stream, stream, ford, trees, road, road. He stopped cranking. With a black grease pencil he carefully circled two blurry shadows beside the white thread of a road. Next to the circles he placed question marks. Road, road, road, road, trees, trees, trees. His eyes felt hard as shells, sore as bruises. Trees, trees, trees, trees. Wherever he put circles on the film there the air force would make holes in the ground" (40).

27   The first motion picture was shot from an aeroplane in 1909 (Epstein). Eddie Rickenbacker describes the making of "An Aeroplane Movie Show" (October 1918) in Chapter 33 of his memoir (321, 323–34). See Virilio, *War and Cinema*, for the "the aerialization of human vision and the cinema" (46) and Esposito on "the 'dream factory' … in the process of crystallization" in the early aviation era (Esposito 204).

28   The war would go on, "wearing down the life-energies of millions" (Gilbert 460), but the end was becoming visible. Hindenberg's appeal for an immediate armistice on October 3 "was a confession to the world—and to the German people themselves—of defeat" (Hart, *World War I* 266-7).

29   "The peculiar conditions of special glory [that] surround the RFC in Faulkner's mind continually recur in his aviation fiction …. flyer's wings are a special and coveted symbol of masculinity in Faulkner's fiction" (Weber 3), and in his social life too. Blotner recalls that in Charlottesville in 1957, Faulkner could often be seen "idly turning over a matchbox housed in a small metal holder decorated with RAF wings" (B 1636).

Wounded Flyer

"The war hurt Faulkner."

—Marshall J. Smith, 1931

Faulkner used poem XXX from *A Green Bough* as the epigraph to *Soldiers' Pay*. The setting is the "gray November earth" of 1918 and the scene is the return of the soldier:

The hushed plaint of wind in stricken trees
Shivers the grass in path and lane
And Grief and Time are tideless golden seas—
Hush, hush! He's home again. (53)

Faulkner's actual homecoming in early December, 1918, was nowhere near this somber, at least as his brother John (Johncy) describes it in his memoir, *My Brother Bill*:

Bill got off the train in his British officer's uniform—slacks, a Sam Browne belt, and wings on his tunic. He had on what we called an overseas cap, a monkey cap that was only issued to our men if they had served overseas. A part of the British uniform was a swagger stick and Bill had one, and across his arm a trench coat .... All of our own returned soldiers saluted Bill in his Sam Browne belt and monkey cap. To them it meant he had been overseas and they saluted an overseas man. They turned up their noses at our own officers who had not been over and refused to acknowledge them in any way.

I liked to walk around the Square with Bill on account of all the salutes he received. I was only seventeen at the time. (139)

Yet more was going on in Faulkner's soul than his little brother could have known. One imagines Faulkner, as he stepped down from the train, scanning the crowd not only for his mother, father, and little brothers Dean and Johncy but also for the spectral figures of Cornell Franklin and Estelle Oldham Franklin, now living in Hawaii. If only they could have seen him in that flying officer's uniform.[1] He also had his brother Murry in mind who was recuperating in a French hospital after being wounded in the Argonne Forest in one of the war's final battles. In Faulkner's later writing about the soldier's return, one feels the pressure of such darker moods. In *Flags in the Dust*, according to

Simon Strother's second-hand report from the African-American underground, RAF flyer Bayard Sartoris, having seen his twin brother leap from his burning aeroplane and fall to his death in France, disembarked from the train in Jefferson, Mississippi, out of uniform and almost completely unnoticed. "'Jumped off de wrong side and lit out th'ough de woods .... Jumpin' offen de bline side like a hobo. He never even had on no sojer-clothes. Jes a suit, lak a drummer er somethin'" (FL 546). As Faulkner settled more deeply into being home again, he began to experience something of Bayard's "mourning and melancholia" (Adamowski) while projecting an aura of secret and untellable experiences.

The opening of *Soldiers' Pay* also imagines the soldier's return as having had more dignity than Faulkner's own. Wounded RAF pilot Lieutenant Donald Mahon first appears in the novel through the eyes of Cadet Lowe, who seems to channel the memory of Faulkner's own "embryo" status in the spring of 1918 when Faulkner described to his mother some of the wounded soldiers he had seen in New York and New Haven:

> [5 April 1918, New Haven] I'm sorry Jack couldn't have been in New York. I walked down Fifth Avenue to 66th St. and saw the convalescent French and British officers. The lobbies and Mezzanine floors of the hotels are full of them, with their service stripes and wings and game legs and sticks .... I saw a French flyer with only one arm and a Croix de Guerre with two palms, which is about as high as a Frenchman can go and live. (TH 45–6)

> [28 April 1918, New Haven] At the Oneco hotel tonight there was a wounded British "Tommy" with a Distinguished Conduct Medal and a stiff leg. (TH 54)

Awed by their wounds and stoic bearing, Faulkner was beginning to absorb their extreme experiences (as he imagined them) and stiff legs into the deepest fantasy of himself, a process he captures in Cadet Lowe's acknowledgment that his own fascination with the pilot officer whom he encounters on the train is sustained by a sense of his utter distance from him: "He saw a belt and wings, he rose and met a young face with a dreadful scar across his brow. My God, he thought, turning sick [....] Had I been old enough or lucky enough, this might have been me, he thought jealously" (SP 17–18). Throughout the novel Mahon reflects the sorrow and envy, dread and fascination of those who circulate around him. All are captivated by the image of the wounded pilot, the image "whose internal thrust ... precipitates" their thoughts, and thus the novel itself, "in a fictional direction" (Lacan, "Mirror" 2).

Soldiers' Pay

Lieutenant Mahon was shot down in Flanders in March 1918 and he has long been presumed dead. (So Faulkner had imagined his own death on the Western Front and the sorrow of those who loved him.) In April of 1919, with the Easter season, the pilot who had been missing in action suddenly reappears on a train full of demobilized soldiers heading south from Toronto and Buffalo. (Faulkner had been on one of these trains where the first notion of the novel was likely conceived.) Mahon is blind and barely knows his own name as the train carries him and his escorts home to a small Georgia town (one much like Oxford and Jefferson, Mississippi in its Yoknapatawphan atmosphere). He is a resurrection, it seems, bearing his wound visibly, a "dreadful scar across his brow" (SP 17). "A military death's-head is central to Faulkner's first novel," Richard Godden observes (*An Economy* 228n), the sign of the war's ugly and enduring violence. After a brief hiatus to welcome him home, the community surmises that the wound is irreparable and resumes its suspended mourning rites. "Life contracts and death is expected/ As in a season of autumn" (Stevens, "The Death of a Soldier"). A body is carried "clumsily" from the house as a Boy Scout bugler plays taps. A procession follows the coffin past "shabby negro stores and shops" ("Well, Jesus! We all gwine dat way some day. All roads leads to de graveyard") and it is laid in the ground amid "all the excruciating ceremony for disposing of human carrion" (SP 236–7).[2]

As he fades slowly into a second death, Mahon's jagged scar reminds everyone of his suffering. It also marks the presence of a psychic wound—a radical splitting of the subject—to be read in modern psychological terms. As Mahon's doctor explains,

> He is practically a dead man now. More than that, he should have been dead these three months were it not for the fact that he seems to be waiting for something. Something he has begun, but has not completed, something he has carried from his former life that he does not remember consciously. (SP 122)[3]

Throughout the novel Mahon marks the space of subterranean mental process. Only near the end, on the threshold of death, does he remember what trauma had long foreclosed. He suddenly becomes himself again within the narrative coherence of a memory, opens his eyes, and tries to explain to his father what he has just seen and relived. He was on patrol, flying solo, when he was shot up by a burst of machine-gun bullets streaming from a diving aeroplane he never even saw except as a shadow. In the process of bringing Mahon's story up from the depths, it is as if the novel discovers a way for the pilot to witness and narrate his own death in the skies over Flanders:

> I never knew I could carry this much petrol, he thought in unsurprised ubiquity, leaving a darkness he did not remember for a day he had long forgot, finding that the day, his own familiar day, was approaching noon [….] Then suddenly it was as if a cold wind had blown upon him. What is it? he thought. It was that the sun had been suddenly blotted from him. The empty world, the sky, were yet filled with lazy spring sunlight but the sun that had been full upon him had been brushed away as by a hand. In the moment of realizing this, cursing his stupidity he dived steeply slipping to the left. Five threads of vapor passed between the upper and lower planes, each one nearer his body, then he felt two distinct shocks at the base of his skull and vision was reft from him as if a button somewhere had been pressed. His trained hand nosed the machine up smartly and finding the Vickers release in the darkness he fired into the bland morning marbled and imminent with March.

Sight flickered on again, like a poorly made electrical contact, he watched holes pitting into the fabric near him like a miraculous small-pox and as he hung poised firing into the sky a dial on his instrument board exploded with a small sound. Then he felt his hand, saw his glove burst, saw his bared bones. Then sight flashed off again and he felt himself lurch, falling until his belt caught him sharply across the abdomen, and he heard something gnawing through his frontal bone, like mice. You'll break your damn teeth, there, he told them, opening his eyes.

His father's heavy face hung over him in the dusk like a murdered Caesar's. He knew sight again and an imminent nothingness more profound than any yet, while evening, like a ship with twilight-colored sails, drew down the world, putting calmly out to an immeasurable sea. "That's how it happened," he said, staring at him. (SP 234–5)

Until the irruption of this scene from one of the novel's darkest spaces, Mahon merely sits in a chair in his father's house, mute, blind, opaque, unconsciously ruminant, casting a shadow over the agitated lives of those who circulate around him. Like his precursors the Shade of Pierrot and the Spirit of Autumn in Faulkner's play *The Marionettes* (1920) (see below), or the poet-tramp of the prose poem "Carcassonne," Mahon is an inert dreamer who "supplies a background in a single tone against which the succeeding action takes place, like a veiled mirror. Without moving or speaking he dominates the whole scene" (Faulkner, *The Marionettes* 37).[4] To his unfaithful fiancée, Cecily Saunders, Mahon is the returned war hero to whom she remains glamorously though ambivalently engaged. Perhaps she never loved him, and now she is drawn to another man who has never stopped wooing her. Besides, she is disgusted by Mahon's ghastly scar and warned by her mother that she would regret a marriage to an impotent man. To the Rector, his father, Mahon is the dead son miraculously resurrected. To Julian Lowe, Mahon reflects the erotic prestige of the pilot officer and the beautiful martial death only a flyer like him can achieve. To Emmy, the young housekeeper, Mahon is the remnant and wreckage of the wild, faun-like boy she loved in the days before the war when they roamed the woods together. By virtue of these psychical investments, Mahon is taken up into the soul of the community. Diffusing himself throughout the novel's complex of social relations, presiding over the field of erotic competition, contaminating desire with the remorse evoked by his dying, he is like the Fisher King of James Frazer and Jessie Weston, or the primal father of Freud's *Totem and Taboo*, the signifier of the group's erotic relation with an essentially absent yet strangely potent figure of proscription and authority. In this capacity Mahon is the fit object of an intense ambivalence of feeling, his scar the sign of a collective—and unconscious— animosity.[5]

Of all such transferences of emotion, none is more significant (both to the novel itself and to Faulkner's creative development as a literary artist) than that of the widow, Margaret Powers, for whom Mahon is a symbolic incarnation of her husband, Lieutenant Richard Powers, who died in the trenches, shot in the face "at point-blank range" by a private in the platoon he commanded. (Margaret does not know how he died). No one in the home community, except for its veteran soldiers, has any understanding at all of the war's ferocious violence. The novel's primal scene of the war is a fratricide, marking a pattern of tensions that traverses all of Faulkner's writings about war. A young soldier, Dewey Burney (from Mahon's home town), believes he has seen a cloud of poison gas forming itself in the dawn mist. Someone "screams Gas" and panic spreads throughout the disintegrating platoon as Lieutenant Powers and Sergeant Madden attempt to restore discipline and order.

> Powers and Madden sprang among them as they fought blindly fumbling and tearing at their gas masks, trampling each other, but they were powerless. The lieutenant laid about him with his fists trying to make himself heard and the man who had given the alarm whirled suddenly on the fire-step, his head and shoulders sharp against the sorrowful dawn.
>
> "You got us killed," he shrieked shooting the officer in the face at point-blank range. (SP 142)

Dewey does not survive the war and his mother mourns him in the second half of the novel where the hideous image of Powers' "face briefly spitted on the flame of a rifle" strikes at the reader aggressively in recurrent yet unpredictable intervals (SP 142, 147, 160, 168, 209). So the novel strives to absorb the shock effects of a trauma it is compelled to repeat.

The novel's deep engagement with the war's ugliness works itself out in terms of these extraordinarily complex social patterns traceable to Mahon's central figure. The case of Margaret Powers is especially fascinating in this respect since she is also Faulkner's first major fictional exploration of "stream-of-consciousness" subjectivity, a uniquely modernist fusion of symbol, myth, and psychopathology. As such she is Donald Mahon's fundamental counterpart, a subject traversed by unconscious processes, an object too of central fascination. Sometimes she is a strikingly sexual, "Beardsleyan" seductress, a "white and slim and depraved" (SP 31) *femme fatale* with long dark hair, long legs, and a red mouth. At other times she is maternal and affectionate: "when he was beside her she took his face in her hands and kissed him. He put his arms around her, and she drew his head between her breasts. After a while she stroked his hair and spoke" (SP 54). In her radical subjectivity, however, she invariably belies the "emotionally-charged fictions" (Freud, "Letter to Wilhelm Fliess" 216) the novel's other characters (along with the primary narrative voice of the novel) generate about her.

No one else knows that she has suffered the trauma of bereavement though it is marked by the scar she also bears. About this the text is insistent: "the red scar of her mouth," "her mouth was like a scar," "her pallid face [...] scarred with her mouth" (SP 32, 40, 42). The emotional past works its way through her in a movement parallel to Mahon's invisible drive toward self-presence, and, in marrying Mahon just before he dies, she "acts out" her role in the archaic plot that impels her to preside once again over the death of a husband.[6]

As a figure of the death to which Mahon is betrothed, Margaret is given an uncanny stylization. "She was dark" (SP 22). "They watched her until her dark dress merged with shadow beyond the zone of light" (SP 167). "She evaded her blanket and reaching her arm swept the room with darkness" (SP 33). Smoking cigarettes and expelling smoke from her mouth and nostrils, she is a postwar version of Hawthorne's "Rappaccini's Daughter," a woman "to be touched only with a glove, nor to be approached without a mask. As Beatrice came down the garden path, it was observable that she handled and inhaled the odor of several of the plants, which her father had most sedulously avoided" (Hawthorne 391–2). So Margaret walks in the rector's garden, a "black woman [...] among roses, blowing smoke upon them from her pursed mouth, bending and sniffing above them" (SP 197). The women especially intuit her inimical force: Cecily Saunders refers to her as "that black, ugly woman" (SP 110) and accuses her of keeping Mahon shut up like a prisoner, while Emmy accuses Margaret of murder: "'Let me alone! Go away!' she said, fiercely. 'You got him killed: now bury him yourself'" (SP 237).[7]

In one sense there is no transcending the mythological logic: the men who marry her die because she is taboo. But as a principal agent of the novel's modernist "mythical method"—its "manipulation" of "a continuous parallel between contemporaneity and antiquity" (Eliot 177)—she is also a resolutely post-Freudian subject. Like Freud's hysterical patients, Margaret "suffers mainly from reminiscences" (Breuer and Freud 58), both her own and those of a culture whose "mythical methods" continue to control how she can be conceived.[8] The novel in this sense represents her husbands' deaths as just punishment for their acts of sexual violation.[9]

After the U.S. declaration of war, Margaret had accepted a spirited marriage proposal from a young officer about to leave for the front, Lieutenant Richard Powers. The novel represents the passage and repassage in her mind of her highly ambivalent sexual experience during the first three days of their marriage: "it was like when you are a child in the dark and you keep on saying, It isn't dark, it isn't dark" (SP 129). As she replays the scene obsessively, it is as if the knowledge of Powers' death invades the memories of their lovemaking. He was already then a corpse, it seems, as he should have died during the scene of violation.

> Your bones, your mouth hard and shaped as bone: rigid. My body flows away: you cannot hold it. (SP 144)

> (Dick, Dick. Dead, ugly Dick. Once you were alive and young and passionate and ugly, after a time you were dead, dear Dick: that flesh, that body, which I loved and did not love; your beautiful, young, ugly body, dear Dick, become now a seething of worms, like new milk. Dear Dick.) (SP 32)

> How ugly men are, naked. Don't leave me, don't leave me! No, no! we don't love each other! we don't! we don't! Hold me close, close: my body's intimacy is broken, unseeing: thank God my body cannot see. Your body is so ugly, Dick! Dear Dick. Your bones, your mouth hard and shaped as bone: rigid. (SP 144)

> Dick, my love, that I did not love, Dick, your ugly body breaking into mine like a burglar, my body flowing away, washing away all trace of yours (SP 146)

Once the affair was over, she experienced a steadily mounting guilt, misgiving, and hostility. When she feared she was pregnant, she "almost hated Dick," but soon, she claims, he became "a shadowy sort of person" (SP 129). At last she no longer missed him, no longer looked forward "to getting one of those dreadful flimsy envelopes" he continued regularly to send her. Eventually she sends him a letter "call[ing] the whole thing off" (SP 129): "And then, before my letter reached him, I received an official notice that he had been killed in action. He never got my letter at all. He died believing that everything was the same between us" (SP 130). Thereafter she behaves as if she had somehow brought about his death, a death in which she encounters the dreaded evidence of the potency of her own hostile wishes. Her guilt is predicated in this sense on what Freud was so fascinated by in James Frazer's account of magical or animistic thinking, the "belief in the sympathetic influence exerted on each other by persons or things at a distance": "Should a wife prove unfaithful while her husband is away he will lose his life in the enemy's country" (Frazer 22, 25), an archetypal logic as necessary to *Soldiers' Pay* as to Homer's *Odyssey* and Joyce's *Ulysses*.[10]

Margaret's marriage to Donald Mahon is the culmination of a process of mourning driven by the obsessive self-reproaches of a woman who believes herself to have been responsible for the death of her husband. These self-reproaches are justified, for "there was something in her—a wish that was unconscious to herself—which would not have been dissatisfied by the occurrence of death and which might actually have brought it about if it had had the power" (Freud, *Totem and Taboo* 60). It is her compulsion both to repeat and to undo an original death wish that finds in Mahon a clear object of her ambivalence. Again she marries, again her husband dies. Again she is a bride, again a widow. Ostensibly an act of atonement, the marriage is also a screen for another death wish.

With Mahon dead and buried, her long work of mourning and melancholia is accomplished: "She felt freer, more at peace with herself than she had felt for months. But I won't think about that, she decided deliberately. It is best just to be free, not to let, it into the conscious mind" (SP 241). Thus she disappears from the novel, a Persephone returning as a bride to join her dead lovers, or a Eurydice failing back into Hades, as Joe Gilligan chases a fast-receding figure:

> He stopped at last, actually weeping with anger and despair, watching her figure, in its dark straight dress and white collar and cuffs, become smaller and smaller with the diminishing train that left behind a derisive whistle blast and a trailing fading vapor like an insult, moving along twin threads of steel out of his sight and his life. (SP 247)

Margaret Powers is the key figure in Faulkner's fictional analysis of the complex of individualized perspectives that array themselves around the wounded flyer Donald Mahon. She is traceable in this sense to Faulkner's fascination, beginning in December 1918, with the effects of his own RAF uniform, and the limp and other wounds he sometimes displayed, upon his mother Maud, Estelle, Estelle's parents, Faulkner's own father and brothers, his friends, and everybody else in town who had thought of him as a bum of No 'Count (Wasson). It was as if Faulkner had adopted the Christlike wounded warrior persona not only to produce but also to study, formally and psychologically, the effects of admiration, awe, hostility, resentment, jealousy, and fantasy-work in a surrounding community of souls.[11]

The Marionettes

In 1920 Faulkner enrolled in the University of Mississippi "as a returned veteran for whom the ordinary admission requirements had been waived" (B 248). During that time he wrote *The Marionettes: A Play in One Act*—"hand-printed, -decorated, and -bound, during his association with the drama group at the University of Mississippi" (Polk, "William Faulkner's *Marionettes*" 247). Candace Waid isolates the logic by which the play's narrative unfolds. "The events of Faulkner's symbolist play are depicted as the drunken reveries of Pierrot, who is always present as a sleeping figure on stage while his dreams take shape on the page in an enacted plot of seduction" (Waid 1). This symbolist play reads as a kind of dramatic sketch for *Soldiers' Pay*, the novel in germination.

As the play opens, Pierrot "appears to be in a drunken sleep, there is a bottle and an overturned wine glass upon the table, a mandolin and a woman's slipper lie at his feet …. He does not change his position during the play" (Faulkner, *The Marionettes* 2, 3). Throughout he is the central erotic focus of the spurned lover, Marietta, whose sole raison d'etre, it seems, is "to watch him, beautiful in slumber" (35), or perhaps in death. It is as if Pierrot, along with his shadow, The Spirit of Pierrot, is present at his own funeral in order to witness the bereavement of the lover, Marietta, who will thus also die of "sorrow" (35). As Waid has observed of the play's concluding visual tableau (see p. 55 for Faulkner's ink-drawn illustration), in this dream world Pierrot "gazes into the reflective space of the oval looking glass that vertically balances and visually echoes the slab-like bier demarcated by the supine and seemingly dead female body" (Waid 2).

As the dream unfolds, Marietta is the sole object of Pierrot's coercive seduction. "Her hands are clasped upon her breast, her eyes are fastened upon Pierrot, she is like a sleep walker while Pierrot continues to sing, weaving his song like a net about her" (24):

Plunge your fingers in her hair,
Spin and weave moon madness there,
Spin your dreams within her head
And let them dance in her white bed
Till all her dreams are fever hot,
Rout peace until she knows it not;
But only madness in the head,
Desire to follow where I lead. (27)

Hypnosis serves some fantasy of revenge, for at the moment of Marietta's maximum captivation (Lacan's "captation" would perhaps be the more resonant term here) Marietta is abandoned:

> Will he turn back where she awaits him in her rose bower, or will he go on? Ah, he goes on, his young eyes ever before him, looking into the implacable future. Perhaps a new, stronger love has called him away, perhaps he is fallen upon by wild beasts while traversing a dark forest, or perhaps, while crossing a stream, he slipped and was drowned. Yet she, among her dried rose stalks, waits for him to come along the sky; she waits in vain. There was none to fly to her when he fell, only the ripples of his fall to whisper across the pool. (34–5)

Many critics have read the play biographically. Writes Lothar Hönnighausen, "suffering from the disorientation of a 'lost generation,' out of place in his own hometown, and unhappily, seemingly hopelessly in love, the sensitive young Faulkner evidently thought he had found in Pierrot an appropriate persona to reflect his own melancholy" (132). Judith Wittenberg notes the "symbolic importance" of Pierrot (along with many cognate figures in Faulkner's work) as a "vehicle for Faulkner's romantic fantasies of himself as a wounded hero" (Wittenberg 46). And Judith Sensibar observes that "The physical resemblance between Faulkner's drawings of Marietta and Estelle would have been instantly apparent to the readers and buyers of Billie Faulkner's play" (Sensibar, *Faulkner and Love* 218).

Such readings situate the play in relation to the "Estelle complex" that runs through all of Faulkner's aviation fictions. We should recall that, even if, as Sensibar claims, "At twenty-one, [Faulkner] did not need or want a wife" (*Faulkner and Love* 320), the scene of the failed elopement of Bill and Estelle, and the subsequent wedding of Estelle and Cornell Franklin in the spring of 1918, was played out for Faulkner as a searing public humiliation. In what Lacan has termed "the struggle for recognition .... the fight to the death for pure prestige" (Lacan qtd. in Borch-Jacobsen 21), Faulkner, as a matter of life and death, needed to join the war as an officer and to come back with something substantial, to come back even, if necessary, as a corpse to be flung at Estelle's feet (who's sorry now?). As the first-person narrator of Faulkner's prose sketch, "The Kid Learns," puts it (in the *New Orleans Sketches*, May 31, 1925): "Competition is everywhere: competition makes the world go round. Not love, as some say. Who would want a woman nobody else wanted? Not me. And not you. And not Johnny" (86). Johnny for his troubles wins only an assignation with "Little sister Death" (91).

Another of Faulkner's pilots, an American Air Force Captain, has been through this passion play himself, as he describes it in conversation with the old general in *A Fable*:

> "because a girl had stood me up and I thought I knew why. I mean, who it was, who the guy was. And you know how it is: you think of all the things to do to get even, make her sorry; you lying dead right there where she's got to step over you to pass, and it's too late now and boy, wont that fix her—"

"Yes," the old general said. "I know."

"Sir?" the captain said.

"I know that too," the old general said.

"Of course you do—remember, anyway," the captain said. "Nobody's really that old, I don't care how—" going that far before he managed to stop himself. "I'm sorry, sir," he said. (FA 923)

What Waid has called "the tableau of a looked-upon death" in *The Marionettes* (Waid 2) remained highly cathected (to use the Freudian period language) throughout Faulkner's narrative memories of his RAF experience.

War Stories, Hangar Flying, Sopwith Camels

When Faulkner returned from the war, he drank and he dreamed. He wrote and he acted out. Sometimes he held a cane and walked with a limp. He put on a kind of "antic disposition," his mourning and melancholia seeming more than a little irrational at times. With Estelle married to another man and soon to be the mother of two children, something was indeed rotten in the world to which he had returned. "Why did Faulkner limp? Why did he lie about nonexistent wounds all of his life? Why did he assert false identities so aggressively?" asks Michael Grimwood (35). Before providing any personal answers, Lewis Simpson pursues the matter across a broad cultural terrain, citing the legend of the "small-town youth" who discovers "the great world" and the Great War:

> In what has become the classic form of the refined legend, it is about an American boy who finds the meaning of the war through the transforming power of a wound, which may be physical or psychic but is always primarily psychic. His wound is his badge of membership in the "lost generation" of the post-war wasteland, a sign, we might say, of the damnation by which he will live. (Simpson xiv)

For Faulkner, as a member of this lost generation, there had to be a wound, and he put himself in the place of the wounded soldier in order to experience, as fully as he could, imaginatively and emotionally, one of the most powerful expressions of the age. "Beyond the dual aims of imitation and parody," Donald Kartiganer reflects, "I suspect Faulkner believed that in some strange way he had successfully appropriated the war ... by the sheer power of his imaginative empathy" (Kartiganer 632), an empathy also sustained by his own genuine suffering. Grimwood's claim that Faulkner's "bogus war souvenir was a deliberate lie, designed to incite pity and envy among friends and neighbors" (Grimwood 39), therefore, needs careful qualification.[12] As we bring up the light on the social effects of Faulkner's impersonations, putting the given presentation of the wound within its particular social scene (when we can), we find that Faulkner's masquerade was not so much deliberate as compulsive, while to say he was lying (and to leave it at that) would be to obscure the situation of the military veteran who returns home and feels the pressure "to produce experiences worth telling" (Johnson 273). Hemingway's classic story, "Soldier's Home," about the home audience's radical inability to comprehend the soldier's nerve-strain and humiliation, is worth reading again in all these respects.

Still, soldiers returning from military service need stories and Faulkner had no shortage of them. "Multiple, overlaid, palimpsestic," some of his oral tales would also become "written performances and displays based in his life as he both lived and imagined living it" (Watson, *William Faulkner: Self-Presentation* 37, xiii). One of the first ones he told was about an Armistice Day joy ride ending with the aeroplane crashing through a hangar at RAF Camp Borden, pilot, crock of bourbon, and plane suspended from the roof upside down.[13] Faulkner told the story to his brother Murry upon their first meeting after the war:

> I asked him what he thought about flying airplanes. "Nothing to equal it," he replied. Then I asked him if he had had a crackup or experienced any other untoward event in his flying. "Yes," he said, "I did, as a matter of fact. The war quit on us before we could do anything about it. The same day they lined up the whole class, thanked us warmly for whatever it was they figured we had done to deserve it, and announced that we would be discharged the next day, which meant that we had the afternoon to celebrate the Armistice and some airplanes to use in doing it. I took up a rotary-motored Spad with a crock of bourbon in the cockpit, gave diligent attention to both, and executed some reasonably adroit chandelles, an Immelmann or two, and part of what could easily have turned out to be a nearly perfect loop." "What do you mean—part of a loop?" I asked. He chuckled and replied, "That's what it was; a hangar got in the way and I flew through the roof and ended up hanging on the rafters." (Murry Falkner 90–1)

Faulkner's brother John also keeps the story in circulation in his own memoir. In his version the French Spad is replaced by the British Camel:

> When he got off [the train] we saw that he was limping. As soon as we greeted him and got him in the car he told us that some of the graduating class had gone up to celebrate getting their wings and he had flown his Camel halfway through the top of a hangar. The tail of his ship was still outside and they got Bill down from inside the hangar with a ladder. (John Faulkner 139)[14]

Faulkner's urgency to establish his bona fides as a military aviator, especially in the eyes of his younger brothers, helps to account for the manner in which the effeminate flight trainer, the Curtiss Jenny, was overlaid, in double exposure, by genuine front-line war machines in the course of these tellings and retellings. Two things are clear: "All student pilots in Canada, even those at the School of Aerial Fighting at Beamsville, flew only one aeroplane: the Curtiss Jenny" (Harrison 24). And: "What can be definitely established is that absolutely no Sopwith Camels, a front-line fighter aircraft, were in Canada in 1918" (Weber 6). The Jenny was the plane that would have been "inverted" by the young RAF cadet on Armistice Day.[15]

John Faulkner, perhaps with Bill's help, found a way to explain his brother's "graduation" from training machines to Camels in the following way:

> They sent Bill to primary training in Toronto on Canucks, ships about like the Jennies we used to train our pilots. He graduated from them and went on to fighter training on Sopwith camels, the orneriest airplane ever built. (135)

> I remember how quickly Bill learned [to ride a bicycle]. He was the first of us who did. I think it was his sense of balance that helped him live through flying Camels in the First War, for there never was a more tricky airplane built than a Sopwith Camel. (89)

> Bill was bound to have been a good pilot with the RFC, else he would never have got by flying Camels. (168)[16]

The legendary Camel certainly assumed a central place in the Faulkner brothers' collective investment in the mythology of the war. As Lewis Simpson has observed, Faulkner "and his brothers, all licensed pilots, had a 'common and everlasting love' for airplanes. Caught up in the wonder and adventure of flying, they took equal delight in aerial techniques and in the mechanics of fallible, at times cantankerous, flying machines" (Simpson xii). The Camel was the *ne plus ultra* of cantankerousness, as John Faulkner well knew:

> They had rotary engines and were placarded against a left-hand spin at anything less than three thousand feet. It took that long to get one out once it got in.
>   The whole engine turned. The prop was bolted onto it. The back end of the crankshaft was fastened to the first station of fuselage frame and a mixture of gasoline and castor oil was fed into the engine through a hollow crankshaft and hollow piston rods. Immediately you landed one of them you headed lickety-split for the bathroom. (John Faulkner 135)

Faulkner's stepson, Malcolm Franklin, also believed that his "pappy" had flown Camels in the war:

> A good friend, Captain Vernon Omlie, owner of a hangar at the then small municipal airport at Memphis, Tennessee, encouraged Faulkner to begin flying once more. First of all it would be necessary to obtain a flying license. He had not flown since his World War I days and the flying of a Sopwith Camel. (Franklin 102)

Faulkner's close identification with the Sopwith Camel was also central to the bond he forged with the aviators he knew in Memphis and New Orleans. And if Camels were in

Figure 6.1 Sopwith Camel.

service only on the Western Front and at the RAF bases in England, Faulkner sometimes needed to shift the location of his flying tales accordingly. In 1934, for example, as Blotner recounts, Faulkner spent much time with fellow-aviator E. O. Champion. "They talked flying all the time, Champ always eager to listen. Faulkner told about flying Sopwith Camels in England, how they threw castor oil so badly that you could hardly see to land. He would watch pilots bust them up every day, he said" (B 856).

As Joel Williamson has noted, Faulkner loved to indulge in "'hangar flying' with other aviators. The amount of time spent in the air was small compared to the time spent talking about flying and telling flying stories in the small lounges that were often tucked into the corners of hangars. It gave him a special entree, too, into a grand airshow at the New Orleans airport in February, 1934" (Williamson 242). Eventually his circle of fellow hangar flyers would include real combat aviators Joseph Blotner and Frederick Gwynn whom Faulkner met in Virginia in 1957. Faulkner, in Blotner's account, "was the chief of the hangar-flying squadron that clustered near the coffee-making equipment" (B 1662). And sometimes, "sitting in Fred Gwynn's office during those coffee-and-hangar-flying sessions, we had told war stories" (B 1711). The Sopwith Camel was the special "model" of their regard for the war service Faulkner wished to be associated with in their presence. They called themselves The Squadron and they had their own special room.

The attention we had devoted to the wars we ourselves had served in took a different form. Fred and I had decided to obtain miniatures for the Squadron

Room: a Sopwith Camel for him, a TBF torpedo bomber for Fred, and a B-17 Flying Fortress for me. Thus far we had managed only the Camel, which Fred and I had laboriously assembled, painted, and mounted, to Mr. Faulkner's seeming pleasure. This model-making was something we had not done since boyhood. We had done it now with a combination of fun and some nostalgia but without solemnity, though the Squadron had come to mean a good deal to us. That evening, after our trip to the Civil War battlefields, the Faulkners gave a Squadron dinner out on the terrace at Rugby Road. (B 1671)

The Camel is the essential link, too, in what would become the stakes-raising fusion of two apocryphal events, the training accident in Canada and the crash-landing during combat on the Western Front. A particularly clear instance of the synthesis of the two appears in an article by Laurence Stallings, "Faulkner in Hollywood," published in the *New York Sun* on September 3, 1932.

William Faulkner has been in Hollywood working with Howard Hawks on a story of war pilots …. Faulkner, at 19, joined the Canadian air force. After two hours instruction in France he went out with a squadron for combat. He was in a Camel. Camels rarely banked to the right, and could be turned to the left only after first making the motions for a right bank. The German who engaged him evidently knew this. "No matter how many motions I'd make," he says, "that German knew all along which way I'd have to turn. I'd kick her rudders and do what was best, but he'd be hanging there waiting. I'd know it before I'd looked on account of tracer bullets going through my wings. After a little of this I couldn't turn at all. I notice then I didn't have any ailerons. I ran along the ground about a hundred miles an hour. Suddenly I turned the other way and ran just as fast. Then it turned over."

"Did you get the engine in your lap?" I asked him.

"No," said Faulkner pleasantly. "I came to hanging from the belt …. I never did figure out how I broke my legs."

Faulkner is a taciturn man. (Stallings 27–8)[17]

Faulkner told such aviation stories in multiple versions over many years, their tones ranging from comical and absurd to tragic and haunting depending on the setting, genre, or audience. With Theresa Towner and James B. Carothers, who are discussing the daredevil Ginsfarb in Faulkner's "Death Drag" in this instance, we can say of the protagonist of such tales that "Faulkner does not mean him for a hero but for a survivor" (Towner and Carothers 108), a survivor, once again, despite his injuries, somehow "landing in luck." In "Death Drag" as in "With Caution and Dispatch" (651), not so much "the innocent mischances of plotting" (Crews 177) as a higher presiding force places the collapsible object or entangling structure in just the right position to absorb the flyer's impact and render his crash survivable: "'Providence knew … that he deserved justice, so Providence put that barn there with the rotting roof'" (Faulkner, "Death Drag" 202).

When women were a part of Faulkner's audience, as they often were, the stories of his own "acts of pure individual recklessness" (Kartiganer, "'So I'" 634) could be likened to the plumage of the peacock: conceited and a little absurd—to be sure—but an unmistakable sign of what he intended to be an alluring masculinity, "the classic hallmarks" of which were "youth … risk, traumatic accidents, and high mortality" (C 14). "Men who take big chances can reap big sexual rewards. Warriors or gladiators or barnstormers who lead short lives can still broadcast their genes" (C 50), the airplane, even if only conjured in words and images, serving as "the ultimate dating machine" (C 51). The medium is the message: the antic verbal stunts and the "can-you-top-this mentality" (C 169) of the hangar flyer are the primary forms of his aerobatic performances.

Pilot Dean C. Smith explains that the risk-taking mentality was implicitly encouraged by the institutional hierarchy of flight assignments in the First World War Air Force:

> The highest rating was pursuit, followed by bomber, observation, and finally Corps d'Arme—the aerial direction of artillery fire, reconnaissance, and liaison flying under the control of ground forces. Almost without exception cadets aspired to a pursuit rating …. Barracks rumor had it that wild daredevil pilots were wanted for combat fliers, while instructors were supposed to be steady and conservative. I wanted to be a fighter pilot, ergo, I would be wild. I made my plans with care. It was important for my purpose to select a time when my antics would attract maximum attention and have the greatest shocking-power. (Smith 62, 72)[18]

Faulkner sometimes conveyed the impression that he had been in line for such training as a pursuit (fighter) pilot or had in fact been one in the war. "The flying heroes of the war had been hard-living and nonchalant in their recklessness, and perhaps their behavior gave us our standards" (Smith 141). And of course many of the best pilots of the war were dead. Faulkner's "recklessness" was his way of saying that he could easily have been among them. As Joel Williamson reflects, "he had flown his plane with such daredevil verve—by his own account—as to establish that he would have been valorous in battle and, ultimately, either victorious or dead" (Williamson 185).

Faulkner's oral aviation tales reflect "the passionate desire peculiar to man to impress his image in reality" (Lacan, "Aggressivity" 22), a desire Faulkner was fully conscious of, if not always in the midst of his tellings, at least as he recollected them in tranquility. As he wrote to his stepson Malcolm Franklin on December 5, 1942 (from Warner Bros. Studio, Burbank, CA), "it's a strange thing how a man, no matter how intelligent, will cling to the public proof of his masculinity: his courage and endurance, his willingness to sacrifice himself for the land which shaped his ancestors" (SL 166). Phil Stone's biographer Susan Snell points out that the Oxford community had many reasons in the late spring of 1917 to be "suspicious regarding the masculinity" of both Stone and William Faulkner (Snell 7). In December 1918 and the months and years following, the mystique of military aviation, the uniform, the wounds, the stories, the silences—all constituted unanswerable "public proof of his masculinity," and patriotism.[19]

It is clear that many people believed that Faulkner, "the old fighter pilot with the Nobel Prize," had done the things he claimed or had written about in his stories, and at least one young Second World War pilot, Dan Brennan, writing of himself in the third person here, cursed him for it:

> He had gone over to England in 1940 and discovered courage and honor and love and death were easier in thought and in books. "Damn you, Faulkner," he thought lying in a hospital in Norfolk with a cannon shell wound in his leg. "Damn you, and your war stories.".... the young man... had stopped being young the night the Junkers 88 shot him down .... You better not get me into the next war, damn you, Faulkner. (LG 50)

Faulkner's words could enter deeply into the souls of his listeners. His lover in Hollywood, Meta Carpenter Wilde, also gives vivid testimony in this respect:

> Sleep overtook me and I dreamed of William Faulkner in an airman's helmet flying low in a warplane over a foreign land, and of great caves open to the sea and the howling wind, and of my own hands—not those of the woman in Bill's poem— moving thunderously over a piano keyboard. (Wilde and Borsten 41)

> He talked easily about his own training as a flier with the Canadian Royal Air Force during World War I and of the combat missions he had flown overseas.
> "When I crashed," he said, "I thought I'd never fly again."
> "Oh, Bill.".…. "You crashed?"
> "Flying a mission in France."
> I put my hand on his sleeve and we stood looking at each other as cars streaked by. "Were you badly injured?"
> "There's a silver plate in my skull." He tapped his head over an ear and grinned.
> "The sterling in my head is worth more than I am down at the Oxford bank."
> That night and for long years after, I believed that William Faulkner had been shot down out of the skies over the French countryside. I had no reason to doubt it until some time after his death when I learned that Bill had never been sent overseas from Canada and therefore could not have been shot down in a plane. Faulkner had told the "shot down" story to many people. (Wilde and Borsten 46)

As Wilde seems to be confirming, though Faulkner often "confined his own deeds to comic flamboyance," "zany theatrics, gallant pratfalls" (Kartiganer, "'So I'" 632), he could also imply, primarily by his silences and his darker moods, that he had experienced painful and haunting combat experiences. Blotner recounts an episode from Faulkner's time in New York in 1921 (when he was writing "Love," to be discussed in the next chapter):

> One evening John Joice told his wife that he had invited Faulkner to join them for dinner. She could converse with him in French, he said. When Faulkner arrived,

he made a vivid impression on her. "He was just back from the war and, in fact, he had a cane and walked with a limp. He was dressed in a light beige mackintosh, a dusty dark brown hat and a pipe. He was generally nice looking with dark brown eyes and hair."

Taking her husband at his word, Mrs. Joice immediately began speaking French. Had he been wounded, she asked. He replied that "he had just been released from the hospital and had a metal disc close to his hip." It was only a good deal later that Mrs. Joice learned that Faulkner had done his RAF service in Canada. As she recalled that evening, however, she remembered that "he did nothing to dispel my illusion that he was a wounded hero returning from France." (B 323–4)

Of Faulkner's time in New Orleans in 1924, Blotner also notes that "most of the new friends he made … remained convinced for years that his airplane accident had left him with a silver plate in his head. They could see that he drank heavily. Soon the impression was general that this alleviated the pain from these wounds" (B 369). Estelle added in interview (February 18, 1965): "after a few drinks, he would tell people anything" (B 371, 59).

The Public Biographies

It was as a wounded combat flyer that Faulkner met Sherwood Anderson in New Orleans in 1924. Anderson fictionalizes the encounter in "A Meeting South":

He was small and delicately built but after he got in [the R.A.F.] he turned out to be a first-rate flyer, serving all through the War with a British flying squadron, but at the last got into a crash and fell. Both legs were broken, one of them in three places, the scalp was badly torn and some of the bones of the face had been splintered …. A silver plate had been set under the skin. (Anderson, "A Meeting" 402, 407)

Anderson, unlike, say, Faulkner's gay friends Ben Wasson and William Spratling, who knew something about masquerade, certainly believed Faulkner's story and did more than his part to keep it in circulation.[20]

Anderson's essay, "They Come Bearing Gifts," published in *The American Mercury* in October 1930, begins in the following manner: "The two most notable young writers who have come on in America since the war, it seems to me, are William Faulkner and Ernest Hemingway. I knew both men rather intimately just after the war and before either had published. Both were terribly injured in the war" (129). Talk about creating Faulkner's reputation.

As in Anderson's presence, in the biographical sketches that Faulkner's publishers demanded of him in the 1920s and '30s, Faulkner typically assumed "a tone of deadpan, hostile irony" (Meriwether and Millgate, Introduction, *Lion* ix) to ward off the excessively literal-minded curiosity of the public mind. In so doing he was certainly protecting a secret and vulnerable part of himself. For his first book, *The Marble Faun*, a collection of poems published in 1924, Faulkner authorized his publisher in a telegram "TO USE ANY FACTS REAL OR IMAGINARY THAT YOU DESIRE TO USE IN THE BOOK OR ADVERTISING MATTER." In a letter that *Forum* magazine published in April 1930 with "A Rose for Emily," Faulkner seemed to be following his own advice. The "facts" of his war service finally pass into the public record in this vivid, evasive, and pressurized form:

—To the editor

Born male and single at early age in Mississippi. Quit school after five years in seventh grade. Got job in Grandfather's bank and learned medicinal value of his liquor. Grandfather thought janitor did it. Hard on janitor. War came. Liked British uniform. Got commission R.F.C., pilot. Crashed. Cost British gov't £2000. Was still pilot. Crashed. Cost British gov't £2000. Quit. Cost British gov't $84.30. King said, "Well done." Returned to Mississippi. Family got job: postmaster. Resigned by mutual agreement on part of two inspectors; accused of throwing all incoming mail into garbage can. How disposed of outgoing mail never proved. Inspectors foiled. Had $700. Went to Europe. Met man named Sherwood Anderson. Said, "Why not write novels? Maybe won't have to work." Did. *Soldiers' Pay*. Did. *Mosquitoes*. Did. *Sound and Fury*. Did. *Sanctuary*, out next year. Now flying again. Age 32. Own and operate own typewriter. (SL 47)

The style Faulkner adopts here seems that of a telegram, perhaps an aviator's, as in a typical example quoted in David Courtwright's *Sky as Frontier*: "On Trip 4 westbound. Flying low. Engine quit. Only place to land on cow. Killed cow. Wrecked plane. Scared me. Smith" (59). A likely source, meanwhile, for the "£2000" increments of equipment loss, and the spirit of the crashing escapades by which Faulkner seemed to be confessing his "inaptitude" as a pilot, is Carroll Dana Winslow's *With the French Flying Corps* (1917). On the training field of the French flying camp a "pilot lost his head" and control of his biplane both, making "escape almost impossible" for the men who found themselves

in the very path of the onrushing biplane. We thought that at least a dozen would be crushed or else decapitated by the rapidly revolving propeller .... The stupid pilot escaped unscathed... needless to say... was immediately dismissed from the aviation school and sent back to his regiment. His escapade had cost the Government just about £2000! Even had there been no damage to the machine it is doubtful whether any further chances would have been taken with a man of such a temperament. (Winslow 87–8)[21]

In the biographical letter that Faulkner published with "A Rose for Emily" he seemed to be confessing that, while he had "served honorably and faithfully" in the RAF, he was "a man of such a temperament" as Winslow describes.

Perhaps in recoil from the attention he had generated with this letter, "When *The American Mercury* bought 'Honor' for publication in July 1930, Faulkner refused to supply anything at all" (Blotner, SL 48):

TO BEN WASSON [spring 1930], Oxford

Sorry, I haven't got a picture. I don't intend to have one that I know of, either. About the biography. Don't tell the bastards anything. It cant matter to them. Tell them I was born of an alligator and a nigger slave at the Geneva peace conference two years ago. Or whatever you want to tell them. (SL 48)

Faulkner's aggression here is palpable. The reporters and interviewers who were always trying to run him to ground were in no position to understand the truth about his military service. Nevertheless, they all seemed to respect the martial aura he projected (or could not prevent being projected upon him) and considered it authentic. In his interview with Faulkner at his home in Oxford in 1931, for example, Marshall J. Smith, reporter for the *Memphis Press-Scimitar*, describes Faulkner as "dark, small, keenly alive, virile and as he might term it—touched with a little sadness" (LG 6). "In the uniform of a British Tommy this Mississippian fought during the World War," Smith makes a point of noting, before quoting another snippet of Faulkner's notorious military biography:

"War came. Liked British uniform. Got commission R.F.C. pilot. Crashed. Cost British government 2000 pounds ($10,000).
"Was still pilot. Crashed. Cost British Government 2000 pounds. Quit. Cost British Government $84.30. King said, 'Well done.'" (LG 7)

In *The Bookman* version of the interview Smith follows Faulkner's reference to the return of the soldier with an explicit darkening of the tone:

"Returned to Mississippi."
The war hurt Faulkner. It took him time to recover. He painted roofs at the University of Mississippi at Oxford while he tried to regain what the conflict had taken away. (LG 13)

In his interview with Faulkner published in the *Dallas Morning News* on February 14, 1932, Henry Nash Smith tried in his own way

to get him to talk about his experiences with the British air force in France. I had heard that during the war he had been pulled out more dead than alive, from under a couple of wrecked planes. But he didn't have much to say about that. "I just smashed them up," he said. He was interested, however, in the fact that I had come from Dallas to Jackson in a trimotored cabin plane. "I've never ridden in a cabin plane," he said. "I'd like to have a chance to fly one. I was looking at the inside of one some time ago. They don't have the old stick—a steering wheel instead. I guess the plane couldn't be steered by one man's strength—they need a wheel with gears."

But he still refused to say much about the war. (LG 31–2)

The source for what Smith had heard about Faulkner being "pulled out more dead than alive, from under a couple wrecked planes" was likely the interview that had appeared in *The New Yorker* the previous year:

> In 1915 he enlisted in the Canadian air force and went to France. He crashed behind his own lines. He was hanging upside down in his plane with both legs broken when an ambulance got to him. He heard one of the men say: "He's dead all right," but had strength enough to deny this. After he recovered he transferred to the American air force. He has a pilot's license now and sometimes flies a rather wobbly plane owned by a friend in Oxford. After the war he studied about five months in the University of Mississippi. (LG 23–4)[22]

The wounded warrior folklore continued to be written into the public record as definitive historical truth, as in the fascinating exhibit, *Twentieth Century Authors: A Biographical Dictionary of Modern Literature*, edited by Stanley J. Kunitz and Howard Haycraft (New York: H. W. Wilson, 1942). "Every living author in this volume who could be reached was invited to write his own [autobiographical] sketch" (vi). The entry for FAULKNER, WILLIAM, includes the following:

> William was the oldest of four brothers, one of whom became a well-known aviator before he was killed in 1935 …. The First World War woke him from this lethargy. Flying caught his imagination, but he refused to enlist with the "Yankees," so went to Toronto and joined the Canadian Air Force, becoming a lieutenant in the R.A.F. Biographers who say he got no nearer France than Toronto are mistaken. He was sent to France as an observer, had two planes shot down under him, was wounded in the second shooting, and did not return to Oxford until after the Armistice. (Kunitz 439)[23]

Faulkner also observes of himself, hiding the key to his mystery in plain sight, "Except among his intimates, he is silent and unsocial, and has even been called 'insolent'; the fact is that his manner is the result of acute sensitiveness" (Kunitz 439).

"Was a Member of the RAF in 1918" (Faulkner to Malcolm Cowley, January 21, 1946)

The fiasco involving the biographical portion of Malcolm Cowley's *The Portable Faulkner* followed in 1945–6, the entire scene a revelation of how unresolved Faulkner's "acute sensitiveness" to his RAF record remained, some twenty-seven years after he first put on the flying officer's costume. Cowley had wanted to include this description of Faulkner's wartime service:

> When the war was over—the other war—William Faulkner went back to Oxford, Mississippi. He had been trained as a flyer in Canada, had served at the front in the Royal Air Force, and, after his plane was damaged in combat, had crashed it behind the British lines. Now he was home again and not at home, or at least not able to accept the postwar world. (Cowley 72)

Faulkner's objection to this passage, unfolding as a tortuous attempt to distinguish "truth" from "fact," must still make us wince a little, even as we recognize that he is offering us a key to his imagination as a writer of powerful and true fictions:

> But to me it was false. Not factually, I dont care much for facts, am not much interested in them, you cant stand a fact up, you've got to prop it up, and when you move to one side a little and look at it from that angle, it's not thick enough to cast a shadow in that direction. (Cowley 89)

Yes factually it was false of course. Yet as he said at Nagano in 1955, "Truth is a quality which one must accept or cope with. That is, he must accept or spend all his life running from it" (LG 145). Blotner, with his characteristic gentleness, understands, and is not deeply troubled: "There was still no hard factual evidence that he had crashed, let alone flown a military aircraft, but this was apparently too much a part of his own personal myth to be surrendered or repudiated" (B 1202–3). Cowley further explains:

> I wanted to accept that paragraph [in *Twentieth Century Authors*] because I had come to think of Faulkner... as being among the "wounded writers" of his generation, with Hemingway and others. It was hard for me to believe that his vivid stories about aviators in France—"Ad Astra," "Turnabout," "All the Dead Pilots"— and his portraits of spiritually maimed veterans, living corpses, in *Soldier's [sic] Pay* and *Sartoris* were based on anything but direct experience .... I did not dream that my facts were wrong or that Faulkner would question them. (Cowley 71–3)

He began to suspect the truth with Faulkner's letter of January 21, 1946:

Dear Cowley:

Yours at hand. You're going to bugger up a fine dignified distinguished book with that war business. The only point a war reference or anecdote could serve would be to reveal me a hero, or (2) to account for the whereabouts of a male of my age on Nov. 11, 1918 in case this were a biography. If, because of some later reference back to it in the piece, you cant omit all European war reference, say only what Who's Who says and no more:

Was a member of the RAF in 1918.

I'll pay for any resetting of type, plates, alteration, etc. I'm really concerned about the war reference. As I said last, I'm going to be proud of this book. I wouldn't have put in anything at all about the war or any other personal matter. (Cowley 82–3)

In response to which Cowley tells us: "This time I saw the light" (Cowley 83).

Even a decade later, during his visit to Japan, Faulkner's elaboration of the distinction between truth and fact suggests that his aviation secret lay among the deepest layers of what André Malraux, upon reading *Sanctuary* in 1931, recognized as Faulkner's "powerful, and savagely personal world" (Malraux 273):

Truth to me means what you know to be right and just, truth is that thing, the violation of which makes you writhe at night when you try to go to sleep, in shame for something you've done that you know you shouldn't have done. That to me is truth, not fact. Fact is not too important and can be altered by law, by circumstance, by too many qualities, economics, temperature, but truth is the constant thing, it's what man knows is right and that when he violates it, it troubles him. Well, I doubt if he ever does toughen himself, toughen his soul, to where it doesn't trouble him just a little and he'll try to escape from the knowledge of that truth in all sorts of ways, in drink, drugs, various forms of anesthesia, because he simply cannot face himself. (LG 145)

In drink, drugs, various forms of anesthesia: "even if American rumors did not kindly inform us that alcohol was an integral part of Faulkner's personal legend," Malraux reflects (273), it would be important to acknowledge its destructive impact on Faulkner's life and its association with a number of vivid episodes involving Faulkner's display of the aviation wound or story. Blotner tells us that Faulkner's "drinking did produce the equivalent of one or two serious illnesses a year for thirty years. His own euphemism for such an illness was 'a collapse'" (B 720). Faulkner's lover Meta Carpenter saw her share of such collapses, as we've seen, observing too that "Above everyone, I know that William Faulkner was the most private of men and that he suffered from invasions of his fortressed self as from jagged, festering wounds of his very flesh" (Wilde and Borsten 9). "What heartrending, what incurable despair did the drinking hide?" asks Michel Gresset in his Faulkner chronology (Gresset, *A Faulkner Chronology* 33), before answering: "Perhaps nothing can ever say it better than the books themselves" (33).[24]

In reminding us that Faulkner's "bouts of drinking were, in effect, the inevitable results of a disease over which he had little or no control" (7), Tom Dardis, however, contests the view that "Faulkner's drinking problems arose as a response to some inner emotional turmoil or anguish. But Faulkner drank under any and all circumstances, good, bad or indifferent. His behavior had only one explanation: he was an alcoholic" (28). Even so, alcoholics too must sometimes drink "to alleviate the pains of and torments of life" (13), some of which can be identified. In interview with Bruce Kawin in 1976 ("This interview took place in Mr. Hawks's home in Palm Springs, California, on May 24, 1976. He was 79 years old"), Howard Hawks recalled, "He wasn't a constant drunk but he did get—something would send him off on—and he would just drink himself blind" (105). "And also he was a very very shy man. Very shy" (Kawin, "Interview" 123).[25] In an irony of unrelenting and cruel circularity, Faulkner sometimes dealt with a shame "never even past" by sustaining, at considerable psychic cost and often with the help of alcohol, the outward and visible form of the wounded aviator, as if in response to the demand of "a single voice always somewhere saying, 'You must be braver than you may be and are'" (LG 109). (As he admitted to Lauren Bacall in 1954, "When I have one martini I feel bigger, wiser, taller. When I have a second, I feel superlative. When I have more, there's no holding me" [B 1487].) Meanwhile, the claim of the wound, whether to leg or skull, was also a coded confession of this shame, a confession hiding in plain sight and itself a wound in need of healing and sympathy. "'He who lets the truth escape like that,' comments Freud, 'is in reality happy to throw off the mask'" (qtd. in Lacan, "Function and field" 60).

It seems that Faulkner never had a sustained opportunity to throw off the mask of the wounded aviator once and for all in the presence of an ideal and resolute comprehension and forgiveness. In interviews with women in the 1950s, however, Faulkner came close, in speaking as a surviving representative of those who had actually flown, fought, and died in the war. As he had written to Richard Wright in September, 1945, "I think you will agree that the good lasting stuff comes out of one individual's imagination and sensitivity to and comprehension of the suffering of Everyman. Anyman, not out of the memory of his own grief" (SL 201). It was as a First World War "anyman" flyer that Faulkner seemed to be speaking when he responded to interviewer Lavan Rascoe in 1947.

Q: Which World War do you think was tougher?

A: Last war we lived in constant fear of the thing catching on fire. We didn't have to watch all those instruments and dials. All we did was pray the plane didn't burn up. We didn't have parachutes. Not much choice. World War II must have been tougher. (Note: Mr. Faulkner had both legs broken in a plane crash in the First World War). (Rascoe 71)

In her classic interview of 1954, Jean Stein asked:

Q: How much of your writing is based on personal experience?

FAULKNER: I can't say. I never counted up. Because "how much" is not important. A writer needs 3 things: experience, observation, imagination, any two of which, at times any one of which, can supply the lack of the others. With me, a story usually begins with a single idea or memory or mental picture. (LG 248)

In so answering, Faulkner was channeling Louis Kronenberger who, in reviewing *Soldiers' Pay* in 1926, had remarked "on the book's 'rich compound of imagination, observation, and experience'" (qtd. in B 505), giving durable expression to Faulkner's warrant as a military storyteller. On this basis, with "a combination of shyness and defensiveness" and "great internal reserve" guarded by his "epicanthic lids," Faulkner admitted to his interviewer, Cynthia Grenier in 1955, that he was always speaking not so much for himself as for all of the military aviators of his time.

> Q: I imagine from what you've said, and from what's known from your writing and life, that you've taken quite a lot from your own experience to put into your books. Like the parts in your books on aviation for instance. Did those come out of your own experience?

> FAULKNER: No. They came from the imagination and experience of anyone who had much to do with airplanes at that time. (LG 224)

In his compilation and study of Vietnam War oral histories, finally, Mark Baker offers us something wise about how we might understand Faulkner's martial testimony:

> It must be assumed that included here are generalizations, exaggerations, braggadocio and—very likely—outright lies. But if these stories were told within a religious framework, the telling would be called bearing witness. The human imperfections simply authenticate the sincerity of the whole. The apocryphal aspects have more to do with metaphor than with deceit. (Baker xv)

As the interview with Cynthia Grenier suggests especially, it seems to have taken something like three decades for Faulkner to begin to feel that some members of his audience might be capable of such an understanding.

Finally, in a letter to literature professor Dayton Kohler dated January 10, 1950, Faulkner comes clean, although he had been confessing all along in all sorts of ways throughout his published fiction and in other ways. Kohler had published "William Faulkner and the Social Conscience" in *College English*, December 1949, and like Sherwood Anderson twenty years earlier, he began his essay thus: "The war was the conditioning experience William Faulkner had in common with other writers of his generation. He had served in the British Royal Air Force, been wounded in a plane crash, drifted from one odd job to another after his return from France; and he wrote his first novels in the familiar idiom of postwar disillusionment and discontent" (119). Thanking Kohler for his analysis and saying that he agreed with it, Faulkner ends his letter with a p.s.: "re opening. Am proud to have belonged to RAF even obscurely. But had no combat service nor wound" (SL 297).

Still, after this point, there are many examples on the record of Faulkner's reversion—or perhaps regression—to the wounded warrior persona, especially under the extreme pressures of illness, alcohol, or love sickness. In May 1952, he was suffering from severe back pain after another fall from a horse.

> He was trying to control the pain with beer and Seconal, but it gradually grew worse. Then, on September 18, he suffered a convulsive seizure. They took him to

Memphis, to the Gartley-Ramsay Hospital, a fifty-bed psychiatric hospital where Dr. Dick C. McCool, an Ole Miss graduate ten years Faulkner's junior, examined him. Faulkner was able to give a coherent history of his trouble, though he said it had begun with the wartime plane crash which had left him with multiple injuries of the face, limbs, and back. (B 1433–4)

In this period of chronic injuries the doctors sometimes "thought it would be a good idea to have skull x-rays …. to see if there was any evidence for Faulkner's trauma theory. They might also discover what, if anything, this periodic punishment over a span of years had done to his body. The x-rays of the skull were normal" (B 1452–3), and no silver plate was ever discovered.

Notes

1   Faulkner made sure that Estelle would. Estelle's son Malcolm, whom Faulkner would adopt after he and Estelle were married in 1929, recalls one of his earliest childhood memories from about 1927: "As I looked out the window I saw a man dressed in a uniform, holding a bunch of flowers, with a cap, and a cane …. I looked up from my ice cream to see this man come into the kitchen and ask for Miss Cho-Cho [Malcolm's sister]. He had brought her the bunch of flowers he'd been holding all during the recital, and said: "These are for Miss Cho-Cho because she played so wonderfully!" So Cho-Cho came into the kitchen and received the bouquet of flowers from the gentleman in uniform. Later I queried Julia about who this man was. She told me that he wore the uniform on special occasions, and that it was the uniform of a foreign army—that he had been turned down by the American Army at the age of seventeen because of his small size and age. So this is the first recollection I have of William Faulkner: the afternoon he brought my sister a bouquet of flowers. Julia ended the conversation with a statement she delivered with great profundity: 'You know, Mr. Malcolm, Mr. Bill is courtin' your mother'" (Franklin 13–14).
2   For illuminating commentary on the novel, see Brooks; Castille; Kreiswirth 37–69; McHaney, "The Modernism of *Soldiers' Pay*"; Millgate, *Achievement* 61–7; Millgate, "Starting Out in the Twenties: Reflections on *Soldiers' Pay*"; Volpe 49–56; Wittenberg 42–50; Yonce; Lynch; Dougherty; Wulfman; Fichtel, Fujie, and Watson, *William Faulkner* 18–27.
3   "The division of the psychical into what is conscious and what is unconscious is the fundamental premise of psychoanalysis" (Freud, *Ego and the Id* 19).
4   I discuss the dreaming tramp-poet of "Carcassonne" as a war veteran in "War, Labor, and Gasoline in 'Carcassonne.'"
5   Here is Freud on the psychoanalysis of group psychology and Greek tragedy: "A company of individuals, named and dressed alike, surrounded a single figure, all hanging upon his words and deeds: they were the Chorus …. The Hero of tragedy must suffer; to this day that remains the essence of a tragedy. He had to bear the burden of what was known as 'tragic guilt'; the basis of that guilt is not always easy to find, for in the light of our everyday life it is often no guilt at all. As a rule it lay in rebellion against some divine or human authority …. The crime which was thrown on to his shoulders, presumptuousness and rebelliousness against a great authority, was

precisely the crime for which the members of the Chorus, the company of brothers, were responsible. Thus the tragic Hero became, though it might be against his will, the redeemer of the Chorus" (*Totem and Taboo* 218, 219).

6   Writes Jessie Weston in *From Ritual to Romance*, "Not Death but Resurrection is the essential centre of Ritual .... a ceremonial 'marriage' very frequently formed a part of 'Fertility' ritual, and was supposed to be specially efficacious in bringing about the effect desired"—that is, the removal of the curse lying on the dying king, the restoration of his health and virility, and the regeneration of the land (xi, 31). In this sense, Margaret's marriage brings about the renewal of the death wish that accompanies the community's ironical re-enactment of the fertility ceremony. Since the task of the restoration of the waste land has failed, the king must be killed, again (every year).

7   Frederick Crews calls Beatrice an "insecticide maiden" (117). Like Beatrice subjected to the gaze of the voyeur Giovanni, Margaret suffers the gaze of the more brazenly lecherous Januarius Jones: "He saw that black woman in the garden among roses, blowing smoke upon them from her pursed mouth, bending and sniffing above them, and he joined her with slow anticipated malice mentally stripping her straight dark unemphatic dress downward from her straight back over her firm quiet thighs" (SP 197). Margaret succeeds Marietta of *The Marionettes*: "Nothing save death is as beautiful as I am, and I shall wear a jade gown, and walk on the gravel paths in my garden" (49). With "Her black eyes, her red mouth like a pomegranate blossom" (SP 82), Margaret is both Persephone and Clytemnestra. And with their horrible facial wounds, Margaret's husbands, Richard Powers and Donald Mahon, trace the arch of a recognizable destiny mobilized by the transgression inherent in their very sexual being. As she herself warns Joe Gilligan, who would be the third to wed her, "All the men that marry me die, you know" (SP 245).

8   "Psychoanalysis encourages its subjects to live with a reduced burden of memory, closer to the surface of life, where tensions cannot take root and feed off the accumulated energies of the past. Though Freud is commonly thought to have measured neurosis against the ideal of an unimpaired sexual efficiency, it would be more accurate to say that he measured it against an ideal contemporaneity" (Rieff 44).

9   As Faulkner's first sustained foray into psychological realism and the ground of the novel's most convincing exploration and assessment of mental process and motivation, Margaret Powers prefigures the powerfully imagined subjectivities of Temple Drake, Dewey Dell, Addie Bundren, and Rosa Coldfield. As his first important experimental study of the psychological subject and the stream of being and consciousness (as impelled by undercurrents of memory or inhibited by repression) she is also a precursor of Darl, Benjy, Quentin, and Joe Christmas.

10 In "*Sanctuary* and Frazer's Slain Kings" Thomas McHaney shows that Faulkner wove into the novel critical aspects of the opening pages of the one-volume abridgement of *The Golden Bough*. Frazer's discussion of the psychological principles of imitative and contagious magic occurs within that volume's first forty pages.

11 "His earliest known experiments with visual images were self-portraits of himself in masquerade as the wounded officer" (Sensibar, *Faulkner and Love* 218).

12 See Taylor Hagood on "the fraud that haunts about wounds in Faulkner's ancestry, life, and writing" (85), traceable to "the memory of the Colonel and the many conflicting emotions it provoked" (48). The Colonel "brought home with him [from

the Mexican War] ... souvenirs which yet remained in the Fa(u)lkner family: an ornately carved walking stick and a Mexican machete bearing the inscription 'Not to be used for cutting trees'" (47). "[T]he similarity between Faulkner's military experience and subsequent performances are uncanny in their resemblance to the stories surrounding his ancestor" (51). "There is a dashing photograph of the young Faulkner in uniform leaning on a walking stick, and it is delicious to think that it could have been the walking stick the family had inherited from the Colonel's Mexican War experience" (52).

13   Michael Millgate in researching Faulkner's RAF record found "no mention of any such episode in the Toronto newspapers." Nor did any of Faulkner's RAF classmates whom Millgate interviewed "retain any memory of such an exploit or of Faulkner's sustaining any injuries, from whatever causes, during the time they all spent together" (Millgate, "William Faulkner, Cadet" 125). A fellow cadet, Mr. Hinchley, "felt quite convinced that Faulkner could not have done any other flying or been involved in a flying accident. 'If such happened the other cadets on the same floor in the same building would have heard of it'" (Millgate, "Faulkner in Toronto" 198). Following up in 1964, Kenneth L. Weber received confirmation from official historian Frank H. Ellis, author of *Canada's Flying Heritage* (University of Toronto Press, 1964), "that there was no crash on a hangar at Camp Borden on November 11, 1918" (Weber 5).

14   The spirit of the story seemed to be a part of the Faulkner family inheritance. In *Across the Creek: Faulkner Family Stories*, Faulkner's nephew Jimmy Faulkner recalls how, as a kid, he wore bat wings and jumped off the barn to see if he could glide: "I hit the bush headfirst like a bomb released from a dive bomber .... the big rubber bands with which I had attached the wings ... held me dangling upside down a few feet above the ground like a sleeping bat" (59). The "original" aeroplane accident of Faulkner's childhood set the pattern, as we've noted.

15   "The Inverted Jenny" postage stamp was issued on May 10, 1918. Is it possible that Faulkner—pierced by this inverse rarity—had adopted the image as his own private emblem, his muted cry of sarcastic triumph as a member of silent Trystero's empire, "always waiting, waiting," like J. D. Salinger's Laughing Man, "for a decent chance to strike terror and admiration in the nearest mediocre heart"? (Salinger, "The Laughing Man" 62).

16   Leaving the military as a wingless cadet, Faulkner was appointed "to the Honorary Rank of Second Lieutenant in His Royal Air Force" on March 9, 1920 "with effect from the date of his demobilization" (B 289) in January 1919. The RAF uniform he had purchased in Toronto thus enabled him to step into this liminal space in something resembling the proper clothing. The commission itself (which came in the mail without any accompanying uniform or insignia) was "twelve by sixteen inches ... an impressive document .... William Faulkner had his commission framed. After that it hung on the wall of his room in the old Delta Psi house" (B 289). Its visibility must have given him, or imposed upon him, many occasions on which to explain how he could have completed his RAF training after the Armistice and gotten his wings. Brother John's account suggests that Faulkner succeeded in conveying a plausible scenario. "The war ended before Bill could finish his training. But the British government told him and some others that if they wanted to stay and finish their course they'd get their wings and commission. Bill and a few others stayed. They lacked only a few weeks. He received his commission as a lieutenant in His Majesty's

Royal Flying Corps. His commission was signed by George R.I. He had it framed and kept it on his wall when we lived out on the campus. It hung above the mantle over the fireplace" (John Faulkner 135).

17   The aeroplane here (and in such tales as "With Caution and Dispatch") moves as Temple Drake runs in *Sanctuary*: "In the hall she whirled and ran. She ran right off the porch, into the weeds, and sped on. She ran to the road and down it for fifty yards in the darkness, then without a break she whirled and ran back to the house and sprang onto the porch and crouched against the door just as someone came up the hall" (*Sanctuary* 65).

18   "From the time of the Wright brothers, who worried (with reason) about their exhibition fliers, the reckless tendencies of young pilots have concerned their elders" (C 11). Yet "risk-taking and aggressiveness were two sides of the same psychological coin" (C 115), the essential currency of the young fighter pilot. Despite his spectacular solo achievement, Charles Lindbergh, as the prime ambassador of commercial aviation, did more than any other to transform this aviation culture of "extreme and unwarranted risk" (C37) to one of safety checklists and calm, scientific preparation. See especially Courtwright's chapter, "The Protestant Ethic and the *Spirit of St. Louis*" (C 70–88).

19   "For Phil, having to return to New Haven in civilian dress in September ... was not only a disappointment but an embarrassment. Every letter coming from Mississippi reported on another Ole Miss friend in war service .... By Christmas 1917, then especially, Phil stone and William Faulkner felt themselves to be pariahs. When fall classes had opened in New Haven, a slim majority of the students were still civilians— but over a thousand had not returned. Those who had were stung by Captain Edward Reed's November pronouncement that the 'intellectual leaders among the students are just where they ought to be—in France or making ready to go there'" (Snell 98, 99).

20   "It seemed likely that the account he told of crashing a training plane was a somewhat colored, romantic version of what actually happened. None of us who listened to his purported experiences believed half of them. We particularly doubted his account of receiving a leg injury that caused him to limp. 'That's the Count for you. Even a war doesn't stop him from telling tall stories,' said those who heard him" (Wasson 29–30).

21   In the Preface to Volume 1 of *The Lafayette Flying Corps* (1920), James Norman Hall and Charles Bernard Nordhoff are kinder to this class of aviator: "Members of the Lafayette Corps who were not breveted, or who were released from the French service before being sent on active duty, are included in a separate list. Most of the names in this supplementary list are of men who served honorably and faithfully, and who were released because of illness, as the result of injuries received in flying accidents, or because of inaptitude. While always a matter of regret to the pilot, inaptitude is no cause for shame. In the Air Service of any country, the number of men released before receiving the military brevet was always large, sometimes one half of the number enlisted" (ix–x). The word "inaptitude," spelled the same way in French and English, certainly sounds more polite than "ineptitude."

22   Blotner gives an account of a letter he had received from Jean Stein in 1969 in which she remembered some things Faulkner had told her during their brief affair in the early 1950s when Faulkner was bringing *A Fable* to completion: "It seemed to Jean that WF was even going through some sort of identification with the runner. 'In World War I,' he told her, 'I enlisted as an RAF pilot, and when I wasn't flying I drank

almost all the time to forget what we were up against.' Later he added, 'One day the plane crashed. I was pulled out of the wreck, laid on the ground and declared dead. I knew I wasn't dead. They couldn't kill me.' WF's words reminded her of those of the fallen runner: 'I'm not going to die. Never'" (B *189*).

23   The entry also includes evidence of Faulkner's sublime sense of deadpan humor: "*Sartoris* was published in 1929, the same year that its author married Mrs. Estelle (Oldham) Franklin, a widow with two children" (Kunitz 439). Cornell Franklin, of course, was very much alive, and Faulkner would adopt Estelle's children with him, Victoria and Malcolm. Of another comical "obverse reflection" of the truth, from Faulkner's trip to New Orleans in 1926, Blotner reports, "He was amusing during dinner, telling them about a woman in Oxford he was going to marry with the agreement that she would adopt all his illegitimate children" (B 525). See also the abandoned novel *Elmer* (written in Paris in 1925) in which a pilot returns home, "interesting and limping from his rather vain participation in the war," to find that the woman he loved has married another man. "Elmer had a bastard son in Houston" (Faulkner, *Elmer* 360, 359).

24   See also Kartiganer, "Faulkner as Celebrity."

25   Like Wilbur Wright, in the words of his friend "François Peyrey, who had seen more of Wilbur than had others and knew more, he was '*un timide*'—shy, a simple man, but also a 'man of genius'" (M 175).

"Love," *Manservant*, and Faulkner's First Screenplay

"Nerve's gone."

—Faulkner, "Love"

In "William Faulkner's 'War Wound': Reflections on Writing and Doing, Knowing and Remembering," Panthea Reid uncovers an early scene in which Faulkner raised the stakes of his self-presentation as a wounded RAF pilot beyond any sustainable limit. The account comes by way of Estelle's cousin Carolyn Smythe whom Faulkner in 1919 had sent a small hand-printed book, "Poems by William Faulkner for Carolyn Smythe"—"bound and sewn by Faulkner himself (in purple velvet!)." In other words, this was a young woman he was trying mightily to impress.[1] "In early 1919," as Reid tells it,

> a soldier stationed at a nearby camp met Carolyn Smythe in the lobby of Memphis's old Peabody Hotel, but, to the soldier's surprise, Faulkner also showed up walking with a cane, "in uniform and bandaged," with his arm in a sling. He said he had suffered a plane crash in France. Faulkner thought himself dashing. Carolyn found him amusing. Her beau thought he was crazy.

In this astonishing piece of historical uncovering, Reid lays bare the source of the silver plate that Faulkner claimed he bore as a patch over the skull injury he had suffered in the apocryphal aeroplane crash. Her own father, Sergeant John Reid, had suffered a gunshot wound in the war. Part of his skull was caved, and the wound was photographed and discussed in a medical textbook owned by Carolyn Smythe's father, an expert in war surgery.[2] "I suspect Faulkner did read the article" on her father's wound, Reid surmises, "because in the early 1920's his 'war wound' changed. It was no longer a rather vague injury to arm or hip that produced a limp; now he described it as a wound to the skull, covered by a silver plate." The luster of that silver plate must have also owed something to the medal Faulkner would have loved to display on his uniform too, the Silver Star "for gallantry in action against an enemy of the United States," as awarded to "Sergt. John Reid Wounded in France" for genuinely heroic actions under fire.[3]

As it turns out, Faulkner would soon write a story about such a figure as he appeared to be in this scene of 1919 and in many others as the years went by: a wounded and nerve-shot military veteran who may or may not be lying about his combat experience, who strives to hide the shame of his less than fully heroic service in the military institution behind dramatic moods and mysterious gestures, who risks exposure and thus a kind of social death in the erotic struggle for recognition and prestige after the war, and who loves women who are involved with or distracted by men more physically and socially attractive than he—including, especially, men of higher military rank. All of this is the main subject matter of one of Faulkner's earliest and still relatively unknown stories, "Love," first published in *The Missouri Review* in 1988. As the editor of the story Speer Morgan notes in his Afterword, "Faulkner once commented that 'Love' was 'about the first story that I wrote'" (149). "Love" was written in 1921 when Faulkner was living in Greenwich Village and working for Elizabeth Prall in the book section of the Lord and Taylor department store. (Prall would go on to marry Sherwood Anderson and Faulkner would spend much time with them in New Orleans in 1925.)

When the story is noticed at all, it is generally dismissed, according to an unfortunate and clearly obsolete paradigm, as a "minor failure" (Kawin, *Faulkner's MGM Screenplays* xiv) of "appallingly poor quality" (Collins, "'Ad Astra'" 127). In fact the story is fascinating and important not only as a confession of Faulkner's postwar anxieties but as a major scene of self-discovery: Faulkner's RAF experience, his worries, his humiliations, his fantasies, all were rich material in a life that was becoming richly writable. In "Love," at the outset of his career as a writer of prose fictions, his subject is the home community's troubled reception of the military veteran whose story never becomes clear or fully understandable to those who circulate around him. The story thus reads as a kind of first draft of *Soldiers' Pay* while belonging to a rich mass of early prose textuality that also includes "Landing in Luck," *The Marionettes*, "Moonlight," "Nympholepsy," "The Hill," and "Carcassonne," works written in the first few years after the Great War and set in the remembered emotional past of Faulkner's experience as a spurned lover, RAF cadet, and military veteran. This "aviation matrix" also extends through *Elmer, Flags in the Dust*, the war stories of the 1930s, *Pylon*, a host of Hollywood treatments and screenplays, and *A Fable*.

A war pilot with an obscure service record, Bob Jeyfus returns to his hometown and becomes engaged to a beautiful and erotically dangerous young socialite, Beth Goreham (aptly sur-named), who apparently has selected him as a lover from out of an extremely competitive field. "Then they were talking about Beth's young men and her latest acquisition, which she called her air force" (131). Everybody in Beth's country-club crowd, however, is sure that Jeyfus is lying about having been an aviator in France and they resent him besides as an interloper who "kept talking and using his tales to jimmy himself into places" (131). (Does "Jeyfus" echo "Dreyfus," a man resented for the position he has come to occupy, a man falsely accused of being a liar and publicly crucified?) A mysterious aviator known as "the Major," however, may be in a position to know the truth about Bob Jeyfus's war record. This Major, "a cold man, with bronze skin and silver temples and ice-colored eyes, who fell into easy, immaculate attitudes of a distracting weariness that were a challenge to women young and old" (124), is a decorated American ace, a volunteer who had flown with the French long before the United States entered the war in April, 1917.[4]

This Major, "the man in the wicker chair" (123), like Donald Mahon of *Soldiers' Pay*, is a still point at the center of a magnetic field of attraction and frenetic activity. A man of few words, he believes that "Language is just the smoke that rolls away from what a man has done" (131), his reticence only adding to the potency of his erotic effect. "At dinner there was the usual complement of women come to flutter about the Major" (129), and with food and drink "the Major talked willingly enough in his weary, impeccable manner, but as he talked the women began to look at him with that growing identical expression of exasperation which sooner or later all women developed in his presence" (129). "All women," including Beth Goreham, are in love with this taciturn and mysterious man who looks beautiful in his uniform.

The narrative, focalized at one point through the perspective of a housemaid who is also obsessed with the Major, flows into the Major's vacant room in order to zoom in on "a battered pigskin dispatch case stencilled with a few cryptic letters and numerals which the maid did not know was the designation of a French Nieuport squadron which had enjoyed a certain sentimental notoriety in 1916 and until it was assimilated by the United States Forces" (125). The truth about Jeyfus is contained within this dispatch case and it will soon be revealed. Meanwhile, during a dinner party hosted by Beth's parents, a difficult conversation unfolds:

"He was with the French," her father said. "You might have known him."

"I might," the Major agreed. "There were other squadrons, you know. If he could pass for a territorial. Besides the escadrille Lafayette. Was that his squadron?"

"I really don't know," Beth's mother answered in a baffled, hopeless tone, "What difference does it make now?"

"None at all," the Major agreed.

"Of course it doesn't," Beth's father said, "The war's over now."

"If it only were," Beth's mother said.

"Now, don't go blaming him on the war," her father said, "Do you think it makes any difference to her whether he was in it or not?"

"I don't know," her mother answered. "I know so little about what she does."

Beth's father presses the issue:

"But this Jeyfus. Been around her for six months, now. I thought at the time that he was leading a pretty aimless sort of life to have gone through as much shot and shell as he claims to have. But Beth and her gang ate it up, of course, from the start. And I liked the boy, too. But there's one thing I won't stand for." The Major looked at him quickly and found him hammering the arm of his chair in a mild and snuffy caricature of rage, like the rage of a Pekingese without the dog's shrillness. "And that's a liar. I won't have Beth—I won't have—"

"Steady all," the Major said. He put his cigarette into the tray. "They think he's lying, do they?"

The other had subsided. He was lighting the cigar. "What would you think? Of course, a lot of it was too technical for us. But someone proved a date on him, and nobody can find where he was in 1918 at all, and he was inconsistent in another instance. In fact, he seems to have an alternate for every incident of the whole damn war that has fallen into the personal knowledge of anyone from about here who went to France. But he sticks to the fact that he was a noncommissioned pilot in a French squadron in 1916 and '17—which obviously nobody can disprove on him on this side. I can't see why he didn't claim rank and make a good job of it. He explains that by saying that the French didn't give commissions to foreigners. While I have you in my own house to refute that."

"Well, mine was *pour le sentiment*," the Major said. "But why bother to prove the boy up? What good will it do?"

The other smoked a while. "I don't know how it began. I don't think anybody deliberately set out to do it. But he kept talking and using his tales to jimmy himself into places, until someone caught him in a minor discrepancy. Even that would have blown over, if Beth hadn't jumped in and taken his part. She started all the hurrah defending him, dragging it up again when everybody else would have let it drop. And now, when I stopped at the Club this afternoon to pick up Clara, they told me that Hamilton over at Claybrook had got a machine over there and that without letting Jeyfus know what was up, they were going to ask him over there and at least find out if he could fly or not."

"What?" the Major said. "Ah, the devil. Why can't they let the boy alone? This afternoon, you say?"

"If he was lying, what do you think Beth will do?"

"She'll throw him over," the other answered promptly, "Like a hot potato." (131–5)

There follows a scene of excruciating suspense, narrated, as in "A Rose for Emily," by an anonymous member of a community that is aware and a little ashamed of its own cruelty and curiosity. The group arranges and then stands back to watch the ultimate public test of Jeyfus's credibility:

When we noticed him again he was walking across the field, toward the ship .... He went up to the ship and put his hand on one of the wires and stood there, with his head sort of down and his back to us. The pilot that flew it over came up and handed him a helmet and a pair of goggles and said something to him, but he didn't move, and Beth shook his arm, but still he didn't move. Mac said, "Maybe he wants a passenger." …Then she went to the machine and the pilot came and helped her into the front seat and she stood up in it and cursed Mac just like a man. Then Jeyfus took his hand off the wire and went to the other seat and sort of fumbled at it.

"Ten to one," Mac says. Jeyfus held onto the edge and raised his foot and fumbled at the step like a drunk man trying to find a stirrup. "Hundred to one," Mac says. The rest of us were quiet. I swear, I felt kind of sick.

"Wait," Jeyfus says, before Beth could answer. He pulled himself up, slow, and he stood there, above us, not looking at us. Beth had turned and she was looking at him. "Bob," she says, "Bob!" After a while Jeyfus says, kind of like this: "Nerve's gone," he says.

His voice was like a voice speaking up a ventilator on a boat. A sound not coming from anywhere, just in your ear all of a sudden. "1916," he says, "It's in the book. Look in the book."

"Come on," Hamilton says, "Let's go have a drink." Even Mac didn't say anything, and we went back to the house. (144)

From one angle, the scene might represent Jeyfus's ingenious and breathtaking escape from exposure as a fraud. If he really never was a flyer at all, claiming that the war had shattered his nerves would be a perfect way to undermine any realistic expectation that he could ever fly again. The story is subtle and profound in showing that some of the people, in taking him at his word, understand that the psychic wounds of war can continue to endure in the souls of its survivors in this way. Others, however, are sure that Jeyfus has been resolutely exposed. "I hate to see a young liar get caught" (144) says one of the observers. But he also seems to understand that lying about one's war service can be a sign of dreadful internal pressures and deep humiliations. For many soldiers, shame is one of the enduring psychic wounds of war.

Beth is torn up by the scene but she is also convinced that Jeyfus, whom she had just married in a quick legal ceremony, is a liar, and that the Major, to whom she now erotically turns, has also been lying on Jeyfus's behalf:

"Now I hope you're satisfied," she said, "Liar!" And later, when he [Jeyfus] called at the house, she sent the wedding license down to him, wadded into an envelope with a furious command to leave town and never try to see her again, and now she danced in the expiring flareup of that fury while the Major watched her from the porch, and a moment later, leaving her partner in the center of the floor, she rushed into the moonlight where the Major stood.

"Take me home," she said.

"Look here," the Major said, "This Jeyfus—"

"Damn you," Beth blazed, beating him on the arm with her fists, "Will you take me home." (145)

The Major then reveals and tries to make Beth understand the truth about Bob Jeyfus that the old Nieuport squadron papers in the "battered pigskin dispatch case" helped him to remember:

"I daresay he is not very proud of some of it."

"What part of it?" she said. Her eyes were dark and intent. "Was he yellow?"

"Worse than that," the Major said. "He was a cook once."

"Oh," she said, staring at him. He could see the muscles in her forearms tautening, although her hands were hidden at her sides, and the bosom of her dress beginning to rise and fall jerkily, and he moved quickly and drew a chair up. "No," she said, "Tell me."

"He was one of my pilots. He crashed badly, hung upside down in his machine for three hours until a barrage lifted and they got him out. When they reached the Poste with him they thought he was dead, and they laid him with the other bodies for the burial party to fetch after dark. It happened that the bodies were lying on a slope, and his head was lower than his feet, and when the burial party came along they found that he was not dead still, though whenever they raised his head to the level of his feet he seemed to go out again. He was that way for two days, lying with his feet higher than his head until the surgeons got his chest shored up again. He said he was conscious all the time, and when he was about again, naturally his nerve was gone. So I sent him back. The French had permitted us to function as a unit, for sentiment, but a man too—yellow, sick, what you will—to fly, but able to peel potatoes, was not sentiment. So they gave him a cross with palms and a potato knife and apron. And that's all."

"Oh," Beth said. (145)

Bob Jeyfus, that is to say, was decorated with the *Croix de Guerre*, a legendary honor, and then promptly and permanently grounded.

The French "spirit" of this seeming absurdity is described by Clyde Balsley in one of the primary documents of the air war of 1914–18, *The Lafayette Flying Corps*, edited by James Norman Hall and Charles Bernard Nordhoff (Boston and New York: Houghton Mifflin, 1920). The two volumes of this work give a complete service history of the Corps and its American volunteers and include personal letters and excerpts from separately published memoirs. The Hall and Nordhoff volumes were the ultimate "dispatch case" for Faulkner's researches at this moment of his history as a war writer. Balsley was "the first American aviator to be severely wounded—for France" (Hall and Nordhoff v. 2, 66), and we recall that Victor Chapman died while attempting to bring him oranges in the military hospital where Balsley lay in bed for many weeks, his intestines having been "pierced in nearly a dozen places" by the fragments of an exploding bullet.[5]

Then I saw the heavy, black hair, the great arms, and the sincerest eyes in the world. When I put them all together, I gave a groan of joy. It was Victor Chapman, flown over from Bar-le-Duc …. "Anything I can get for you, old man?" he said.

"You bet," said I. "They won't let me have any water." The way I kept moistening my lips finished the appeal.

"How about oranges?" he said, and turned to my doctor, just at that moment come in.

"*Bien*," answered the surgeon, with a shrug; "but there are not any to be had in the village."

"Guess we'll fix that," said Victor. "I'll get those oranges if I have to fly to Paris." (Hall and Nordhoff v. 2, 65)

The next morning, as he woke from his "hot, drugged sleep," Balsley became aware of a "deep hush" in the room.

I felt the eye of every man upon me. Then I saw for the first time that my captain was not alone. The major and colonel were with him. Suddenly the colonel stepped forward.

"In the name of the Republic," he began—he took from his pocket a large box— "I confer upon you le *Médaille Militaire* and la *Croix de Guerre.*"

"For me?" I asked. "What for?"

The figure in its horizon blue gathered as if about to spring.

"*Pourquoi?*" His light, racing syllables slowed solemnly. "You are the first American aviator to be severely wounded—for France." (v.2, 66)

As Balsley reflected afterwards, "It was strange that this cool, efficient colonel should have commended my struggle rather than my performance! No, not strange. That was the spirt of this whole country" (Hall and Nordhoff v. 2, 66). The oranges did arrive the following day, but they were brought by Elliott Cowden, for Victor Chapman was dead. "He then showed me the clipping. On his way to the hospital at V—– with a bag of oranges for a wounded friend" (v.2, 67).

In "Love," the Major acknowledges Jeyfus's *struggle rather than his performance* with a brief look and comment, knowing too that it would be almost impossible to explain the truth of Jeyfus's history to those, like Beth, who might have little appreciation for anything but straightforward narratives and positive scores from the war front. Here Jeyfus finally receives the recognition that only one who has also been at the Front can confer.

[The Major] looked around at Beth and at the man whom she was dragging by the hand, who paused in the doorway and made him a sheepish, flat-handed salute.

"Is this him?" Beth said.

"Well, Corporal," the Major said, "I see you're still having trouble with that heart."

"Yes, sir," the man answered.

"Is that him?" Beth said.

"Yes," the Major answered. Beth turned and slapped her husband across the mouth.

"Now I hope you're satisfied," she said, "Liar!" (146)

The line, "'*Well, Corporal,' the Major said, 'I see you're still having trouble with that heart,*'" represents the key moment in which the soldier Jeyfus is finally recognized in the truth of his being, as it was in the war and as it remains in the after-war. A source for this element of the story, and more, is Major Charles Biddle's *The Way of the Eagle* (New York: C. Scribner's Sons, 1919), also mentioned and excerpted in the Hall and Nordhoff volume (Biddle, we'll recall, is a key source for "Landing in Luck" as discussed in Chapter 5 of this book). In June 1918, Biddle was "made Commanding Officer of the 13th Aero Sqdn., a new chasse squadron being formed" (217), but in a letter to his parents he expresses his great worry, for there are "fifteen perfectly green men in the squadron" (219) and he fears they will be killed during their first missions. A novice pilot "really cannot learn the game in less than six months at the front ...."

Take some of the great French pilots as an example of service at the front: Guynemer was there two and a half years; Fonck has been at it for more than two years and so had Deullin, and I could mention many others" (219). On August 15, 1918, he notes that

> One of my men has had to quit due to heart trouble, as he fainted one day while playing baseball and I found out that he had fainted once before in the air but had said nothing about it. I got Col. N—- (an expert) to examine him and he said he should never fly on the front, so I am sending him off with a recommendation that he be used as an instructor on the ground …. The man has had the same trouble for years and that he was ever passed for the Air Service is remarkable. (238)

The Major's sympathetic acknowledgment of Jeyfus's "heart trouble" surely bears Biddle's signature here. In placing his story in the constellation of the Lafayette Escadrille, Faulkner was reflecting the spirit of its history and the memoirs, stories, and letters of James Norman Hall, Victor Chapman, Dana Carol Winslow, James McConnell, and others from that group of American volunteers who had flown for France (as he of course had done only in his dreams).

Interlude: Canadian RAF Captain Arthur "Roy" Brown

As previous chapters in this book have noted, pilot memoirs and letters from France are full of references to hearts, nerves, and souls "strained," "shocked," or "shattered" by the realities of the war, including the deaths of comrades in accidents or combat; the violence witnessed, suffered, or perpetrated in the course of regular duty; the hunkering down in shelters to avoid the nighttime Gotha bombing raids; the sheer exhaustion of relentless patrols over enemy lines, for weeks and months on end, at high altitudes and in extreme cold.[6] Victor Yeates describes Tom Cundall's state of nearly constant fear in the final months of the war, and his constant wish to avoid "the nervous tension of flying a long way over Hunland; things happened so suddenly, and there was always the chance of meeting a Hun circus anything up to fifty strong. Only to be over there was a strain to war-tired nerves, and was cumulative in its effect" (Y 312). Near the end of his service Cundall's spirit burns so low it almost goes out completely:

> He had never known such utter boredom and weariness, such mental numbness. It was worse than his fits of rage and fear; for then he knew at least that he was alive and wanted to be alive: but now he knew nothing. It was unlikely that he would ever again find anything worth doing. Both action and inaction were intolerable. Grey time pressed on his brain and nerves like an ache. (Y 360)

Alan Bott describes hospital wards "loaded with broken and nerve-shattered men" (Bott 257): "I can imagine no more wretched state of mind than that of a man whose nerves have just been unbalanced by close shaves from gun fire" (Bott 257). Mick

Mannock's is perhaps the most forthright of all the pilots' diaries and memoirs in speaking of his own more or less constant nervous fatigue as a combat flyer:

> Over the lines today on Parry's bus. Engine cut out three times. Wind up. Now I can understand what a tremendous strain to the nervous system active service flying is. However cool a man may be there must always be more or less of a tension on the nerves under such trying conditions. (Mannock 49)
>
> I turned away and landed here with my knees shaking and my nerves all torn to bits. (Mannock 75)

Billy Bishop recalls a time when his commander forced him to go on leave. "When I reached England, however, I found I was in a very nervous condition. I could not be still" (Bishop 141). "For the only time in my life it entered my thoughts that I might lose my senses in a moment, and go insane" (Bishop 161). Even Eddy Rickenbacker, for whom aerial combat was the greatest experience of his life, remarks on "how tightly strung were the nerves of these boys of twenty who had for continuous months been living on the very peaks of mental excitement" (Rickenbacker 360) as combat pilots in his squadron. And though Manfred von Richthofen confesses in his memoir, "I like that feeling [of aerial combat] for it is a wonderful nerve stimulant" (Richthofen 61), he was not exempt from nervous exhaustion, including nausea, disorientation, and depression, especially after he suffered a serious head wound on July 6, 1917 (Gibbons in Richthofen 185–211).

From the aviation narratives of the First World War that I have read, Canadian RAF Captain Arthur "Roy" Brown emerges as a true man of sorrows and self-knowledge, nervous, sick, and yet also eminently sane and ultimately heroic. In these respects he resembles the type of war pilot Faulkner imagined he would have been as he thought himself into the souls of Bob Jeyfus, Donald Mahon, Bayard Sartoris, and David Levine. Brown was thought for a time to be the one who had killed Manfred von Richthofen, *Der Rote Kampfflieger*, an honor he did not especially welcome or value. His nausea in response to the whole affair is a sign of protest against the war and the grievous moral injury he suffered in it. In Floyd Gibbons' *The Red Knight of Germany: The Story of Baron Von Richthofen Germany's Great War Bird* (1927), the principal combatants, as he narrates the fateful day of their encounter, wake up in radically different states of health. "On the morning of April 21, 1918, two young men rolled out of their wartime bunks in France and took a look at the weather" (Gibbons 266). Richthofen's "eyes were clear, his nerves were steady; he both ate and slept well. He felt fine" (Gibbons 266). His antagonist, Captain Roy Brown, was

> twenty-four years old and a war bird of the Royal Air Force. He awoke with a sick stomach and shattered nerves. He had been living for the past month mainly on brandy and milk and fighting in the air daily on that diet. He was almost all in .... His physical condition was bad. Fourteen months of the strain and uncertainty of constant air fighting—more than a year of hairbreadth and hair-raising escapes from death—long days and longer nights in the shell-torn war zone, with ears, eyes, and sensibilities shocked by recurrent concussions of high explosive—these, plus

irregular hours and diet, exposure to inclement weather and the daily spectacle of death, suffering, and destruction had left an indelible stamp upon the brain, bone, and flesh of this war bird whose youth had been one of peace and tranquility with never a thought of war.

His nervous system was disorganized, and his stomach was in revolt. He should have been in hospital or some convalescent rest camp back home in Canada …. When Brown was not in the air, he was in bed, soothing the jumpy nerves, doping the bolshevik tummy, and pegging himself with brandy and milk for nourishment. Then up again, twice a day, into the flying boots and togs, and into the air on regular patrol. (Gibbons 267–8)

There follows the story of the Richthofen Jagdgeschwader descending upon a British observation squadron with Richthofen himself hovering above. The Red Baron then "singled out" (in his own official phrase) a Sopwith Camel trailing behind the British R.E.s at very low altitude. This was piloted by (the beautifully named) novice Canadian pilot Lieutenant Wilfrid May who, flying his first mission, was told to stay out of trouble and learn as much as he could by watching. May, contrary to orders (and in a manner feared by Major Biddle as commander of his squadron of green pilots), fired on an aeroplane piloted by Richthofen's cousin, Lt. Wolfram von Richthofen (future architect of the Gernika terror bombing of 1937).[7] The Red Baron then swooped down upon May for the kill.

Meanwhile, Roy Brown's Camel squadron, as Gibbons tells the story, diving from above "with the wind screaming through every strut and bracing wire" and "guns roaring and motors wide open" (Gibbons 273), appeared out of nowhere to save young May's life. A single .303 bullet, fired whether by Brown, infantry machine-gunner Cedric Popkin, or somebody else in Popkin's Australian Imperial Force anti-aircraft company, struck Richthofen in the heart.[8]

Richthofen managed a rough landing and died with the words "kaput" on his last breath, according to the Australian soldiers who arrived on the scene within minutes. Medical examiners found that the bullet had penetrated "from the right armpit and resurfaced next to the left nipple" (Richthofen 127), shredding the Red Baron's lungs and heart.[9]

As Richthofen's body lay "in state in one of the English tent hangars at Bertangles …. [a]ll English airmen who could be present viewed the remains and paid their respects in silent admiration for a brave foe" (Gibbons 280). The following day, his coffin "covered with floral tributes," the German hero was buried with full military honors. (A silent film of the funeral, photographs of the crashed airplane, and Richthofen's dead face, are viewable on the internet.) Roy Brown, however, "kept away from the tent, the guns, and the wreckage. Comrades came to his quarters to tell him he had done a bully fine job. He preferred not to talk about it" (Gibbons 281). The edition of Richthofen's memoir includes a letter Brown wrote to his parents soon after:

My stomach has been very bad recently and the doctor says if I keep on I shall have a nervous break-down and has ordered me to stop active service flying …. It is a terrible thing when you think of it that they should examine a body to see who should have the credit of killing him. What I saw that day shook me up quite a lot as it was the first time I have seen a man whom I know I had killed. If you don't shoot them they will shoot you so it has to be done. Shall write again soon.

Love to all

Roy. (Gibbons 211)

Gibbons includes a coda, as to this section do I: "Today, at thirty-three years of age, the man who killed Richthofen lives at No. 8, Morse Street, Toronto, and is engaged in business. He has a wife and three children, and has completely recovered his health" (281). No evidence has yet come to light that Brown during his recovery ever came into contact with Shrevelin McCannon, "Captain, Royal Army Medical Corps, Canadian Expeditionary Forces, France, 1914–1918. Now a practicing surgeon, Edmonton, Alta" (Faulkner, *Absalom, Absalom!* 315).

The Major and His Manservant, Das

When Major Hugh returned from the war he brought a manservant home with him named Das. Das is a figure Faulkner seemed to have pulled out of the laboring class of anonymous colonial workers who did the menial jobs in the massive French aviation camps during the war.[10] An American flyer, quoted in the Hall and Nordhoff history, describes them thus: "There are about three thousand men in the camp counting mechanics and quantities of Annamites. These latter act as servants, make roads and do the dirty work generally" (Hall vol. 2, 9). Another American flyer notes that "the cleaning up and digging is left to Arabs and Indo-Chinese (Annamites). Each of our rooms has an Annamite valet who sweeps the floor and brings our coffee in the morning" (Hall vol. 2, 23). In his memoir *High Adventure*, James Norman Hall recalls that whenever an aeroplane crashed in a training accident, "Annamites appeared on the spot to clear away the debris and take it to repair-shops, where the usable portions were quickly sorted out" (15–16). Dana Carroll Winslow gives additional perspective to the role of the Annamites in the general operations of the French flying services:

> There are over three hundred men training. The repair-shops are like a large manufacturing plant. Five hundred mechanics are continually employed there. Among these are little Indo-Chinese, or "Anamites," as the French call them, who have come from distant Asia to help France in her struggle for liberty. As French citizens they are mobilized and wear the military uniform, but their tasks are usually of the monotonous, routine variety. (Winslow 25)

None of the Annamites is ever named or individually identified in the materials I've just cited, but Faulkner imagines and dignifies one of them at least in the figure of Das, "a slight man whom any wind might blow away, save that of destiny" ("Love" 130).

Das, moreover, suffers the first realistic version on the fictional record of the notorious scalp wound Faulkner had already attributed to himself in real life, as in the Carolyn Smythe episode discussed above.

> "Das?" the Major said. "I found him. Under a muck of twisted rails and crossties, where a bomb fell. I got there before the Zeppelin was out of sight. It was one of the first ones, the one they brought down near Compiegne." In those days he was in charge of an ambulance section and so titleless and somewhat equivocal beyond the range of the knowledge that he had bought the ambulances out of his own pocket, when he had found Das with his head laid open in a debris of twisted steel and recent earth still reeking a little of explosive—a slight man in a denim overall looking up at him out of wild, soft eyes, patient and uncomplaining—a victim of the white man's incomprehensible penchant for concerted and noisy violence. ("Love" 129)

In "Love," it is as if the scalp wound has been lifted literally from the pages of the surgical textbook (owned by Carolyn Smythe's father) to be laid over and sutured into Das's cranium: "his scalp turned back like a page in a book. I could see the veins, and the blood pumping a little" ("Love" 129–30). "In time Das' head had healed," but his casualty card "said Wound in the head" ("Love" 130).

Das is there at the origin story of the Major's transfiguration, his transcendent passage from ambulances to Nieuport single-seaters:

> The next year, 1916, his new patron tired of blood at second hand and, having laid siege to the Quai d'Orsay with the indomitability which was a part of his character, was taught to fly and permitted to organise and equip a chasse squadron and to choose his own personnel. "And Das came with me," the Major added. "He didn't have any status at all, now—he was officially dead—but his ghost was permitted." (130)

In a narrative rich with doubles, shadows, and mirror images, Das, like Jeyfus, Major Hugh, and Beth Goreham is a private autobiographical inscription "hidden within the fabric of the work … what Roland Barthes would have called a 'biographeme'" (Gresset, *Fascination* 4): "His face was thin, of a pale coffee color, with high cheekbones and eyes faintly almond-shaped, of a wild, soft brown" ("Love" 128).[11]

As highly condensed (auto-) representational figures, the main characters in "Love" are composites of people real, fictional, and historical, a complex of figures and relationships through which Faulkner moved freely in his imagination in order to experience and understand things from every possible angle of subjectivity. Major Hugh, as an ideal figure conjured out of the French-American romance with the Lafayette Escadrille, is also traceable, I suggest, to the man who had displaced Faulkner with Estelle and yet with whom he also experienced a mysterious identification: Cornell Franklin, as Faulkner saw him and imagined Estelle and the town of Oxford seeing him before and during their wedding in April of 1918.

(Beth's father, clearly, is also modeled on Estelle's father, "Major" Oldham.) Let the image of Cornell Franklin at his wedding with Estelle Oldham on April 18, 1918, stand in for all that Faulkner was up against that spring. Judith Sensibar gives a vivid account:

> Cornell, resplendent in his white dress uniform [that of a Major in the National Guard of Hawaii], complete with masses of gold braid and a saber, met Estelle and her father at the altar. At the ceremony's completion the bride and groom exited together under an arch of glinting crossed sabers .... Estelle and Cornell cut the first piece [of the wedding cake] with Cornell's sword .... The local papers reported effusively on the wedding ceremony, decor, dress, and food, all of which defined for the Oldhams perhaps the most important day in their public lives. Estelle's contemporaries, even in their nineties, still described it as the most memorable wedding they ever attended. There are no surviving photographs to document the event. (Sensibar, *Faulkner and Love* 334–5)

No matter: If we had been there we "could not have seen it this plain" (Faulkner, *Absalom, Absalom!* 155).

Sensibar reminds us too of these special features of the young Major (young, though seven years older than Estelle and Faulkner):

> As president of his class, he was popular with men and women. (324)
> he was a formidable figure, accustomed to having his way. Like Thomas Sutpen, whom he resembled somewhat... (324)
> Voted "Most Likely to Be a Millionaire" by his Ole Miss Law School class in 1914... (326)
> With his quick mind, charm, and expertise at bridge and on the polo fields ... (326)
> Besides maintaining an average that hovered between A and B plus, he was a campus leader. (326)
> Cornell throve on athletic competition and lots of socializing. (326)
> Besides belonging to three sports teams, he was a member of numerous campus social clubs including The Outlaws. (326)
> In 1913 Cornell had graduated as president of his undergraduate class. (326)[12]

Faulkner, in the great competition for Estelle's love, a competition that extended from before the war to the first several years after it, wrote *Soldiers' Pay*, a novel based not merely on psychology and "the narcissistic preoccupations of an ideal self" but on "anthropology" (Gresset, *Fascination* 45), that is, on the study (following Freud's *Totem and Taboo* and Frazer's *The Golden Bough*) of the group's erotic relation with a wounded though strangely potent figure of mystery and authority (the wounded flyer Donald Mahon). Early reviews of the novel assumed that the novelist was an aviation combat veteran (Inge, *William Faulkner: The Contemporary Reviews* 9–16). We also know that *Soldiers' Pay* "greatly impressed"

Howard Hawks who "had followed [Faulkner's] work ever since" (Kawin, *Faulkner's MGM Screenplays* xxvi). When in 1932 "most of the producers did not want to work with Faulkner ... [considering] him unreliable if not incompetent," Hawks "proved to have some special interest in him" (Kawin, *MGM* xxv). And Hawks, like Meta Carpenter, and, for a considerable time, Malcolm Cowley, Jean Stein, and Joseph Blotner (*An Unexpected Life* 172), believed that Faulkner had been a flyer in the Great War.

That is why Faulkner turned to the story "Love" in order to develop the material for his first screenplay, "Manservant." He was hired because he was expected to know something valuable about the conduct of the war in the air. As Kawin reminds us, "every script he wrote for MGM was centrally concerned with aviation, usually in the context of World War I" (xxii). "Love," along with many other narratives of the aviation matrix that forms itself at the beginning of his career as a writer, thinks through and represents the matter of the wounded veteran and his transferential fantasies and relationships at deep levels of psychological subtlety and complexity. Something of the intensity of the pressure of this situation, as originally experienced by Bill Faulkner and Bob Jeyfus in the spring of 1919, might be suggested by what seems the reinscription of the notorious head wound into the figure of himself Faulkner presented to Hollywood upon his arrival there on May 7, 1932: "As [Samuel] Marx remembers it, Faulkner walked into his office with a 'bloody gash' on his forehead" (Kawin, *MGM* xxiii).

As it turns out, Faulkner would not meet Howard Hawks for another two months. Hawks would go on to work with Faulkner on and off for more than two decades, but in this brief, pre-Hawks Hollywood period, Faulkner was truly on his own, and the pressures converging on him seem to have been immense, and violent, as the stigmata of the "bloody gash" on Faulkner's forehead suggests. Faulkner immediately went AWOL in response to his first assignment, a Wallace Beery script that he was asked "to doctor." He returned a week later from (as he claimed) a sojourn in Death Valley (where Faulkner generally felt he always resided during his time in California, judging from his letters and his story "Golden Land").

Marx, no doubt nonplussed, simply asked Faulkner to develop an original film script on any idea he wanted. At this moment, facing the abyss, Faulkner turned to the short story he had written in 1921 in order to extract from it, in a process that can only seem weirdly tortured, something he would call *Manservant*, in which he presents the rudiments of what he hoped would be a serviceable screenplay. It's a bizarre scene, and a rich opportunity to speculate.

Bruce Kawin describes *Manservant* as "a maudlin and contrived failure. The file includes no reader's reports, indicating that *Manservant* was never remotely considered for production. Yet Faulkner seems to have found the story interesting and so cannot be accused of deliberately attempting to pass off inferior work on MGM" (*Faulkner's MGM Screenplays*, 1). *Yet Faulkner seems to have found the story interesting.* Strangely, the interesting part of the story—the most confessional and personal part— is what the screenplay, *Manservant*, represses and excludes in order to constitute itself as something that could be structured like a film. But of course it fits: Faulkner, masquerading as a screen writer, turned to "Love," a story about a man who may or may not be an imposter, in his inaugural Hollywood crisis.

The early film "system," as David Trotter discusses it in *Cinema and Modernism*, implied a certain pressure on the screen writer "to produce complete and coherent narratives for a rapidly expanding and diversifying audience. The narrator system was an industrial necessity" (Trotter 54). "Love" seems part of something prior to "the film system" in this sense, or perhaps part of something far ahead of that system in its challenge to film's representational possibilities. Perhaps someone will make a film version of "Love" someday that will do justice to its origins in Faulkner's early, pre-published, and holographic archive of experimental and radically personal works of art. In his attempt to imagine "Love" as a film, Faulkner stripped away the most intimately personal dimension of the story, or at least those aspects of it that might identify him in relation to his deepest aviation secret. What's left are mere traces and residues of that violent process of revision and censorship, signs of that "strategy of obliquity and indirection" that Peter Lurie has identified as central to "American obscurantism" more generally. The essential triangle of the Major (now named Nigel Blynt), Beth (now Judy), and Das (along with a sub-cast of maids and servants) survives into the film script. But Jeyfus does not, or rather, if spectral absence is also a form of spectral presence, Jeyfus (standing in for the military veteran with whom Faulkner deeply identified) and his aviation story are there in hiding, beneath the figure of the mute and slightly comical Oriental manservant, a man-child who prostrates himself at the feet of the lovers and willingly drinks the love potion he knows is contaminated with a fatal dose of rat poison.

The tableau recalls a pantomime out of *The Marionettes*, as Faulkner struggles to describe in words what must be rendered visually as in a silent film:

> Blynt and Das and the poison drink, which Das knows is poison and Blynt does not. Das knows that if he were to tell Blynt the drink is poison, Blynt would not believe him. And he knows that if he pours it out, the maid will know that something went wrong and she will merely fix another one tomorrow and continue to fix them until the time when Das will not be there. His only hope is to get Blynt to leave the house. (27)

Etc. The scene continues to be described in such a manner in many more words, such passages bearing the signature of that famous Faulknerian epistemology that leads inexorably toward formidable complexities in its drive to account for what people know and when and how they came to know it.

> Blynt is puzzled and worried. He is worried about Das, too. He knows that Das has been trying to tell him something but he doesn't know how much Das knows or suspects. (27)

But Das soon dies and the script comes to an end ON SHIP:

> Judy and Blynt—they are married. They are taking Das's ashes back to the home
> which he had not seen in fifteen years!

THE END

If, in this "secondary revision" of the primary material, the narrative does indeed
appear to have coherence and meaning, "that meaning," in Freud's words from *The
Interpretation of Dreams*, "is as far removed as possible from [its] true significance"
(490), which can only be found in the earlier, forgotten story originally written as
"Love."

"Love": A Biographical Coda

At the Greenwood Arts Festival a young woman told me that her parents had
known William Faulkner. When he had returned from Canada wearing his RAF
uniform and wings, he had approached her father and said, "Everybody thinks I
can fly, but I can't. Will you give me lessons?" So Albert Erskine and I had decided
that there was enough new material to justify another, shorter Faulkner biography.
(Blotner, *Unexpected* 237)

"I miss flying," he said sadly to Wasson in the autumn of 1919. Faulkner was fully
conscious of his deception, and he attempted at least a partial repair. Robert R.
"Baby" Buntin, a student at the university soon after the war and a flyer, revealed
many years later that Faulkner had asked him for flying lessons. "Everyone thinks
I can fly," Faulkner explained, "but I can't." He proposed that they "sneak off" to the
airfield so that Buntin could instruct him secretly. Faulkner and Buntin took to the
air, but it soon became clear that Faulkner had little talent for landing an airplane
and the lessons ended. In the early 1930s, however, Faulkner did earn his pilot's
license with a professional instructor in Memphis, but his tendency to botch the
most vital element in flying, coming smoothly to earth again, made him notorious
in the flying fraternity. (Williamson 185)

On February 2, 1933, he had begun taking formal instruction for flying. "When
Faulkner came to me for lessons," Vernon Omlie later said, "he told me not to
say anything about it. He said he wanted to get back his nerve and learn to fly all
over again before anybody knew what he was doing." He was not able to manage
it. But when reporters discovered that a reputed combat pilot was taking lessons,
Faulkner had a double explanation. Not only was he trying to regain the nerve
lost in two plane crashes, but "He says there have been so many radical changes

in planes and flying since he was a Canadian 'leftenant' that he has to learn all over again …. "I had quite a time with Bill," Omlie told another pilot and mutual friend. "He had trouble getting the feel of the controls. He had to learn to use the instruments, not the seat of his pants, but he still tried to do it the old way, trying to get the old feel back, but he couldn't." …. Then, on April 20 [1933], he soloed, going aloft for three-quarters of an hour. (B 795–7)

Notes

1   "Faulkner produced several hand-lettered booklets in the 1920s" (Collins, Introduction, *Mayday* 5), some of which he sold and some of which he gave as romantic gifts, including to Carolyn Smythe, Estelle, and Helen Baird, whom he met in Pascagoula, Mississippi, and wished to marry in 1926. "He made a little book for her, a forty-eight-page allegorical novelette which may have grown from stories told on those sunny afternoons. He gave it the title he had meant for his first novel: 'Mayday.' The protagonist was another of his wounded-soldier heroes: Sir Galwyn of Arthgyl …. Bound in with the story were colored drawings he had made" (B 511). Faulkner would also dedicate his novel *Mosquitoes* (1927) "To Helen, Beautiful and Wise."

2   Robert Jackson, whom I thank again here, tracked down the textbook. The photos are reprinted in my essay "Faulkner and the RAF Canada, 1918."

3   Faulkner's head wound was classically overdetermined. His brother Murry had suffered a head wound in the war and he was decorated for it. The list of famous pilots whose head wounds were noted in the newspapers and histories includes Victor Chapman, Norman Prince, Hobey Baker, Albert Ball, Manfred von Richthofen, and Oswald Boelcke. Lieutenant Thomas Selfridge suffered "a great gash across his forehead" (like Faulkner's Donald Mahon) and a fractured skull in the first fatal aeroplane crash of the motor age (M 192). Charles Hamilton, "the crazy man of the air," "won ten thousand dollars for a round-trip New York-Philadelphia flight" in 1910. He survived sixty-three accidents and "when he died in 1914, he had a plate in his skull, two silver ribs, and pins in his shin" (C 7).

4   Faulkner had imagined such an ideal, "gilded" figure in a poem he sketched out in his RAF notebook and copied in a letter to his father on September 9, 1918:
The Ace

The silent earth looms blackly in the dawning
Sharp as poured ink beneath the grey
Mists spectral, clutching fingers
                The sun light
Paints him as he stalks, huge through the morning
In his fleece and leather, and gilds his bright
Hair. The first lark hovers, singing, where
He flashes through the shining gates of day. (TH 99)

5   Balsley's report is also one of the most harrowing and realistic descriptions of death and suffering in a military hospital that I have encountered in the history of the First World War.

6   "*Chasse* patrols at the Front now often fly at an altitude of 6000 meters (20,000 feet); remaining at this height for two hours at a stretch is very fatiguing and in the end affects the heart, lungs, and nerves" (Hall and Nordhoff v. 2, 45).

7   See Xavier Irujo, *Gernika, 1937: The Market Day Massacre,* after whom I retain the Basque spelling of the town.

8   Debate still circulates about the source of the bullet that killed Richthofen, but the essential answer was hiding in plain sight all along. "**SLAYER OF VON RICHTHOFEN. German Report Translated Lewis Gun as 'Gunner Lewis.'** *In an article on the death of Germany's star aviator ... the Kölnische Zeitung remarked: 'The Wolff Bureau's report attributed the shooting down of Baron von Richthofen to Gunner Lewis, and a number of German journals have helped the gallant gunner to widespread fame—much to the disadvantage of a British airman who says he fired the shot*" (NYT, June 10, 1918).

9   A single bullet through the heart (a wound, however, seldom described by medical examiners) is a common mode of death in the air war as narrated in the popular stories and newspapers of the era. Faulkner's pilot in "The Lilacs" also dies, so he narrates his own "death," from a penetrating heart wound:
"The bullet struck me here, I think
In the left breast [....]
One should not die like this
On such a day,
From angry bullet or other modern way.
Instead, I had a bullet through my heart—" (*A Green Bough* 7–9)

10 Faulkner clearly identified with their condition. As he wrote from Long Branch on July 31, 1918: "Dear Mother .... Did more work yesterday than any Wop or Nigger living" (TH 86).

11 His delicacy resembles Faulkner's own, as sketched, for example, by Sherwood Anderson in the figure of David in his "A Meeting South." See also Faulkner's "Out of Nazareth" (1925), and Edwin Arnold on the figure of "David" across Faulkner's work.

12 Don't you just love the guy?

Pylon: The Last War and the Next

CHRONOLOGY[11]

December 17, 1903: the *Wright Flyer* takes off.

August, 1908: Wilbur Wright demonstrates the *Wright Flyer* in France.

February 20, 1909: F. T. Marinetti, "Manifesto of Futurism."

July 25, 1909: Louis Blériot's flight across the English Channel.

September 29, 1911–October 18, 1912: During the Italian war in Libya, airplanes are used in military reconnaissance and aerial bombing for the first time.

1914–18: First World War.

In June 1918 Faulkner enlists in the Royal Air Force and trains in Toronto. He is demobilized in December 1918, and discharged in January, 1919.

Mussolini's "March on Rome" takes place on October 28, 1922. By August 1925, when Faulkner visits Italy, Mussolini is the dictator of the country. In Faulkner's *Elmer*, written in Paris in the fall of 1925, Elmer, an American war veteran, is accosted by an angry Italian mob and arrested by the Carabinieri for a crime against the State.

Soldiers' Pay, about a wounded aviator, is published on February 25, 1926.

On May 21, 1927, Charles Lindbergh, flying *The Spirit of St. Louis*, lands in Paris before a crowd of 100,000 people.

The Sound and the Fury is published on October 7, 1929.

As I Lay Dying is published on October 6, 1930.

Sanctuary is published on February 9, 1931.

On October 3, 1931, Italian poet Lauro de Bosis, after only seven hours of solo experience, in a plane named *Pegasus*, flies over Rome and Mussolini's headquarters while dropping 400,000 anti-fascist leaflets. Author of a play entitled *Icaro*, he runs out of gas somewhere over the Mediterranean Sea. His body and his airplane are never found.

On February 19, 1932, Faulkner completes the manuscript of *Light in August* and the book is published on October 6.

On January 30, 1933, Hitler becomes Chancellor of Germany. On March 5 he declares there will be no more elections "for a hundred years."

On March 25, 1933, the Memphis *Commercial Appeal* announces that "the writer William Faulkner is learning to fly."

On February 2, 1933, Nazi youth groups burn thousands of books on the Opernplatz in Berlin.

On May 13, 1933, Faulkner buys a Waco-210 monoplane.

On July 16, 1933, Italian Blackshirt leader and Secretary of State for Air, Italo Balbo, leads a squadron of twenty-four seaplanes from Rome across the Atlantic to Chicago, a 6,100-mile flight completed in seven stages.

On November 3, 1933, accompanied by his brother Dean and flight instructor Vernon Omlie, Faulkner flies to New York in his Waco airplane.

On December 14, 1933, William Faulkner passes "the flight check required for the issuance of the private pilot certificate… and he was subsequently issued certificate number 29788. This certificate authorized him to fly single-engine, land aircraft of from 0 to 150 horsepower. Technically, Faulkner was not licenced to fly his own aircraft" (Bostwick 5–6).

In January or February, 1934, Faulkner begins *Dark House* (*Absalom, Absalom!*).

On February 14, 1934, Captain Merle Nelson is killed during an air show in New Orleans at the inauguration of the Colonel A. L. Shushan Airport. Faulkner and Vernon Omlie arrive by aeroplane from Memphis the following day. Faulkner suspends work on *Dark House* and begins to write the novel *Pylon* more or less immediately.

On September 5, 1934, Leni Riefensthal begins filming *Triumph of the Will*. The film opens with shots of clouds above the city, masses of people below, the shadow of Hitler's plane, Hitler emerging from his plane to thunderous applause. The musical accompaniment is by Wagner and the Horst-Wessel Song.

Between November 11 and December 15, 1934, Faulkner sends to Harrison Smith the seven chapters of *Pylon*. The book is published on March 25, 1935. Faulkner resumes work on *Dark House*, now retitled *Absalom, Absalom!*.

On November 10, 1935, Faulkner's younger brother, Dean, crashes and dies in the Waco airplane his older brother had given him.

Absalom, Absalom! is published on October 26, 1936. Faulkner donates the manuscript to support the cause of Republican Spain during the Spanish Civil War.

On April 26, 1937, the Basque town of Gernika (I follow Xabier Irujo in using the Basque spelling) is bombed by the German Luftwaffe Condor Legion and the Italian Fascist Aviazione Legionaria.

In October, 1938, Charles Lindbergh receives the Service Cross of the German Eagle (Verdienstorden vom Deutschen Adler) (Germany Deutsches Reich, 1938), a diplomatic and honorary award given to prominent foreigners, particularly diplomats, who were considered sympathetic to Nazism. Recipients include Mussolini, Franco, and Henry Ford.

September 1, 1939: Germany invades Poland and the Second World War begins.

* * *

The experience of the last war and the omens of the next unite in a warning of what otherwise awaits us.

—Liddell Hart, *Europe in Arms* (1937)

One pair of eyes is not enough.

—Franz Kafka, "The Aeroplanes at Brescia" (1909)

Pylon is based on real events that took place during a three-day air show at the brand new, $4,000,000 Colonel A. L. Shushan Airport in New Orleans during Mardi Gras week, February 1934 ("Big Airport for South" XX8).[2] Faulkner flew in from Memphis with Vernon Omlie on February 15 (B 834), and for the next several days he circulated around the airport with his newspaper friends and accompanied reporter Hermann B. Deutsch as he covered the scene for the New Orleans *Item*. The air show's events included aerial acrobatics, wing walking, parachute jumping, and pylon racing, the daredevil pilots competing for cash prizes in their "oversouped" (PY 880) machines. One of the main draws was Jimmy Wedell who, in a solo exhibition, flew around the pylons at 300 mph in his customized Wedell-Williams Special. The aeroplane was powered by a Pratt & Whitney Hornet, a nine-cylinder, single-row, air-cooled radial engine originally developed for the U.S. military (Hull 197).[3] Wedell, who appears in *Pylon* as Matt Ord, was renowned not only as a pilot but as an aeroplane designer and builder. He broke many an air-speed record in his customized machines, and they were so fast that no one consented to race him anymore (Hull 71–3, 117). When he died in an exhibition crash on June 24, 1934, he left unfinished the aeroplane he had been building in which he had hoped to fly at 450 mph ("Aeronautics: Death of Wedell").

On February 14, Merle Nelson died in a fiery crash on the opening night of the airshow. Faulkner and Omlie, arriving the following day, heard the accounts of the witnesses who could not stop talking about the event. They speculated that Nelson was blinded by the airport's searchlights. He started his aerobatic loop at too low an altitude and flew his "comet plane" right into the ground at full throttle in front of thousands of spectators (B 834, "Stunt Flier Burns to Death in South"). This is the primal scene of the novel.

8:00 P.M. Special Mardi Gras Evening Event. Rocket Plane. Lieut. Frank Burnham

[....]
"Say, what do you suppose happened?"
"Blinded, probably."
"Yair. Blinded."
"Yair. Probably couldn't read his altimeter at all. Or maybe forgot to watch it. Flew it right into the ground."
"Yair. Jesus, I remember one time I was..... " They smoked. (PY 877)

That Faulkner was shocked—electrified—by this event and others that he witnessed at the air show is clear from *Pylon*'s peculiar language and rhythm, its experimental narrative forms, and its plot. The repercussions of the Nelson crash, transfigured by Faulkner into that Special Mardi Gras "Burn Him" Event, warp the novel's narrative contours and generate its overall mood of fascination, apprehension, and terror.

The novel is focalized through the consciousness of the reporter (that is the only name he is given) who is sent out by the editor of a mass circulation newspaper to cover the air races at the new airport. As he wanders around the airport and through the city streets at night—New Valois, Franciana, an uncanny metropolitan labyrinth akin, as I will suggest, to the Surrealists' Paris—the novel's narrative language is commandeered by his "excited impressionism" (Benjamin, "Return of the *Flâneur*" 262), his obsessive notation of all that he sees and hears, an essential effect of which is to make visible, linguistically, what is really being seen and heard for the first time by anybody.[4] A characteristic form of the novel's alienated vision is the composite, the portmanteau word, the neologism: *corpseglare, wirehum, gasolinespanned, pavementthrong, trafficdammed, machinevoice, gearwhine, slantshimmered, typesplattered*—weird, defamiliarizing "machinelanguage" appearing with Joycean strangeness upon the page. As Walter Benjamin observed in an analogous context, the crisis of language "which manifests itself in this way can be seen as an integral part of a crisis in perception itself" (Benjamin, "On Some Motifs in Baudelaire" 189). *Pylon*'s most important function is not only to tell a story, then, but to record, transcribe, interpret, and manage successfully the phenomena of a radical new reality characterized by the relentless "increase in technological artifacts, in power sources, in tempo" (Benjamin, "Theories of German Fascism" 312). According to Benjamin's psychoanalytic theory of repetition, absorption, and assimilation, "the more readily consciousness registers these shocks, the less likely are they to have a traumatic effect" (Benjamin, "On Some Motifs in Baudelaire" 163).

The speed and violence of the aeroplane generate the novel's primary shock effects, their repercussions resonating within a period marked by the rise of global fascism and the technological steeplechase toward total war—"the disaster, toward which without yet being conscious of it apparently, they moved" (PY 892). A key scene of the novel in this respect involves the reporter and pilot Roger Shumann who, in a complex legal maneuver, hijack the lethal aeroplane (Faulkner's spelling throughout the novel) that Matt Ord refused to let them have in the first instance. Shumann's original airplane is old and in disrepair. "Ship's obsolete," Jiggs explains to the bus driver who brings him out to the airport. "It was fast two years ago, but that's two years ago. We'd be O.K. now if they had just quit building racers when they finished the one we got" (PY 783). Ord's machine, in contrast, is brand new and ultra-modern in design.

"Monocoque," Jiggs exclaims when he sees the machine. "Jesus Christ, do you mean—" (PY 924). The machine is

a lowwing monoplane with a big nose and a tubular fuselage ending in a curiously flattened tailgroup which gave it the appearance of having been drawn lightly and steadily through a huge lightlyclosed gloved fist. "There it is," the reporter said.

"Yair," Shumann said. "I see.—Yes," he thought, looking quietly at the queer empennage, the blunt short cylindrical body [....] (PY 922)[5]

After a test flight, with the reporter serving as dead weight to help their flying coffin "ride on a balance" (Faulkner, *As I Lay Dying* 62), Shumann pilots the notorious aeroplane the forty miles over to Feinman Airport so that he can enter himself in the next pylon race (he desperately needs the money). Ord's record-breaking machine takes off and makes the trip in ten minutes, but the word has somehow gotten out—transmitted across the ether apparently—and a large crowd awaits Shumann's arrival at the field: "and by the time he landed you would have thought he was Lindbergh" (PY 925), the mechanic Jiggs tells it later.

At an earlier point in the novel, after their meeting with the Aeronautical Committee in the Superintendent's office, Shumann and the parachute jumper, Jack,

> went out and around toward the hangar, walking now in a thin deep drone from somewhere up in the sun, though presently they could see them—a flight of army pursuit singleseaters circling the field in formation to land and then coming in, fast, bluntnosed, fiercelyraked, viciously powerful. "They're oversouped," Shumann said. "They will kill you if you don't watch them. I wouldn't want to do that for two-fifty-six a month." (PY 880)

As the American aviation arms race revs up its powerful engines, Shumann's hesitation marks a significant moment. All that he represents—the solo aviation exploit and whatever fragile expression of individual freedom and heroic mortality inheres in it—has long been driven into obsolescence by the military squadron and the formation flight of the "soup"-er machines. The "viciously powerful" aeroplanes are there, ostensibly, to defend the nation, but they also menace their own pilots while signaling the presence of an international system organizing itself for an apocalypse. Japan invaded Manchuria in 1931. Hitler took dictatorial power on January 30, 1933. The American mass media—newsprint, magazines, photography, newsreels, radio—is covering the rising global terror with massive daily exposure as the borders of the republic (real, symbolic, imaginary) are felt to be ever more permeable and porous.[6] It is within the expanse of this media environment that we might imagine the visual and sonic effects of the Italian Air Force's spectacular American appearance in July 1933. Italo Balbo, Blackshirt leader and Secretary of State for Air in Mussolini's Fascist Italy, led a squadron of twenty-four seaplanes from Rome across the Atlantic to Chicago, site of the World's Fair in celebration of "A Century of Progress"—a flight of 6,100 miles undertaken in seven stages. Newspapers described "the ecstatic welcome they encountered in Chicago when the squadrons put down on Lake Michigan on 15 July before a cheering crowd of a hundred thousand onlookers" (qtd. in Wohl, *Spectacle* 93–4). Motorcades, parades, banquets, receptions, and even honorary degrees followed. "Saluted by nineteen cannon shots fired from the warship *Wilmette* and escorted by thirty-six American fighters, the Italians took off for New York on the morning of the 19th" (Wohl, *Spectacle* 95). Then "Balbo and twenty of his pilots were flown to

Washington, D.C., where the most senior of them were invited to a luncheon at the White House hosted by President Roosevelt" (Wohl, *Spectacle* 96). Although Balbo boasted in response to the crowd's feverish welcome that "Anti-Fascism Here [is] a Myth" (*New York Times*), "heavy security forces had been mobilized in Chicago and New York to forestall the possibility of embarrassing anti-Fascist demonstrations" (Wohl, *Spectacle* 101–2).

Given the escalating arms race amid ever-louder displays of martial rhetoric worldwide,[7] it was impossible not to have somewhere in mind "at least some conception of the next war," as Walter Benjamin felt in 1930 while reviewing a book by Ernst Jünger. Jünger and his fellow Freikorps members were already referring to the Great War as merely the *First* World War (Benjamin, "Theories of German Fascism" 313). When Faulkner was writing *Pylon* in 1934—he would set the novel one year into the future—global fascism was spreading, international tensions were being revived, Italy was preparing to invade Ethiopia in an effort to enhance its military prestige, Germany was no longer disguising the pace of its rearmament, Spain was expanding its air force to exert control over the Mediterranean, and the world was openly preparing for another war (Hart, *Europe in Arms* 100–16 and passim). "The most noticeable sign, perhaps … of the armament race now in progress throughout Europe," observes Hart in 1936, "is the number of new military aerodromes—there are forty more than at the end of 1934. Some of the great motor factories, too, show large extensions for the building of aircraft. The British Air Force is fast, if not furiously, expanding to a formidable scale" (Hart 67).

In representing Faulkner's alienated fascination with the scene of militarized aviation in the 1930s—its machines, systems, people, its sonic, visual, and phenomenological effects—the reporter is the novel's primary photosensitive surface and echo chamber.[8] He is employed by the main city newspaper but he operates as a radically singular free agent. He immerses himself in "the one hundred percent image space" (Benjamin, "Surrealism" 217) of the New Valois metropolis, extending from its old French Quarter to the ultra-modern suburban airport built as "a spade-shaped peninsula out into Lake Pontchartrain" (Gordon 26). Faulkner bases the novel upon "the strength of his precise reaction" (Adorno 70) to this urban space, its relation to a given consciousness, "the inner man, the psyche, the individual" (Benjamin, "Surrealism" 217). The novel's analytical power is inherent in this focalized subjectivity, its latent, perhaps even unconscious refusal to accede to the era's "extremely positive negation of the individual's freedom of thought and expression" (Hart, *Europe in Arms* 2).

Incomparable witness to the rise of European fascism in the 1920s and '30s, Benjamin characterizes the emerging global political crisis in 1929 in the following terms: "Mistrust in the fate of literature, mistrust in the fate of freedom, mistrust in the fate of European humanity, but three times mistrust in all reconciliation: between classes, between nations, between individuals. And unlimited trust only in IG Farben and the peaceful perfecting of the air force. But what now? What next?" (Benjamin, "Surrealism" 216–17).[9] So contemplates "the reader, the thinker, the loiterer, the *flâneur* … types of illuminati just as much as the opium eater, the dreamer, the ecstatic"

(Benjamin, "Surrealism" 216).[10] This quality of "profane illumination" (217) is also what makes the novel *Pylon* so rich in augury and prophetic images, so "alive to reverberations of the future" (André Breton qtd. by Benjamin, "The Work of Art" 131n).

As the novel unfolds the reporter tries to get behind a scene dominated by the vivid display of the awesome machines, and thus he takes up with the air show's principal performers (as he is drawn to them), an itinerant set of barnstormers joined together in a radically unconventional arrangement, one woman living openly with three men—two of whom she sleeps with alternately—and one child of doubtful paternity. The reporter is obsessed with this erotic collective and tries to insinuate himself into its very center.[11] He also comes to identify with their workers' struggle for a larger percentage of the gate receipts and for improvements in their working conditions given the extreme dangers inherent in their employment. Against the flyers stands Colonel Feinman, after whom the airport has been named, along with the economic and political class who run the metropolis.[12]

In the pauses between aerial events, the reporter sees the crowd

> slowing and clotting before one of the temporary wooden refreshment booths which had sprung up about the borders of the airport property as the photographs of the pilots and machines had bloomed in the shop windows downtown for some time before he began to realise that something besides the spectacle (still comparatively new) of outdoors drinking must be drawing them. (PY 873–4)[13]

They seem willing to wait for it with supreme patience.[14] Meanwhile the "the voice of the amplifyer, apocryphal, sourceless, inhuman, ubiquitous and beyond weariness or fatigue" (PY 801) unfolds its ceaseless running commentary on what the crowd is watching with its own eyes without, perhaps, fully grasping what it all means. The future is on display, a future that will see the regular death of pilots and passengers in civil aviation and the advent of the "viciously powerful" modern air weapon based on "the idea of being bombed from the air" (Hart, *Europe in Arms* 12). Writes Liddell Hart in 1936, the dangers from these new instruments may "have already outstripped our powers of comprehension" (Hart, *Europe in Arms* 142). Yet even if one possessed an understanding as acute as Hart's of the era's "ever-accelerating process of rearmament and progress of invention … the onlooker, although he may see most of the game, is not allowed a whistle" (Hart, *Europe in Arms* viii).

In accordance with the novel's uncanny "compulsion to repeat" (Freud, *Beyond the Pleasure Principle* 13), the primary event recurs as a series of mediated repercussions:

> a gust of screaming newsboys ….swirled about him, screaming: in the reflected light of the passing torches the familiar black thick type and the raucous cries seemed to glare and merge faster than the mind could distinguish the sense through which each had been received: "Boinum boins!" **FIRST FATALITY OF AIR** "Read about it! Foist Moidigror foitality!" **LIEUT. BURNHAM KILLED IN AIR CRASH** "Boinum boins!" (PY 811)[15]

This, then, is Faulkner's stunning figure for the cultural logic of modernity: the phallic pylons, the revolving airplanes, the mesmerized crowd gazing skyward, the inevitable smashing of machines, the burning of the pilot's corpse, the front-page, bold-face publicity. All along the metallic voice of the amplifyer narrates the scene, invading the reporter's brain. The voice runs on into the night as the searchlights rove. In the words of the brave anti-fascist flyer, Lauro de Bosis, it would do no good to "deplore the excesses" of this new system organized by mechanized circular motion operating under "two new conditions—air power and motor power" (Hart, *Europe in Arms* 90). "Its excesses *are* its logic" (qtd. in Mudge 3).[16] The mechanism of the rotating drive-shaft of engine and propeller repeats itself on a larger scale in the circulating aeroplanes around the pylons at the aerodrome (race course). At night "the long sicklebar of the beacon [sweeps] inward from the lake, to vanish at the instant when the yellow eye came broadside on" (948). This is the system's sweeping eye, "the grim Spectator himself" (PY 912).[17] The essential pattern of intense circulation around a close circuit "leads to an overwhelming question" (Eliot) whose answer is always the same: "the lightning speed of the projectile toward its explosion [is] the ultimate argument of reason" (Virilio, *Speed* 43–4).

The essential psychological effect of this spectacle is a quasi-spiritual paralysis of the volitional faculties. The crowd out at the airport, as in the streets of New Valois, where, as Michael Millgate notes, "the theme of that year's Mardi Gras parade [February 1934] was 'The Conquest of the Air'" (Millgate, *Achievement* 145), appears as "a static curbmass of amazed confettifaces" (810), "a static human mass" (813). Straining to catch a glimpse of the rapid machines above, the crowd is wrenched into awkward attitudes or pushed into cramped spaces:

> Then he saw Jiggs, the pony man, the manpony of the afternoon, recoiled now into the center of a small violent backwater of motionless backturned faces. (PY 812)

> the gaped and upturned faces… choked the gangway. (PY 933)

> Then the voice was drowned in the roar, the snarl, as the aeroplanes turned the field pylon and, followed by their turning heads along the apron as if the faces were geared to the sound, diminished singly out and over the lake again. (PY 934)

> Once inside, Jiggs paused, looking swiftly about, breasting now with very immobility the now comparatively thin tide which still set toward the apron and talking to itself with one another in voices forlorn, baffled, and amazed:
> "What is it now? What are they doing out there now?" (PY 799)

The crowd is fascinated, intimidated, perhaps unconsciously mistrustful of the awesome power that impels it to follow the revolutionary movements "*as if the faces were geared to the sound.*" The sound is the siren of a permanent state of emergency, of what Stanley G. Payne in *A History of Fascism: 1914–1945* describes as "a new sense of the acceleration of history and of the transformation of human society and culture" (24). The "second industrial revolution," he notes, was accompanied by unprecedented technological innovation. It inaugurated the beginning of large-scale electrification and the modern revolution in communication and transportation, with the expansion of telegraph, telephone, and cable lines, of high-speed oceanic vessels, and... the introduction of the automobile, followed by the airplane ....Thus the fin de siecle became the first age of the masses, the emergence of a mass society being paralleled by commercial mass consumption and industrial mass production. This had major implications for the acceleration of a more modern form of politics and resulted in a new mass culture fed by mass media, featuring the introduction of the cinema and the dawning of a new "visual age." Important aspects were the growth of mass leisure for the first time in history, and the beginning of large-scale spectator sports.(23–4)

As Virilio might say, with their invention of the gasoline-powered aeroplane the Wright brothers also invented the mass aerial exhibition, the economic implications of which were quickly grasped by the promoters. At Rheims, France, August 22-9, 1909, notes Robert Wohl, "five hundred thousand people paid attendance, two hundred and fifty thousand on the last day alone. Hundreds of thousands more watched from the surrounding hills. The stock holders of the Companie Générale de l'Aérolocomotion made a clean profit of close to 800,000 francs, over twenty times their initial investment" (Wohl, *Passion* 109). Rheims also marked a new global pattern of "nationalist antagonisms, imperialist rivalries, and mutual suspicion and anxiety" (Wohl, *Spectacle* 258). If, as Wohl observes, "[e]ven the greatest doubters would be convinced that aviation was revolutionizing the concepts we had of the world, of its inter-relationships and its distances ..." (*Spectacle* 72), in France, "the increasingly militarized and conflict-ridden atmosphere" at the turn of the century was based unmistakably on the "the increasing probability of war with Germany" (Wohl, *Spectacle* 17). With Bleriot's flight across the Channel in 1909, as with Count Zeppelin's 240-mile flight in his rigid airship in July 1908, or Santos-Dumont's flight around the Eiffel Tower in 1906, the British too gave expression to a characteristic fear: "England is no longer an island. There will be no sleeping safely behind the wooden walls of old England with the Channel our safety moat. It means the aerial chariots of a foe descending on British soil if war comes" (Lord Northcliffe qtd. by Wohl, *Passion* 42). "The air around London and other large cities will be darkened by the flight of aeroplanes .... They are not mere dreamers who hold that the time is at hand when air power will be an even more important thing than sea power" (an article in *The Daily Mail*, 1906, quoted in Wohl, *Passion* 42).[18]

Meanwhile, the aerial exhibition was an immediate danger to watchers on the ground. "In May 1911, at the moment of the departure of the contestants in the Paris-Madrid race, one of the machines went out of control and killed the French Minister of War, while severely injuring the Prime Minster and the leading patron of French aviation, Henry Deutsch de la Meurthe" (Wohl, *Passion* 133)."[M]oving picture shots of the accident were on view in Paris's cinemas the same afternoon" (Wohl, *Passion* 276).[19]

In Faulkner's view of "the closepeopled land" (936) beneath the aerial spectacle, the crowd remains motionless and transfixed. Only its awe and its "longing" seem to rise up. As Mussolini observed in November, 1923, "Not everyone can fly …. Flying must remain the privilege of an aristocracy; but everyone must want to fly, everyone must regard flying with longing" (qtd. in Wohl, *Spectacle* 49). At the exhibition of airplanes at Brescia in September 1909, Kafka is part of the crowd that watches the great Louis Blériot above:

> Devotedly everybody looks up to him, there is no room in anybody's heart for anyone else. And everybody looks with outstretched neck at the monoplane, as it falls, is seized by Blériot and even climbs. What is happening? Here, above us, there is a man twenty meters above the earth, imprisoned in a wooden box, and pitting his strength against an invisible danger which he has taken on of his own free will. But we are standing below, thrust right back out of the way, without existence, and looking at this man. ("The Aeroplanes at Brescia" 306)

The cramped immobility of the proletarian mass stands in dialectical relationship to the thrilling aerial motion of the incomparable heroes. Moreover, large crowds need to be transported and fed. They require police and military control. As Kafka stands with the hungry masses, he feels the hostility of the organizing committee and notes the ostentatious fashion show of the aristocracy in the expensive balconies. As the show comes to an end with the last light of the day, "We are lucky enough to get a carriage; the coachman squats down in front of us—there is no box—and, having at last become independent existences once more, we set off" (308).[20]

Faulkner notes how the architectural layout of Feinman Airport controls and inhibits the movement of the crowd according to its social and economic gradations. As in an anxiety dream, Jiggs and the reporter move through the airshow's maze, their progress chronically disrupted by sudden gates and barriers. They rush to get where they must be but always have to double back or go around, trapped in an elaborate and "tedious" (Eliot's word) succession of pathways: "[Jiggs] too had no ticket and so though he could pass from the apron into the rotundra as often as he pleased, he could not pass from the rotundra to the apron save by going around through the hangar" (800). The labyrinthine spatial logic extends to the city streets at night as the reporter and his companions "thread […] their way between the blatting and honking, the whining and clashing of gears, the glare of backbouncing and crossing headlight beams" (972). Observes Benjamin, "Moving through this traffic involves the individual in a series of shocks and collisions. At dangerous intersections, nervous impulses flow through him in rapid succession, like the energy from a battery" ("On Some Motifs in Baudelaire" 177). This is a grotesque anti-pastoral, a viciously fragmented social space marked by "the disappearance of the habitat that until then had been considered common: *the disappearance of civilian space*, of the common man's right to space … " (Virilio, *Speed* 99). "The increasing proletarianization of modern man and the increasing formation of the masses are two sides of the same process" (Benjamin, "The Work of Art" 120).

Jimmy Collins gives a harrowing vision of this process of Depression-era proletarianization in his memoir, *Test Pilot* (1935), a book that Faulkner reviewed upon its publication.

> Early on the morning I was to start work at the Ford factory I got on a street car and started for the plant. I had on work clothes and my badge. Long lines of workers sat on either side of me. Across the aisle another long line sat facing me. They sat with hunched shoulders and vacant faces, dinner pails on their laps, eyes staring lifelessly at nothing. The car lurched and jolted along, and their bodies lurched and jolted listlessly like corpses in it. A sense of unspeakable horror seized me. I had forgotten the rubber factories. Now I remembered them again, but I didn't remember anything as horrible as this. These men impressed me as things, not men, horribly identical things, degraded, hopeless, lifeless units of some grotesque machines. I felt my identity and my self-respect oozing out of me. I couldn't become part of that. I couldn't. Not even for a short time. Not even long enough to get into the airplane factory and then to become pilot. Not even for that. I wouldn't. Not for anything. Life was too short. Even cadet status in the army was better. I got off the car at the factory. I watched the men file into the factory. I shuddered across the street. I caught the next car back to town. It was like getting away from a prison I had almost been put into. I went out to Selfridge Field and enlisted as a cadet. (4–5)

As a "Socialist and pacifist," Collins found himself "in a considerable dilemma" (7), but he justified his military service on the basis of his commitment to anti-fascism.

After being discharged from the military he considered taking a job as an advisor to the Chinese Nationalist Air Force. "I would be used as an adviser in their school and factories. But I was a Communist. Would the Chinese Nationalist Air Force, which I would be helping to build up, be used against the Chinese Soviets? Against the U.S.S.R.?" (14). In the end he was saved from making a difficult decision by a phone call. A recruiter for an airplane manufacturer was on the other end of the line, offering him a job "demonstrating one of our new airplanes for the navy" (15):

> "What kind of a demonstration?" I asked warily.
>   "A dive demonstration ....It's a bomber fighter, a second model, first-production job, a single-seater biplane with a seven-hundred-horsepower engine ....So, if you are still free, white, and twenty-one—" (15, 17–18)

Here "the obligation to serve the war machine" (Virilio, *Speed* 104) hides behind the Faustian illusion of free-market choice. Collins would die while dive-testing the experimental airplane before his book was published. (As he read Collins' book, Faulkner must have had an uncanny memory of Bayard Sartoris, test pilot, in *Flags in the Dust*.) *Test Pilot* unfolds as an inside report on the U.S. military's aviation arms race as it prepares itself for the coming world war. Many scenes in the book involve roaring airplanes and crowds of people, described by a narrative sensibility alert to the authoritarian tendencies inherent in the mass spectacle of militarized aviation. Could Fascism happen here in America too?

In *The Fourth Ghost: White Southern Writers and European Fascism, 1930–1950*, Robert Brinkmeyer examines "the ghostly presence of European Fascism" lurking on the American "cultural horizon" in this period (2). Ted Atkinson notes the presence in the 1930s of "a steady stream of articles and books from some of the nation's foremost intellectuals reflect[ing] on the potential rise of a dictator figure playing on fear itself in order to manipulate a desperate populace and to accomplish the rise of fascism in America" (115). Jean Follansbee notes "the growing national unease about the increasing military power of fascist regimes in Germany and Italy" (68) while describing an essential American fear: "Fascism didn't happen here, but in 1936, when William Faulkner published *Absalom, Absalom!*, Americans didn't know that yet" (67). Stanley Payne observes that "the only theoretical precondition for fascism which existed in the Unites States was ethnoracial tension" (350), but despite the presence of the Black Legion and the KKK, or the scientific respect granted in some circles to a uniquely American set of racialist and eugenicist doctrines, there was nothing in America to compare with Hitler's plans for "a revolutionary racial restructuring" (Payne 209) of the globe (the ultimate sphere of *lebensraum*). Two "American Mussolinis" are often mentioned in relation to an indigenous American fascism, Father Charles E. Coughlin, the "radio priest"—yet another case of "the man with the megaphone" (see Phil Smith)—and Huey Long (who sometimes used "sound trucks" to broadcast his message).

> Huey Long–feared in some circles as the American Duce–was the most important in a long line of southern demagogues and in 1934–35 the most important politician in the country after Franklin Roosevelt, but he was a southern populist who sought to promote a kind of egalitarianism, and his Share Our Wealth clubs never developed into a political movement. (Payne 350)

Although these figures were taken seriously by thousands of people, there was something widely recognized as absurd, crazed, and buffoonish in their manner (a quality to be definitively captured in Chaplin's *The Great Dictator* of 1940). Here is Faulkner's portrait of Doc Hines (Joe Christmas's grandfather) in *Light in August*:

> That this white man who very nearly depended on the bounty and charity of negroes for sustenance was going singlehanded into remote negro churches and interrupting the service to enter the pulpit and in his harsh, dead voice and at times with violent obscenity, preach to them humility before all skins lighter than theirs, preaching the superiority of the white race, himself his own exhibit A, in fanatic and unconscious paradox. (343–344)[21]

In *Light in August* Hines' counterpart is Percy Grimm, captain of the Mississippi National Guard (to be reified, perhaps, as "the grim Spectator himself" [PY 912] in *Pylon*, the proscriptive panopticon). Faulkner claimed that in Grimm he had invented the type of the Nazi storm trooper before they actually existed (Gwynn and Blotner 41).[22]

The roots of Percy Grimm are traceable, however, to the 1920s' Fascist Italy. Brinkmeyer notes that, of the group he is studying, including Katherine Anne Porter, Robert Penn Warren, Thomas Wolfe, and Lilian Hellman, "all but Faulkner and McCullers ... traveled to Nazi Germany or Fascist Italy during the 1930s" (23). But Faulkner had made a trip to Italy in 1925, and a key episode from that experience made its way into both "Divorce in Naples" and *Elmer*: the arrest of William Spratling for "a crime against the royal family of Italy ... I had placed a coin on the floor and stamped on the king's face" (Spratling 15).[23] Taking over this experience as his own, Faulkner has Elmer be arrested by "two gendarmes in swallow-tail coats and broad short hats—Napoleons" (*Elmer* 423)—as worn by the *carabinieri*, Mussolini's fascist police force. Of "Divorce in Naples" and an analogous character named George, Massimo Bacigalupo, in a fascinating article, observes, "Faulkner's insistence on the 'political' nature of George's arrest is significant if we remember that this was Mussolini's Italy, in which the police forces played a large role and 'disrespectful' foreigners would be easily suspect" (323–4). Bacigalupo puts us on the trail here of the Fascist on a Bicycle as we eventually encounter him in *Light in August*'s Percy Grimm. "Grimm rammed the pistol back into his holster and flung the boy aside and sprang onto the bicycle, with never a break in motion" (*Light in August* 738), as he rides off to kill and castrate Joe Christmas.

> It is notable that [Faulkner's] future rival Hemingway had been in Rapallo in 1921 and again in February 1923 and had given his account of the place in a powerful story, "Cat in the Rain," which is as stark as Faulkner's paragraph is lush. Faulkner was willing to be enchanted by the siren sea. When Hemingway returned to the region in 1927, he wrote another story that is an implicit indictment of Mussolini's Italy, "Che Ti Dice La Patria?"(originally, "Italy, 1927"). The climax of this is an ominous confrontation with a corrupt Fascist militiaman, reminiscent of the mood encountered by Faulkner and Spratling, although not ending in detention. (325)

Turning to Hemingway's story, we read: "On the flat road we passed a Fascist riding a bicycle, a heavy revolver in a holster on his back. He held the middle of the road on his bicycle and we turned out for him. He looked up at us as we passed" (229).

In *Pylon* one encounters the comparable type of petty fascist when the parachutist Laverne Shumann is

> arrested by three village officers one of whose faces Shumann remarked even then with a violent foreboding–a youngish man with a hard handsome face sadistic rather than vicious, who was using the butt of a pistol to keep the mob back and who struck at Shumann with it with the same blind fury. They carried her to jail, the younger one threatening her with the pistol now; already Shumann realised that in the two other officers he had only bigotry and greed to contend with, it was the younger one that he had to fear—a man besotted and satiated by his triumphs over abased human flesh which his corrupt and picayune office supplied him. (PY 909)

This is the sexual fascist as one encounters him in Klaus Theweleit's study of the Freicorps' *Male Fantasies:* "Then he began to struggle and scream again, cursing now, screaming at Laverne, calling her whore and bitch and pervert in a tone wild with despair until the engine blotted it" (912).[24] Primarily in Shumann, Jiggs, and the reporter, Faulkner represents the character of a certain robust popular disrespect and derision for such small-scale despots (they always begin as small-scale despots until—as Marx put it in *The Eighteenth Brumaire of Louis Napoleon*—the social struggle "creates circumstances and relationships that make it possible for a grotesque mediocrity to play a hero's part" [6]).[25]

The key example of what fascism called "the Leadership Principle" in *Pylon* is Colonel Feinman, who, a figure of the International Jew and Powerful Capitalist, becomes the object of a certain degree of racist vitriol even as he himself generates the echoes and rhymes, the trappings, of a certain fascist imagery and style. In a classic essay Kenneth Burke prepares the ground for accepting the logic of the image that fuses opposites into its very structure. In his review of Hitler's *Mein Kampf*, he observes: "Nowhere does this book, which is so full of war plans, make the slightest attempt to explain the steps whereby the triumph of 'Jewish Bolshevism,' which destroys *all* finance, will be the triumph of '*Jewish*' finance" (Burke 196). Faulkner too understands the mysterious operations of such a weird condensation and displacement: "Then he can see that it is two faces which seem to strive ... in turn to free themselves one from the other, then fade and blend again" (Faulkner, *Light in August* 491–2). The blending agency that double-exposes the images of Joe Christmas and Percy Grimm does the same with the International Jew and the Fascist Leader. As Jiggs boards the bus which will take him out to the airport, he opens a newspaper:

> It spread its pale green surface: heavy, blacksplotched, staccato: Airport Dedication Special; in the exact middle the photograph of a plump, bland, innocently sensual Levantine face beneath a raked fedora hat; the upper part of a thick body buttoned tight and soft into a peaked lightcolored doublebreasted suit with a carnation in the lapel: the photograph inletted like a medallion into a drawing full of scrolled wings and propeller symbols which enclosed a shieldshaped pen-and-ink reproduction of something apparently cast in metal and obviously in existence somewhere and lettered in gothic relief:

FEINMAN AIRPORT
NEW VALOIS, FRANCIANA
DEDICATED TO
THE AVIATORS OF AMERICA
AND
COLONEL H. I. FEINMAN, CHAIRMAN, SEWAGE
BOARD

THROUGH WHOSE UNDEVIATING VISION AND UNFLAGGING
EFFORT THIS AIRPORT WAS RAISED UP AND CREATED OUT OF THE

WASTE LAND AT THE BOTTOM OF LAKE RAMBAUD AT A COST OF ONE MILLION DOLLARS

"This Feinman," Jiggs said. "He must be a big son of a bitch."

"He's a son of a bitch all right," the driver said. "I guess you'd call him big too."

"He gave you guys a nice airport, anyway," Jiggs said.

"Yair," the driver said. "Somebody did."

"Yair," Jiggs said. "It must have been him. I notice he's got his name on it here and there."

"Here and there; yair," the driver said. "In electric lights on both hangars and on the floor and the ceiling of the lobby and four times on each lamppost and a guy told me the beacon spells it too but I don't know about that because I don't know the Morse code."

"For Christ's sake," Jiggs said. (PY 783–4)

A Google keyword search at this point of "Shushan Airport" turns up the page of one Blake Pontchartrain, a certain self-styled "New Orleans Know-It-All," who explains:

Abraham Lazar Shushan, President of the Orleans Levee Board, was indicted in 1939 for income-tax evasion, improper use of WPA labor, theft of material, mail fraud, accepting kickbacks, conspiracy to defraud, etc., etc..: After the scandal, the Orleans Levee Board prudently decided to change the name of the airport. But you can't imagine what a difficult task it was. Abe Shushan had decided to immortalize himself by putting his name on any and everything in the airport. And where he couldn't find a place big enough for his name, he used his initial: on doors, in lavatories, in floor tiles, on the sides of the buildings, in the pavement and even in the pattern of the gardens outside. Everywhere you went you would see S's .... Shushan had often boasted it would take $50,000 to $100,000 to remove all signs of himself from the airport. ("Blake Pontchartrain")

In Mussolini's Rome, the *fasces* of the Roman Empire, the official symbol of the regime, is being reproduced everywhere, though, as Payne notes, in 1928 Mussolini ordered it removed from Italian garbage carts (120). "Over this presided the individual cult of the Duce .... He was constantly photographed–in cars and airplanes, skiing, riding horseback, even working bare-chested in the harvest" (120). If Feinman does not come across as especially robust, physically, he is a shameless self-promoter in the same vein. In a letter to his publisher, Harrison Smith, in late December 1934, Faulkner writes, "The 'Feinman Airport' is the Shushan Airport of that place, named for a politician .... Shushan Airport has a lot of capital S's about it, and an air meet was held there" (SL 86). In *Pylon*, Feinman's inflated personal style is denoted by the purple-and-gold color scheme and the letter F, stamped onto the innumerable flags and pennons that dominate the airshow's visual field. The airport runways, apron, and rotundra are also laid out on the F pattern. The hallway of the rotundra features huge murals of Lindbergh and other heroes of

> the furious, still, and legendary tale of what man has come to call his conquering of the infinite and impervious air. High overhead the dome of azure glass repeated the mosaiced twin Fsymbols of the runways to the brass twin Fs let into the tile floor [...] monogrammed into the bronze grilling above the ticket-and-information windows and inletted friezelike into baseboard and cornice of the synthetic stone. (PY 799–800)[26]

Outside, "the bright vague pavilionglitter beneath the whipping purple-and-gold pennons" (PY 786), and everywhere "the purple-and-gold guards" watch over "the throng huddled in the narrow underpass beneath the reserved seats" (PY 799). Perhaps the "puny inexhaustible" voices of the throng may be "still talking" under there (Faulkner, "Address" 119), but up above and all around in the open air only the roar of the airplanes and the amplified voice of the announcer can be heard. The sounds can also be heard inside the deserted steel hangar as the race begins:

> The first starting bomb went—a jarring thud followed by a vicious light repercussion as if the bomb had set off another smaller one in the now empty hangar and in the rotundra too. Within the domed steel vacuum the single report become myriad, high and everywhere about the concave ceiling like invisible unearthly winged creatures of that yet unvisioned tomorrow, mechanical instead of blood bone and meat, speaking to one another in vicious highpitched ejaculations as though concerting an attack on something below. (791)

Faulkner's review of Jimmy Collins' *Test Pilot* extends this conception of the "unvisioned tomorrow" by exposing Futurism's essential nihilism and mysticism and draining it absolutely of its triumphalism. The aviation arms race has been nothing but "'*the arming of the race' toward the end of the world*" (Virilio, *Speed* 152, his emphasis):

> Perhaps they will contrive to create a kind of species or race like they used to create and nurture races of singers and eunuchs, like Mussolini's Agello who flies more than four hundred miles an hour ....I would watch them, the little puny mortals, vanishing against a vast and timeless void filled with the sound of incredible engines, within which furious meteors moving in no medium hurtled nowhere, neither pausing nor flagging, forever destroying themselves and one another, without love or even copulation forever renewing. (332–3)

There is still room for the aviation hero in this vision, but for Faulkner he resembles not Lindbergh nor Balbo nor Mussolini's Agello but Lauro de Bosis, Johnny Sartoris ("Then he thumbed his nose at me like he was always doing and flipped his hand at the Hun and kicked his machine out of the way and jumped" [*FL* 280]), and Roger Shumann, who "without any rudder or flippers and looking down on the closepeopled land and the empty lake" (PY 309), makes a split-second decision as his aeroplane disintegrates all around him. With a last supreme effort of control, he steers out over the water to avoid crashing into the grandstand full of people. He falls free of the machine and disappears into the water.[27]

Notes

1   Compiled with the help of Gresset's *A Faulkner Chronology*, Payne, Wohl, and others.
2   This chapter is based on a revision, woven with fresh material, of my essays "Faulkner's *Pylon*: The City in the Age of Mechanical Reproduction," "*Pylon* and the Rise of European Fascism," and "Faulkner, Adorno, and 'the Radio Phenomenon,' 1935." I would like to express my gratitude to the original editors of this work, Bruce Tucker, Peter Lurie, Julian Murphet, and Stefan Solomon.
3   "In the 1920s and 1930s there was much private investment in racing aircraft, which eventually gave rise to the innovations allowing high-powered all-metal monoplane fighter aircraft such as the Supermarine Spitfire. The drive for profitable airliners brought similar advances to bombers" (Ledwidge 17). Ledwidge cites historian David Edgerton in this context on "'military and civil leapfrogging'" (17).
4   "The Surrealists' Paris, too, is a 'little universe.' ... where ghostly signals flash from the traffic, and inconceivable analogies and connections between events are the order of the day" (Benjamin, "Surrealism" 211).
5   Captain Bogard, as we've seen, looks at Claude Hope's torpedo boat—"the long, narrow, still, vicious shape" of it, with "a machine gun swiveled at the stern" and "its single empty forward-staring eye"—in the same way: "and he thought quietly: 'It's steel. It's made of steel.' And his face was quite sober, quite thoughtful, and he drew his trench coat about him and buttoned it, as though he were getting cold" ("Turnabout" 493).
6   Such fears were more acute in England of course but the analogy was becoming increasingly relevant to the American situation. Observed Liddell Hart in 1936, "This island, if now less of an island strategically—because the air has bridged the sea—is more than ever an island politically .... Will England stand rocklike amid the totalitarian tide until that tide ebbs?" (*Europe in Arms* 1).
7   "Men are once again talking and singing, with a martial fervour that sends a chill through a sober listener" (Hart, *Europe in Arms* 11).
8   See Karl Zender on "the power of sound" in the novel. For recent strong readings of *Pylon*, see Murphet's *Faulkner's Media Romance* and Jay Watson's *William Faulkner and the Faces of Modernity*.
9   See Borkin, *The Crime and Punishment of I. G. Farben.*
10 In "The Return of the *Flâneur*" (1929), Benjamin notes "the extent of the prevailing resistance to *flânerie* in Berlin, and ... with what bitter and threatening expressions both things and people pursue the dreamer. It is here, not in Paris, where it becomes clear to us how easy it is for the *flâneur* to depart from the ideal of the philosopher out for a stroll, and to assume the features of the werewolf at large in the social jungle—the creature of whom Poe has given the definitive description in his story 'The Man of the Crowd'" (265).

11 Robert Wohl observes that "the triad of two men and a woman would become a standard fixture of the Hollywood aviation film" in the 1930s (*Spectacle* 121). The reporter's voyeuristic fascination with this triad produces an additional dimension of intense psychological complexity. Watch *The Lives of Others* (2006) for a recent filmic example of such perverse absorption. See also John Duvall, *Faulkner's Marginal Couple.*

12 Another "theme that would figure prominently in the aviation movies of the 1930s: the conflict between the daredevil pilots of the heroic period of flight and the businessmen, bureaucrats, and engineers who were increasingly coming to dominate the aviation industry" (Wohl, *Spectacle* 135).

13 Jack Holmes, Laverne Shumann's "other" husband, injures his leg when he slams into one of these "jerrybuilt refreshment booths when landing his parachute" (887). Here, as throughout, Faulkner's essential narrative attitude combines nightmare fascination with relentless irony.

14 The world's first major public exhibition of powered "heavier than air" flight was held in Rheims, France, in August 1909. By 1913 there had been so many pilot deaths in such exhibitions that, "to attract customers," the promoters of the Moisant International Aviators exhibition "posted the portraits of their pilots who had been killed while performing" in previous air shows (Wohl, *Passion* 206).

15 "**STUNT FLIER BURNS TO DEATH IN SOUTH**: Captain W. Merle Nelson of Hollywood, stunt flier, was burned to death at 9 o'clock tonight when his small comet-plane crashed to earth and was destroyed by fire at the Shushan Airport here .... The pilot's body was burned beyond recognition" ("Stunt Flier Burns to Death," 11). Faulkner was drawing from Homer's *Odyssey*, Stuart Gilbert's *James Joyce*, and the "Aeolus" chapter of Joyce's *Ulysses* in writing this scene. I discuss Faulkner's deployment of Joycean "mythical methods" (as Eliot termed them) in Zeitlin, "*Pylon*, Joyce, and Faulkner's Imagination."

16 On October 3, 1931, de Bosis, after only seven hours of solo experience, in a plane named *Pegasus*, flew over Rome and dropped 400,000 anti-fascist leaflets across the city, including on Mussolini's headquarters. See Mudge *passim* and the *New York Times* articles "Anti-Fascist Flier" and "Flier Leaves Story."

17 In Faulkner's intertextual allegory the cyclops beacon is associated with Feinman/ King Minos. The airport is the island of Crete. The streets of New Valois and the torturous airport pathways that wend "like a tedious argument/ Of insidious intent" (Faulkner uses Eliot's "The Love Song of J. Alfred Prufrock" as the title of *Pylon*'s sixth chapter) are the Daedalean labyrinth. Shumann is Icarus.

18 See Wohl's discussion of the fantasy fiction of Rudolf Martin and H. G. Wells in *Passion* 69–96: "Martin was so excited by the military implications of Wright's machine that he sought to mobilize public opinion in Germany in favor of its purchase. At the end of 1908 he suggested that, given the relatively inexpensive cost of the Flyer and the facility of its construction, it would be possible to invade England with a fleet of 50,000 airplanes, each carrying two men. Though the English press scoffed at this idea, the joke lost some of its humor when Blériot successfully flew the Channel seven months later" (Wohl, *Passion* 81).

19 The image sequence of this crash at Issy-les-Moulineaux in May 1911—aviation's Zapruder film—can be seen at Wohl, *Passion* 277.

20 "The return from the airdrome after the first day of the competition", wrote Georges de Lafrète on 9 September 1909, had been "terrible". Because of insufficient tramway

service, twenty thousand people had been forced to make the fifteen-kilometer trip by foot amidst thick dust caused by automobiles. "I met elegant women walking while clinging on to their husband's arm, on the verge of exhaustion. Peasant carts, requisitioned at sky high prices, transported as many as fifty people. Clearly, the masses had been carried away by aviation" (qtd.in Wohl, *Passion* 297n).

21 Victor Klemperer describes the sound of Hitler's voice in a diary entry of March 10, 1933: "The never ending propaganda in the street, on the radio, etc. On Saturday, the fourth, I heard a part of Hitler's speech from Königsberg. The front of a hotel at the railway station, illuminated, a torchlight procession in front of it, torchbearers and swastika flag bearers on the balconies and loudspeakers. I understood only occasional words. But the tone! The unctuous bawling, truly bawling, of a priest" (5). See my "Faulkner, Adorno, and 'the radio phenomenon,' 1935."

22 Grimm, like "these trailblazers of the *Wehrmacht*," Ernst Jünger and others, whose book Benjamin reviews in "Theories of German Fascism" (1930), "could almost give one the impression that the military uniform represents their highest end, their heart's desire" (313). See also Faulkner to Cowley on September 20, 1945: "If I recall him aright, he was the Fascist Galahad who saved the white race by murdering Christmas. I invented him in 1931. I didn't realize until after Hitler got into the newspapers that I had created a Nazi before he did" (Cowley 32).

23 Mussolini's "March on Rome" took place on October 28, 1922. When Faulkner made his visit to Genoa and Rapallo in August 1925, Mussolini was dictator of the country.

24 "I don't want to make any categorical distinction between the types of men who are the subjects of this book and all other men" (Theweleit 171). Barbara Ehrenreich elaborates: "Theweleit refuses to draw a line between the fantasies of the Freikorpsmen and the psychic ramblings of the 'normal' man: and I think here of the man who feels a 'normal' level of violence toward women (as in, 'I'd like to fuck her to death') ... the man who has a 'normal' distaste for sticky, unseen 'feminine functions' ... the man who loves women, as 'normal' men do, but sees a castrating horror in every expression of female anger ... or that entirely normal, middle-class citizen who simply prefers that women be *absent* from the public life of work, decisions, war. Here Theweleit does not push, but he certainly leaves open the path from the 'inhuman impulse' of fascism to the most banal sexism" (xv).

25 "With his inner ear [Hitler] always listened to the voice of mockery; and if anyone at court wished to ruin the career of an officer, he had only to whisper, in the right quarter, that his intended victim had referred to Hitler as 'the corporal'" (Trevor-Roper 62).

26 See Wohl on the ubiquity of the military metaphor, "the conquest of the air," during the first decades of flight. "The conquest of the air followed naturally from the conquest of colonial peoples, the exploration of the earth, and the penetration of the seas by submarines. The urge to dominate, to master, to conquer ... " (Wohl, *Passion* 228).

27 "Ben Grew, 40, veteran parachute jumper of Chicago, and his pilot, Charles N. Kenily, 27, Marion, Ohio, fell 2000 feet to their deaths in Lake Pontchartrain before many of the spectators had settled in their seats .... Kenily jumped from the plane before it struck the water. His body was not found near the plane" ("Two Fliers Killed at New Orleans").

Coda: Faulkner and Jimmy McCudden at the Savoy: *A Fable*

He had never heard of a recess in war. But then, he knew so little about war; he realized now that he knew nothing about war,

—*A Fable*

In *A Fable*, a young British RAF pilot, a Jew, "so young in breathing that he wouldn't be nineteen for another year yet," has been trying to write a letter to his mother for some days now, but he is ashamed of his uniform and doesn't have any stories worth telling. For him—Second Lieutenant Gerald David Levine—it is

> already too late, gazetted not into the RFC but into the RAF. Because the RFC had ceased to exist on April Fool's day, two days before his commission came through: whereupon that March midnight had seemed to him a knell. A door had closed on glory; immortality itself had died in unprimered anti-climax: not his to be the old commission in the old glorious corps, the brotherhood of heroes to which he had dedicated himself even at the cost of that wrench to his mother's heart; not his the old commission which Albert Ball had carried with him into immortality and which Bishop and Mannock and McCudden still bore in their matchless records; his only the new thing not flesh nor fowl nor good red herring [....] (FA 747)

Levine's uniform reflects the RAF's degraded condition in May 1918. He wears

> not the universal tunic with RFC badges superposed on the remnants of old regimental insigne which veteran transfers wore, and he didn't even own the old official Flying Corps tunic at all: his was the new RAF thing not only unmartial but even a little epicene, with its cloth belt and no shoulder-straps, like the coat of the adult leader of a neo- Christian boys' club [....] (FA 746)

The earlier Royal Flying Corps pilots and those of the famous Lafayette Escadrille wore magnificent and highly individualized costumes, including scarves, jackets, pants, and boots, ensembles that were anything but "uniform." But the feeling of being "too late" is not only about sartorial style though Levine isn't quite able to articulate the matter clearly to himself. His mind is mixed and uncertain as he struggles unsuccessfully to negate a recognition of the war's ugliness. If he has missed out on "glory and valor" forever (FA 747) that is not only because the RAF has succeeded the RFC, but because he is growing up to realize that war is nothing but killing and the hideous waste of human lives. Moreover, the generals on both sides of the line are meeting secretly to plot the slaughter of their own troops, who have banded together to stop the war, and to stop war, forever.[1] For these soldiers "No-man's Land is no longer in front of us. It's behind us now" (FA 960). Thus are they entrapped on the killing field and annihilated by their own armies' shell-fire. This is the primal scene of the novel, a pure revelation of war's evil and insanity.[2]

Perhaps this is all too much for one eighteen-year-old embryo pilot to grasp: "he knew so little about war; he realized now that he knew nothing about war" (FA 749). But knowledge is seeping into him, eating its way into his inner organs of feeling and apperception with the novel's most profound and uncanny image, that of the sidcott slowly being consumed by the invisible smoldering of white phosphorous. The sidcott (named for its inventor, Sidney Cotton) is the heavy body-suit synonymous with open-cockpit flying, the air-man's anti-uniform that includes boots and goggles, "maps, gloves, helmet, and scarf," with a "knee pocket" where Levine keeps his pistol (FA 761). In one of the novel's many tableaux of crucifixion, Levine stands before his aeroplane's own machine guns in order to demonstrate on his own body whether it is true that, in accordance with the generals' conspiracy, live ammunition has really been replaced by dummy wood-pellet tracer bullets. "He bowed his head a little and crossed both arms before his face and said, 'All right'" (770). His superior officer, Captain Bridesman, fires the machine guns and Levine feels

> the hard light stinging [...] bitter *thock-thock-thock-thock* on his chest and the slow virulent smell of burning cloth before he felt the heat.
> "Get it off!" Bridesman was shouting. "You cant put it out! Get the sidcott off, damn it!" Then Bridesman was wrenching at the overall too, ripping it down as he kicked out of the flying boots and then out of the overall and the slow invisible smoldering stink. (FA 770)

Burning phosphorous sinks into the tufted, dense, and gathered material of the sidcott and thus into the "stuff" of Levine's romantic martial soul. "I'll put it in the incinerator and meet you at the hut," Levine says, but instead "he went to the latrines; it would be pitch dark inside," the better to gaze at the hideous phenomenon of a life slowly being consumed by a war for which Levine can no longer sustain any "fine feelings" or "heroic emotions" (Sassoon, *Memoirs* 112):

> It was dark and the smell of the sidcott was stronger than ever inside. He put the flying boots down and unrolled it but even in the pitch dark there was nothing to see: only the slow thick invisible burning; and he had heard that too: a man in B Flight last year who had got a tracer between the bones of his lower leg and they were still whittling the bone away as the phosphorus rotted it; Thorpe told him that

next time they were going to take off the whole leg at the knee to see if that would stop it. (FA 771–2)

At this late point in what has become a deep psychological depression, in which Levine seems to know that he is on the verge of suicide, he thinks of his mother and then a memory emerges, seeming to come up from the fumes and the glow of the burning sidcott. Newly commissioned as a pilot in the RAF, he was at the Savoy Hotel in London with a couple of his flying mates when they saw Jimmy McCudden walk in. This was perhaps the most beautiful vision of his life. He saw McCudden as he himself wished to be seen by his mother,

> she the woman for whom [...] he was to seek garlands or anyway sprigs of laurel at the cannon's mouth. He remembered, it was the only time, he and two others were celebrating their commissions, pooled their resources and went to the Savoy and McCudden came in, either just finished getting some more ribbons or some more huns, very likely both, in fact indubitably both, and it was an ovation, not of men but of women, the three of us watching while women who seemed to them more beautiful and almost as myriad as angels, flung themselves upward like living bouquets about that hero's feet; and how, watching, they thought it whether they said it aloud or not: "Wait." (FA 776)

The memory contains everything that Levine had ever loved or dreamed about being a flying officer, and it all now slowly burns away, the halo of romance now "grown phosphorescent with that steady decay which had set up within his body on the day of his birth."[3]

Alone in his room "he unrolled the sidcott; at first there had been a series of smoldering overlapping rings across the front of it, but now it had become one single sprawling ragged loop spreading, creeping up toward the collar and down toward the belt and across toward each armpit, until by morning the whole front would be gone probably" (FA 776–7). This vision of death, war, and despair overflows the limits of his traumatic comprehension and spreads across the entire novel "like the remorseless unhurried flow of spilled ink across a table cloth" (FA 838) or the blood of the priest who impales himself upon the Christ-corporal's bayonet, "the sweet thick warm murmur of it pouring suddenly from his mouth" (FA 1009).

Faulkner's strange, post-holocaust, post-H-Bomb novel of the First World War seems to harbor a premonition of mass murders to come. Richard Godden observes that "that the word 'Jew' is unused in *A Fable*, though the concept of the Jew is everywhere, and everywhere in hiding" (172). "Jew," in this sense, is a silent "nomination which indicates that its bearer is marked for death by the state. Why then is 'Jew' a banned term, discoverable everywhere in hiding? To recognize that each citizen and every enlisted man is either Semitic or conceptually so, and is therefore killable by a militarized regime, for the greater good of its economy, *is* unbearable" (190–1). At the University of Virginia in 1957, Faulkner put the matter of Levine's suicide in this way: "This is dreadful, terrible, and I won't face it even at the cost of my life—that was the British aviator" (Gwynn and Blotner, *Faulkner in the University* 62). Keen Butterworth, in conversation with Shelby Foote, helps us to grasp the meaning of what is explicitly unsaid in the novel. Foote told Butterworth about a conversation he had with Faulkner about Levine's suicide.

> For example, he told Faulkner, there seemed to be no real reason for the young pilot to commit suicide. Faulkner hesitated, then asked Foote what the pilot's name was. Foote said, David. Faulkner said, No, he meant his last name. Foote thought for a moment, then said that he could not remember, but that the pilot was a Jew. Yes, Faulkner said, That's it! He's a Jew. (Butterworth 43)

The Photograph

When the war ended for Faulkner at the RAF base in Toronto, the chance to wear a sidcott in an open-cockpit fighter plane was forever lost. But it seems the thought of one might have been on his mind in those times he described in his letters: being "called at some such hour as four o'clock A.M., made to stand shivering on an aerodrome, waiting for enough light to go up and freeze by. Flying is a great game, but I much prefer walking in the winter. Still, I wouldn't take anything for my little four hours" (November 19, 1918; TH 132). On November 22 he writes to his mother, "I am certainly going to be glad to get home. This weather is awful. I came down the other day, so cold that I had to be lifted out of the machine, could scarcely stand it. It is Mississippi for me!" (TH 133). Faulkner was still a long way—months and years of reading and thinking away—from the kind of understanding of sidcotts and the real conditions of war that Levine achieves at the cost of his life in *A Fable*. For now Faulkner actually seems content with and proud of the RAF uniform in which he was famously photographed on more than one occasion. In one of these photos (reproduced in *William Faulkner: Early Prose and Poetry* 12 and as Figure 9.2 in this book), Faulkner stands "in the uniform of the British Air Force," cigarette in mouth, right hand in pocket, left hand holding a cane pitched slightly at an angle, RFC wings pinned over his right breast pocket. This was quite possibly taken by his mother Maud (Sensibar, *Faulkner and Love* 198). "On the back of the photograph someone—perhaps Miss Maud—wrote, 'Lt. Bill. 2/11/19'" (B 238). Michael Millgate adds a crucial note, citing one of Faulkner's fellow RAF cadets whom he had interviewed: "Mr. Monson noticed immediately that [the photo] had been reversed in printing, showing the 'wings' over the right breast-pocket instead of the left. He added that Faulkner would not have been issued with such a uniform but would have had to buy it for himself (interview, October 24, 1964)" (Millgate, "William Faulkner, Cadet" 131n).

Faulkner's motivation for dressing up in such a way on that particular occasion probably had something to do with his need to absorb yet another blow to his masculine dignity, and thus to reassure himself, and his mother, that he could still unfurl the necessary plumage in order to attract a mate, including the one who had already left him for another man. "A day before the new RAF photo had been taken, the Oldhams had received a cablegram from Honolulu. On February 8 [1919] a baby had been born to Major and Mrs. Cornell S. Franklin. They named her Melvina Victoria DeGraffenreid Franklin" (B 239).

The essential image he assumed for his mother, now perhaps for her own camera, had been self-consciously sketched out for her several months before. His letter to her from Long Branch, Ontario, in August 1918, admits there is something affected and playful in the pose he wants to project, but he also knows it will appeal very strongly to his mother's aesthetic sensibilities, social pride, and patriotism. "As soon as I can, Ill send one in my summer clothes, and one standing beside a 'plane, you know, egregious; with one hand resting caressingly and protectively upon its knee cap" (TH 89). The word "egregious" is striking in this context: "bad, blatant, or ridiculous to an extraordinary degree [....] conspicuously and outrageously bad or reprehensible; 'a crying shame'; 'an egregious lie'." But perhaps the pose was egregious only in its prematurity, given Faulkner's youthful vision, in the early days of his training, of a future reality that he fully expected to experience. This verbally described future photo of himself beside an aeroplane will have to compensate for the more modest one he now encloses in the letter, a photo of himself as a Cadet (though, he adds in ink on the bottom margin, in the exalted yet now vanished "Royal Flying Corps," not the RAF; see *Early Prose and Poetry* 5 and Figure 4.4 in this book):

> So I went down last night and had these taken. I've got four. I'm sending you one apiece, and grandfather one. They are not much, for this is my "rookie" uniform and was literally thrown at me. I'll not get my sure enough one until I get to the S. of A.—school of gunnery, aerial fighting, etc.—when my eight weeks are up. As soon as I can, Ill send one in my summer clothes. (TH 89)

From the beginning the aviation pose signified the cadet's intimate link with his mother, a special way of performing for her, an admission that this was how he desired to be seen by her because he also knew she desired and indeed fully expected to see him in this way too. "Maud's faith in 'Billy,' as she always called him, was total and absolutely unshakeable," writes Joel Williamson. "When so many others easily and confidently pronounced him a failure, she insisted that he was a genius and that the world would come to recognize that fact" (Williamson 164). Judith Sensibar offers further valuable insight into this matter:

> One photograph Faulkner sent to his mother from his RCAF training camp in Canada showed him posing beside "his plane," which he never flew. Maud, the realist, believed and did a painting of this trick photograph. When, in the 1960s, she agreed to sell this painting, Faulkner forbade her, saying it was "too personal." At that point in his life, judging from his letters to Malcolm Cowley, he appears to have been embarrassed by this particular early imposture. (Sensibar, *Faulkner and Love* 218)

Maud would use the image, whether a word picture or an actual photo (I have not been able to locate), as the basis of a painted portrait that interviewer James Dahl, in 1953, saw in her living room,

> a small painting, of a pilot in military uniform, standing in front of his plane. I asked if the pilot was Faulkner, knowing of his flight training with the R.C.A.F. during World War I. "Yes, that's Billy in his uniform, and with his plane. He sent me a photograph and I painted the picture from it" [....] "My portraits here are mostly done from photographs." (Dahl 1027)

Figure 9.1 Painting of William Faulkner in his RAF uniform.

Five years later, Dahl wrote to her

> about doing a copy of the painting of Faulkner in his R.C.A.F. uniform, the one I had seen in her living room. This she agreed to do [....] I could still see the portrait in my mind's eye (the flyer was recognizable as Faulkner) and I was very happy at the prospect of getting it. But, that was not to be. Only a few weeks after we agreed on the copy price, I got a letter with this message: 'I received your letter with the $5 [a deposit on the $15 selling price] and the request for a copy of the painting of Billy. Billy has just gotten back from Europe, and says he prefers my not selling the picture of him, as he feels it too close and personal. I am very sorry and am enclosing the check for $5 you sent. (Dahl 1030)

Figure 9.2 William Faulkner in his RAF uniform.

Clearly, the image of "the flyer recognizable as Faulkner" was an icon within the family's store of sacred images. Just weeks before the end, in June 1962, Faulkner "walked down to Cofield's studio and gave him the Kodak snapshot of himself in the RAF uniform for half a dozen copies" (B 1827), as if intending to preserve the image for its flight with him to eternity.

Notes

1   See Godden, Mariani, Matthews, Urgo, and Jay Watson for especially illuminating commentary on the novel.

2   "Each country whose frontiers are consumed by carnage is seen tearing from its heart ever more warriors of full blood and force. One's eyes follow the flow of these living tributaries to the River of Death [....] One of the pale-faced clairvoyants lifts himself on his elbow, reckons and numbers the fighters present and to come—thirty millions of soldiers. Another stammers, his eyes full of slaughter. 'Two armies at death-grips— that is one great army committing suicide'" (Barbusse 2–3).

3   "*The flesh is dead living on itself subsisting consuming itself thriftily in its own renewal will never die for I am the Resurrection and the Life*" (Faulkner, "Carcassonne" 896–7). The genealogy of this scene in *A Fable* is traceable to the immediate postwar period and to Faulkner's RAF demobilization. See my essay, "War, Labor, and Gasoline in 'Carcassonne.'"

Works Cited

Adamowski, T. H. "Bayard Sartoris: Mourning and Melancholia." *Literature and Psychology* 23 (1973): 149–53.

Adams, Henry. *The Education of Henry Adams*. 1918. New York: Modern Library, 1946.

Adorno, Theodor. *Minima Moralia: Reflections from Damaged Life*. Trans. E. F. N. Jephcott. 1951. London: Verso, 1978.

"Aeronautics: Death of Wedell." *Time Magazine* (July 2, 1934).

Allen, Hervey. *Toward the Flame: A War Diary*. New York: Farrar and Rinehart, 1926.

Anderson, John D. *The Grand Designers: The Evolution of the Airplane in the 20th Century*. Cambridge, UK: Cambridge University Press, 2018.

Anderson, Sherwood. "A Meeting South." 1926. *The Portable Sherwood Anderson*. Revised edition. Ed. Horace Gregory. New York: Viking, 1972. 397–409.

Anderson, Sherwood. "They Come Bearing Gifts." *The American Mercury* 21, 82 (October 1930): 129–37.

"Anti-Fascism Here a Myth, Balbo Says." *New York Times*. July 24, 1933.

"Anti-Fascist Flier Believed Drowned." *New York Times*. October 8, 1931.

Aristotle. *Poetics*. Trans. Malcolm Heath. Japan: Penguin Books, 1996.

Arnold, Edwin T. "The Last of the Shropshire Lad: David West, Faulkner, and Mosquitoes." *Faulkner Studies* 1 (1991): 21–41.

Atkinson, Ted. *Faulkner and the Great Depression: Aesthetics, Ideology, and Cultural Politics*. Athens and London: University of Georgia Press, 2006.

Babbitt, George F., ed. *Norman Prince: A Volunteer Who Died for the Cause He Loved*. Boston and New York: Houghton Mifflin Company, 1917.

Bacigalupo, Massimo. "New Information on William Faulkner's First Trip to Italy." *Journal of Modern Literature* 24, 2 (2000/2001): 321–5.

Baker, Mark. *Nam: The Vietnam War in the Words of the Men and Women Who Fought There*. New York: Berkley Books, 1983.

Barbusse, Henri. *Under Fire*. Trans. W. Fitzwater Wray. 1916. New York: Dutton, 1926.

Barthes, Roland. *Mythologies*. Trans. Richard Howard. 1957. New York: Hill and Wang, 2012.

Basso, Hamilton. "William Faulkner: Man and Writer." *Conversations with William Faulkner*. Ed. Thomas M. Inge. Jackson, MS: University Press of Mississippi, 1999. 3–8.

Bellah, James Warner. *Gods of Yesterday*. New York: D. Appleton and Co., 1928a.

Benjamin, Walter. "On Some Motifs in Baudelaire." *Illuminations*. Ed. Hannah Arendt. Trans. Harry Zohn. New York: Harcourt, Brace & World, 1968. 155–200.

Benjamin, Walter. "The Return of the *Flâneur*." *Walter Benjamin: Selected Writings Volume 2, Part 1, 1927–1930*. Trans. Rodney Livingstone and Others. Eds. Michael W. Jennings, Howard Eiland, and Gary Smith. Cambridge, MA: Belknap Press of Harvard University, 2005. 262–7.

Benjamin, Walter. "Surrealism: The Last Snapshot of the European Intellectual." *Walter Benjamin: Selected Writings Volume 2, Part 1, 1927–1930*. Trans. Rodney Livingstone, Edmund Jephcott and Others. Eds. Michael W. Jennings, Howard Eiland, and Gary Smith. Cambridge, MA: The Belknap Press of Harvard University Press, 1999. 207–21.

Benjamin, Walter. "Theories of German Fascism: On the Collection of Essays *War and Warriors*," edited by Ernst Jünger. Trans. Jerolf Wikoff. *Walter Benjamin: Selected Writings Volume 2, Part 1, 1927–1930*. Trans. Rodney Livingstone and Others. Eds. Michael W. Jennings, Howard Eiland, and Gary Smith. Cambridge, MA: Belknap P of Harvard UP, 2005. 312–21.

Benjamin, Walter. "The Work of Art in the Age of Its Technological Reproducibility." Second Version. *Walter Benjamin: Selected Writings Volume 3, 1935–1938*. Trans. Edmund Jephcott, Howard Eiland, and Others. Eds. Howard Eiland and Michael W. Jennings. Cambridge, MA: Belknap Press of Harvard University, 2002. 101–33.

Benjamin, Walter. "The Work of Art in the Age of Mechanical Reproduction." *Illuminations*. Ed. Hannah Arendt. Trans. Harry Zohn. New York: Harcourt, Brace & World, 1968. 219–53.

Berg, A. Scott, ed. *World War I and America: Told by the Americans Who Lived It*. New York: Library of America, 2017.

Biddle, Major Charles J. *The Way of the Eagle*. New York: C. Scribner's Sons, 1919.

"Big Airport for South." *New York Times*, February 4, 1934: XX8.

Bishop, Major William A. *Winged Warfare*. New York: George H. Doran Company, 1918.

Blake Pontchartrain: New Orleans Know-It-All. www.bestofneworleans.com/dispatch/2004-05-18/blake.html

Blotner, Joseph. *Faulkner: A Biography*. One-volume edition. New York: Vintage, 1991.

Blotner, Joseph. *Faulkner: A Biography*. 2 vols. New York: Random House, 1974.

Blotner, Joseph, ed. *Selected Letters of William Faulkner*. New York: Random House, 1977.

Blotner, Joseph. *An Unexpected Life*. Baton Rouge: Louisiana State University Press, 2005.

Borch-Jacobsen, Mikkel. *Lacan: The Absolute Master*. Trans. Douglas Brick. Stanford: Stanford University Press, 1991.

Borges, Jorge Luis. "On Exactitude in Science." *Collected Fictions*. Trans. Andrew Hurley. New York: Penguin Books, 1999. 325.

Borkin, Joseph. *The Crime and Punishment of I.G. Farben*. New York: Free, 1978.

Bostwick, Walter I. "William Faulkner and Aviation: The Man and the Myth." Unpublished M. A. Thesis, Florida Atlantic University, August 1981. http://fau.digital.flvc.org/islandora/object/fau%3A10890

Bott, Alan. *Cavalry of the Clouds*. Garden City, NY: Doubleday, Page, and Co., 1918.

Brennan, Dan. "Interview with Dan Brennan, 1940." *Lion in the Garden: Interviews with William Faulkner 1926–1962*. Ed. James B. Meriwether and Michael Millgate. New York: Random House, 1968. 42–51.

Breuer, Joseph, and Sigmund Freud. *Studies on Hysteria. The Standard Edition of the Complete Psychological Works of Sigmund Freud*. Trans. and Ed. James Strachey. London: Hogarth Press, 1966. Vol. 2.

Brinkmeyer, Robert H., Jr. *The Fourth Ghost: White Southern Writers and European Fascism, 1930–1950*. Baton Rouge: Louisiana State University Press, 2009.

Brooks, Cleanth. "Faulkner's First Novel." *Southern Review* 6 (1970): 1056–74.

Broughton, Panthea Reid. "An Interview with Meta Carpenter Wilde." *The Southern Review* 18 (October 1982): 776–801.

Burke, Kenneth. "The Rhetoric of Hitler's `Battle." *The Philosophy of Literary Form: Studies in Symbolic Action*. Baton Rouge, Louisiana: Louisiana State University Press, 1941. 191–220.

Butterworth, Keen. *A Critical and Textual Study of Faulkner's* A Fable. Ann Arbor, Michigan: UMI Research Press, 1983.

Buttitta, Anthony. "William Faulkner: That Writin' Man of Oxford." *Saturday Review of Literature* 18 (May 21, 1938): 6–8. *Conversations with William Faulkner*. Ed. M. Thomas Inge. Jackson: University Press of Mississippi, 1999. 9–14.

Campbell, James. "Combat Gnosticism: The Ideology of First World War Poetry Criticism." *New Literary History* 30 (Winter 1999): 203–15.

Castille, Philip. "Women and Myth in Faulkner's First Novel." *Tulane Studies in English* 23 (1978): 175–86.

Chapman, John Jay, ed. *Victor Chapman's Letters from France*. New York: Macmillan, 1917.

Cobb, Humphrey. *Paths of Glory*. New York: Viking, 1935.

Collins, Carvel. "'Ad Astra' through New Haven: Some Biographical Sources of Faulkner's War Fiction." *Faulkner and the Short Story: Faulkner and Yoknapatawpha, 1990*. Ed. Evans Harrington and Ann J. Abadie. Jackson: University Press of Mississippi, 1992. 108–27.

Collins, Carvel. "Introduction." *Mayday*. By William Faulkner. Notre Dame and London: University of Notre Dame Press, 1976. 1–41.

Collins, Jimmy. *Test Pilot*. New York: Sun Dial Press, 1935.

Cornish, Paul. "Expanding Bullets." *International Encyclopedia of the First World War*. https://encyclopedia.1914-1918-online.net/home.html

Courtwright, David T. *Sky as Frontier: Adventure, Aviation, and Empire*. College Station, Texas: Texas A&M University Press, 2005.

Cowley, Malcolm. *The Faulkner-Cowley File: Letters and Memories 1944–1962*. New York: Penguin, 1966.

Crews, Frederick. *The Sins of the Fathers: Hawthorne's Psychological Themes*. New York: Oxford University Press, 1966.

Dahl, James. "A Faulkner Reminiscence: Conversations with Mrs. Maud Falkner." *Journal of Modern Literature* 3 (April 1974): 1026–30.

Dardis, Tom. *The Thirsty Muse: Alcohol and the American Writer*. New York: Ticknor & Fields, 1989.

Dillon, Richard T. "Some Sources for Faulkner's Version of the First Air War." *American Literature* 44 (January 1973): 629–37.

Dougherty, Kimberly. "'A Death Like the Rebel Angels: Cather and Faulkner Expose the Myth of Aerial Chivalry in *One of Ours* and *Soldiers' Pay*." *The Faulkner Journal* 31 (Spring 2017): 67–87.

Douglas, Ann. *Terrible Honesty: Mongrel Manhattan in the 1920s*. New York: Farrar, Strauss and Giroux, 1995.

Douhet, Giulio. *The Command of the Air*. Trans. Dino Ferrari. 1921. Copyright, 1942, by Coward-McCann, Inc. *USAF Warrior* Studies. Ed. Richard H. Kohn and Joseph P.

Harahan. Washington, D.C.: Rpt. Office of Air Force History, 1983. First edition 1921. Second edition 1927.

Driggs, Laurence La Tourette. *Heroes of Aviation*. Boston: Little, Brown, and Company, 1919.

Duffy, Enda. *The Speed Handbook: Velocity, Pleasure, Modernism*. Durham: Duke University Press, 2009.

Duvall, John N. *Faulkner's Marginal Couple: Invisible, Outlaw, and Unspeakable Communities*. Austin: University of Texas Press, 1990.

Eliot, T. S. "*Ulysses*, Order and Myth." *Selected Prose of T. S. Eliot*. Ed. Frank Kermode. London: Faber, 1975. 175–8.

Ellis, Frank H. *Canada's Flying Heritage*. Toronto, Ontario, Canada: University of Toronto Press, 1954.

Epstein, Sonia Shechet. "First in Flight: The Wright Brothers and 'Aviation Cinema.'" http://www.scienceandfilm.org/articles/2783/first-in-flight-the-wright-brothers-and-aviation-cinema

Esposito, Fernando. *Fascism, Aviation and Mythical Modernity*. Trans. Patrick Camiller. Basingstoke, UK: Palgrave Macmillan, 2015.

Falkner, Murry C. *The Falkners of Mississippi: A Memoir*. Baton Rouge: Louisiana State University Press, 1967.

Fant, Joseph L., III, and Robert Ashley, eds. *Faulkner at West Point*. New York: Random House, 1964.

Fantini, Graziella. "Faulkner's *War Birds/A Ghost Story*: A Screenplay and Its Relationship with Faulkner's Fiction." *RSA Journal: Rivista di Studi Nord-Americani* 12 (2001): 67–77.

Faulkner, Jim. *Across the Creek: Faulkner Family Stories*. Jackson and London: University Press of Mississippi, 1986.

Faulkner, John. *My Brother Bill: An Affectionate Reminiscence*. New York: Trident Press, 1963.

Faulkner, William. *Absalom, Absalom!* 1936. *William Faulkner, Novels 1936–1940*. New York: Library of America, 1990. 1–315.

Faulkner, William. "Ad Astra." *Collected Stories of William Faulkner*. New York: Vintage, 1977. 407–29.

Faulkner, William. "Address upon Receiving the Nobel Prize for Literature." *Essays, Speeches and Public Letters*. Ed. James B. Meriwether. Updated Edition. New York: Modern Library, 2004. 119–21.

Faulkner, William. "All the Dead Pilots." *Collected Stories of William Faulkner*. New York: Vintage, 1977. 511–31.

Faulkner, William. *As I Lay Dying*. *William Faulkner: Novels 1930–1935*. New York: Library of America, 1985. 1–178.

Faulkner, William. "Carcassonne." *Collected Stories of William Faulkner*. New York: Vintage, 1977. 895–900.

Faulkner, William. *Collected Stories of William Faulkner*. New York: Vintage, 1977.

Faulkner, William. "Country Mice." New Orleans *Times-Picayune*, September 20, 1925. *William Faulkner: New Orleans Sketches*. Ed. Carvel Collins. New York: Random House, 1958. 108–20.

Faulkner, William. "Death Drag." *Collected Stories of William Faulkner*. New York: Vintage, 1977. 185–205.

Faulkner, William. "Divorce in Naples." *Collected Stories of William Faulkner.* New York: Vintage, 1977. 877–93.

Faulkner, William. *Elmer.* Ed. Dianne L. Cox. *Mississippi Quarterly* 36 (Summer 1983): 337–460.

Faulkner, William. *Essays, Speeches and Public Letters.* Ed. James B. Meriwether. Updated Edition. New York: Modern Library, 2004.

Faulkner, William. *A Fable.* 1954. *William Faulkner, Novels 1942–1954.* New York: Library of America, 1994. 665–1072.

Faulkner, William. "Forward." *The Faulkner Reader: Selections from the Works of William Faulkner.* New York: Random House, 1954. ix–xi.

Faulkner, William. *Flags in the Dust.* 1928. *William Faulkner, Novels 1926–1929.* New York: Library of America, 2006. 541–875.

Faulkner, William. *If I Forget Thee, Jerusalem.* [*The Wild Palms*]. *William Faulkner, Novels 1936–1940.* New York: Library of America. 1990. 493–726.

Faulkner, William. "Interviews in Japan, 1955." *Lion in the Garden: Interviews with William Faulkner 1926–1962.* New York: Random House, 1968. 84–198.

Faulkner, William. "The Kid Learns." May 31, 1925. *New Orleans Sketches.* Ed. Carvel Collins. New York: Random House, 1958. 86–91.

Faulkner, William. "Landing in Luck." *The Mississippian,* November 26, 1919. *William Faulkner: Early Prose and Poetry.* Ed. Carvel Collins. Boston: Atlantic Monthly Press, 1962. 42–50.

Faulkner, William. "The Life and Death of a Bomber." *Country Lawyer and Other Stories for the Screen by William Faulkner.* Eds. Louis Daniel Brodsky and Robert W. Hamblin. Jackson: University Press of Mississippi, 1987. 61–81.

Faulkner, William. "Love." [*c.* 1921]. *The Missouri Review* 11, 2 (1988): 123–50.

Faulkner, William. *The Marble Faun and a Green Bough.* New York: Random House, 1965.

Faulkner, William. *The Marionettes.* Ed. Noel Polk. 1920. Charlottesville: Bibliographical Society of the University of Virginia, 1977.

Faulkner, William. *Mosquitoes.* 1927. *William Faulkner: Novels 1926–1929.* Library of America, 2006. 257–540.

Faulkner, William. "On Privacy (The American Dream: What Happened to It?)." *William Faulkner: Essays, Speeches & Public Letters.* Ed. James B. Meriwether. New York: Modern Library, 2004.

Faulkner, William. "Out of Nazareth." (April 12, 1925). *William Faulkner: New Orleans Sketches.* Ed. Carvel Collins. New York: Random House, 1958.

Faulkner, William. *Pylon.* 1935. *William Faulkner: Novels 1930–1935.* Library of America, 1985. 775–992.

Faulkner, William. "Review of *Test Pilot* by Jimmy Collins." The uncut text. *William Faulkner, Essays, Speeches and Public Letters.* Ed. James B. Meriwether. Updated Edition. New York: Modern Library, 2004. 328–33.

Faulkner, William. *Sanctuary. William Faulkner: Novels 1930–1935.* New York: Library of America, 1985. 179–398.

Faulkner, William. *Soldiers' Pay.* 1926. *William Faulkner: Novels 1926–1929.* New York: Library of America, 2006a. 1–256.

Faulkner, William. *The Sound and the Fury. William Faulkner: Novels 1926–1929.* New York: Library of America, 2006b. 877–1124.

Faulkner, William. "Turnabout." *Collected Stories of William Faulkner*. New York: Vintage, 1977. 475–509.

Faulkner, William. "Uncle Willy." *Collected Stories of William Faulkner*. New York: Vintage, 1977. 225–48.

Faulkner, William. "Victory." *Collected Stories of William Faulkner*. New York: Vintage, 1977. 431–64.

Faulkner, William. *William Faulkner: Early Prose and Poetry*. Ed. Carvel Collins. Boston: Atlantic Monthly Press, 1962.

Faulkner, William. "With Caution and Dispatch." *Uncollected Stories of William Faulkner*. Ed. Joseph Blotner. New York: Vintage, 1981. 642–64.

Fichtel, Jason D. "'Things Are Back to Normal Again': Reassessing *Soldiers' Pay*." *Fifty Years after Faulkner: Faulkner and Yoknapatawpha, 2012*. Ed. Jay Watson and Ann J. Abadie. University Press of Mississippi, 2016. 46–56.

"Flier Leaves Story of Anti-Fascist Raid." *New York Times*. October 14, 1931.

Flint, R. W. "Introduction." *Marinetti: Selected Writings*. Eds and Trans R. W. Flint and Arthur A. Coppotelli. New York: Farrar, Straus and Giroux, 1971. 3–36.

Follansbee, Jeanne A. "'Sweet Fascism in the Piney Woods': *Absalom, Absalom!* as Fascist Fable." *Modernism/modernity* 18 (January 2011): 67–94.

Franklin, Malcolm. *Bitterweeds: Life with William Faulkner at Rowan Oak*. Irving, TX: The Society for the Study of Traditional Culture, 1977.

Frazer, James G. *The Golden Bough: A Study in Magic and Religion*. Abridged edition. 1922. London: Macmillan, 1987.

Freud, Sigmund. *Beyond the Pleasure Principle. The Standard Edition of the Complete Psychological Works of Sigmund Freud*. Trans. and Ed. James Strachey. London: Hogarth Press, 1966. Vol. 18. 1–64.

Freud, Sigmund. *The Ego and the Id. The Standard Edition of the Complete Psychological Works of Sigmund Freud*. Trans. and Ed. James Strachey. London: Hogarth Press, 1966. Vol. 19.

Freud, Sigmund. *The Interpretation of Dreams. The Standard Edition of the Complete Psychological Works of Sigmund Freud*. Trans. and Ed. James Strachey. London: Hogarth Press, 1966. Volumes 4 & 5.

Freud, Sigmund. "Letter to Wilhelm Fliess (September 1897)." *The Origin of Psycho-Analysis: Letters to Wilhelm Fliess, Drafts and Notes: 1887–1902*. Ed. Mari Bonaparte, Anna Freud, and Ernst Kris. Trans. Eric Mosbacher and James Strachey. New York: Basic Books, 1977. 216.

Freud, Sigmund. "Thoughts for the Times on War and Death." *The Standard Edition of the Complete Psychological Works of Sigmund Freud*. Trans. James Strachey. London: Hogarth Press, 1966. Vol. 14. 275–301.

Freud, Sigmund. *Totem and Taboo. The Standard Edition of the Complete Psychological Works of Sigmund Freud*. Trans. James Strachey. London: Hogarth Press, 1966. Vol. 13.

Fujie, Kristin. "'Two Rotten Tricks': War and Sex in *Soldiers' Pay*." *Mississippi Quarterly* 73, 1 (2020): 35–51.

Fuller, J. F. C. *Tanks in the Great War*. New York: E. P. Dutton and Company, 1920.

Galassi, Jonathan. "Speed in Life and Death." *New York Review of Books* LXI, 11. June 19, (2014): 18–20.

George, David Lloyd. "The Thanks of the Nation." November 1, 1917. www.flightglobal.com/FlightPD-FArchive/1917/1917%20-%201135.PDF.

Gibbons, Floyd. *The Red Knight of Germany: The Story of Baron von Richthofen Germany's Great War Bird*. Garden City, New York: Garden City Publishing Co., 1927.

Gibbons, Floyd. "Wounded—How It Feels to Be Shot." *World War I and America: Told by the Americans Who Lived It*. Ed. A. Scott Berg. New York: Library of America, 2017. 470–83.

Gibson, James William. *The Perfect War: Technowar in Vietnam*. Boston, MA: Atlantic Monthly Press, 1986.

Gilbert, Martin. *The First World War: A Complete History*. New York: Henry Holt, 1994.

Gleeson-White, Sarah, ed. *William Faulkner at Twentieth-Century Fox: The Annotated Screenplays*. New York: Oxford University Press, 2017.

Godden, Richard. *William Faulkner: An Economy of Complex Words*. Princeton, NJ: Princeton University Press, 2007.

Gordon, Alastair. *Naked Airport: A Cultural History of the World's Most Revolutionary Structure*. Chicago: University of Chicago Press, 2004.

Graves, Robert. *Good-Bye to All That: An Autobiography*. 1929. Ed. Richard Perceval Graves. Oxford and New York: Berghahn Books, 1995.

Grenier, Cynthia. "Interview with Cynthia Grenier, 1955." *Lion in the Garden: Interviews with William Faulkner 1926–1962*. Eds. James B. Meriwether and Michael Millgate. New York: Random House, 1968. 215–27.

Gresset, Michel. *Fascination: Faulkner's Fiction, 1919–1936*. Adapted from the French by Thomas West. Durham and London: Duke University Press, 1989.

Gresset, Michel. *A Faulkner Chronology*. Trans. Arthur B. Scharff. Jackson, Mississippi: University Press of Mississippi, 1985.

Grider, John MacGavock. *War Birds: Diary of an Unknown Aviator*. New York: Grosset & Dunlop, 1926.

Grimwood, Michael. *Heart in Conflict: Faulkner's Struggles with Vocation*. Athens, Georgia: University of Georgia Press, 1987.

Gwynn, Frederick L. and Joseph L. Blotner, ed. *Faulkner in the University: Class Conferences at the University of Virginia, 1957–1958*. New York: Vintage, 1965.

Hagood, Taylor. *Faulkner, Writer of Disability*. Baton Rouge: Louisiana State University press, 2014.

Hall, James Norman. *High Adventure: A Narrative of Air Fighting in France*. Toronto: T. Allen, 1918.

Hall, James Norman. *Kitchener's Mob: The Adventures of an American in the British Army*. Boston and New York: Houghton Mifflen Company, The Riverside Press Cambridge, 1916.

Hall, James Norman, Charles Bernard Nordhoff, and Edgar G. Hamilton. *The Lafayette Flying Corps*. 2 Volumes. Boston and New York: Houghton Mifflin, 1920.

Harrison, Robert. *Aviation Lore in Faulkner*. Amsterdam/Philadelphia: John Benjamins, 1985.

Hart, B. H. Liddell. *Europe in Arms*. London: Faber and Faber, 1937.

Hart, B. H. Liddell. *The Real War 1914–1918*. Boston: Little, Brown and Company, 1930.

Hart, B. H. Liddell. *World War I in Outline*. 1936. Yardley, PA: Westholme Publishing, 2012.

Hawthorne, Nathaniel. "Rappaccini's Daughter." *Selected Tales and Sketches*. Ed. Michael J. Colacurcio. New York: Penguin, 1987. 386–420.

Hemingway, Ernest. "Che Ti Dice la Patria?" *The Complete Short Stories of Ernest Hemingway*. The Finca Vigía Edition. New York: Charles Scribner's Sons, 1987. 223–30.

Hemingway, Ernest. "Soldier's Home." *In Our Time.* 1925. Scribner, (1996): 67–77.

Herr, Michael. *Dispatches.* New York: Vintage, 1977.

Hertwig, Benjamin. *Slow War.* Montreal and Kingston: McGill-Queens's University Press, 2017.

Hillary, Richard. *The Last Enemy.* New York: Macmillan, 1942.

"Hitler Proclaims War on Democracy at Huge Nazi Rally." *New York Times.* February 11, 1933.

Hönnighausen, Lothar. *William Faulkner: The Art of Stylization in His Early Graphic and Literary Work.* Cambridge: Cambridge University Press, 1987.

Horkheimer, Max, and Theodor W. Adorno. *Dialectic of Enlightenment.* Trans. John Cumming. New York: Herder and Herder, 1972.

Hughes, Ted. "Hawk Roosting." https://allpoetry.com/Hawk-Roosting.

Hull, Robert. *September Champions: The Story of America's Air Racing Pioneers.* Harrisburg, PA: Stackpole Books, 1979.

Hunt, C. W. *Dancing in the Sky: The Royal Flying Corps in Canada.* Toronto: Dundurn Press, 2009.

Hynes, Samuel. *The Unsubstantial Air: American Fliers in the First World War.* New York: Farrar, Straus and Giroux, 2014.

Inge, M. Thomas. *William Faulkner: The Contemporary Reviews.* Cambridge, UK and New York: Cambridge University Press, 1995.

Inge, M. Thomas, ed. *Conversations with William Faulkner.* Jackson: University Press of Mississippi, 1999.

Irujo, Xabier. *Gernika, 1937: The Market Day Massacre.* Reno & Las Vegas: University of Nevada Press, 2015.

"Italy Is Jubilant at Feat of Fliers." *New York Times.* July 16, 1933.

Jablonski, Edward. *Warriors with Wings: The Story of the Lafayette Escadrille.* Indianapolis: Bobbs-Merrill, 1966.

Jackson, Robert. "The Anatomy of Thrift: Markets, Media, and William Faulkner's Great Depression." *Faulkner and Money: Faulkner and Yoknapatawpha, 2017.* Ed. Jay Watson and James G. Thomas, Jr. Jackson: University Press of Mississippi, 2019. 31–44.

Jackson, Robert. *Fade in, Crossroads: A History of the Southern Cinema.* New York: Oxford University Press, 2017.

Jakab, Peter, and Rick Young. *The Published Writings of Wilbur and Orville Wright.* Washington, D.C.: Smithsonian Books, 2000.

Jameson, Fredric. *The Political Unconscious: Narrative as a Socially Symbolic Act.* Ithaca: Cornell University Press, 1981.

Johnson, Denis. *Tree of Smoke.* New York: Farrar, Straus and Giroux, 2007.

Kafka, Franz. "The Aeroplanes at Brescia." 1909. Trans. G. Humphreys Roberts. *The Penal Colony: Stories and Short Pieces.* Trans. Willa and Edwin Muir. New York: Schocken Books, 1961. 297–309.

Kaplan, Philip, and Richard Collier. *The Few: Summer 1940, the Battle of Britain.* London: Seven Dials, Cassell & Co., 1990.

Kartiganer, Donald. "Faulkner as Celebrity." *William Faulkner in the Media Ecology.* Ed. Julian Murphet and Stefan Solomon. Baton Rouge: Louisiana State University Press, 2015. 67–90.

Kartiganer, Donald. "'So I, Who Had Never Had a War … ': William Faulkner, War, and the Modern Imagination." *Modern Fiction Studies* 44, 3 (1998): 619–45.

Kawin, Bruce F. "Interview with Howard Hawks." *Selected Film Essays and Interviews*. Ed. Bruce Kawin. London: Anthem Press, 2013. 80–128.

Kawin, Bruce F. "Introduction: Faulkner at MGM." *Faulkner's MGM Screenplays*. Ed. Bruce F. Kawin. Knoxville, Tennessee: University of Tennessee Press, 1982. xiii–xl.

Kawin, Bruce F. *Faulkner and Film*. New York: Frederick Ungar, 1977.

Kawin, Bruce F. *Faulkner's MGM Screenplays*. Knoxville: University of Tennessee Press, 1982.

Kawin, Bruce F. "*War Birds* and the Politics of Refusal." *Critical Essays on William Faulkner: The Sartoris Family*. Ed. Arthur M. Kinney. Boston: G. K. Hall & Co., 1985. 274–89.

Kennan, George F. Kennan. *The Decline of Bismark's European Order: Franco-Prussian Relations, 1975–1890*. Princeton, NJ: Princeton University Press, 1979.

Klemperer, Victor. *I Will Bear Witness: A Diary of the Nazi Years, 1933–1941*. Trans. Martin Chalmers. New York: Random House, 1998.

Kohler, Dayton. "William Faulkner and the Social Conscience." *College English* 11 (December 1949): 119–27.

Kreiswirth, Martin. *William Faulkner: The Making of a Novelist*. Athens: University of Georgia Press, 1983.

Kunitz, Stanley J. and Howard Haycraft, eds. *Twentieth Century Authors: A Biographical Dictionary of Modern Literature*. New York: H. W. Wilson, 1942.

Lacan, Jacques. "Aggressivity in Psychoanalysis." *Écrits: A Selection*. Trans. Alan Sheridan. New York: Norton, 1977. 9–29.

Lacan, Jacques. "The Function and Field of Speech and Language in Psychoanalysis." *Écrits: A Selection*. Trans. Alan Sheridan. New York: Norton, 1977. 31–113.

Lacan, Jacques. "The Mirror Stage as Formative of the Function of the I as Revealed in Psycho Analytic Experience." *Écrits: A Selection*. Trans. Alan Sheridan. New York: Norton, 1977. 1–7.

Lacan, Jacques. *The Seminar of Jacques Lacan: Book I: Freud's Papers on Technique 1953–1954*. Ed. Jacques-Alain Miller. Trans. with notes by John Forrester. New York: Norton, 1991.

Laplanche, J. and J.B. Pontalis, *The Language of Psycho-Analysis*. Trans. Donald Nicholson-Smith. New York: Norton, 1973.

Ledwidge, Frank. *Aerial Warfare: The Battle for the Skies*. Oxford: Oxford University Press, 2018.

Lind, Ilse Dusoir. "The Language of Stereotype in 'Death Drag'." *Faulkner's Discourse: An International Symposium*. Ed. Lothar Hönnighausen. Tübingen: Niemeyer, 1989. 127–31.

Lowe, John. "Fraternal Fury: Faulkner, World War I, and Myths of Masculinity." *Faulkner and War: Faulkner and Yoknapatawpha, 2001*. Ed. Noel Polk and Ann J. Abadie. Jackson: University Press of Mississippi, 2004. 70–101.

Lurie, Peter. *American Obscurantism: History and the Visual in U.S. Literature and Film*. New York:Oxford University Press, 2018.

Lynch, Jacqueline Scott. "Postwar Play: Gender Performatives in Faulkner's *Soldiers' Pay*." *The Faulkner Journal* 14 (Fall 1998): 3–20.

Mahieu, Eric. "Georges Guynemer." *International Encyclopedia of the First World War*. https://encyclopedia.1914-1918-online.net/home.html.

Malraux, André. "A Preface for Faulkner's *Sanctuary*." 1933. *Faulkner: A Collection of Critical Essays*. Ed. Robert Penn Warren. Englewood Cliffs, NJ: Prentice-Hall, 1966. 272–4.

Mann, Thomas. "Freud and the Future." 1936. *Essays of Three Decades*. Trans. H. T. Lowe-Porter. New York: Knopf, 1968. 411–28.

Mannock, Major Edward. *The Personal Diary of Major Edward "Mick" Mannock*. [1917–18]. Ed. Frederick Oughton. London: Neville Spearman, 1966.

Mariani, George. *Waging War on War: Peacefighting in American Literature*. Urbana: University of Illinois Press, 2015.

Marinetti, F. T. "The Founding and Manifesto of Futurism." 1909. Trans. R. W. Flint and Arthur A. Coppotelli. *Marinetti: Selected Writings*. Ed. R. W. Flint. New York: Farrar, Straus and Giroux, 1971a. 39–44.

Marx, Karl. *The Eighteenth Brumaire of Louis Bonaparte*. Moscow: Progress Publishers, 1934.

Marx, Leo. *The Machine in the Garden: Technology and the Pastoral Ideal in America*. Malden, Massachusetts: Oxford University Press, 1964.

Matthews, John T. *William Faulkner: Seeing through the South*. Malden, Massachusetts: Wiley-Blackwell, 2009.

McConnell, James R. *Flying for France: With the American Escadrille at Verdun*. New York: Doubleday, Page & Company, 1917.

McCudden, James. T. B. *Flying Fury: Five Years in the Royal Flying Corps*. 1918. Ed. Stanley M. Ulanoff. Bailey Brothers and Swinfen Limited, 1973.

McCullough, David. *The Wright Brothers*. València, Spain: Simon and Schuster, 2015.

McHaney, Thomas L. "Faulkner and Autobiography in Fiction." *Constructing the Self: Essays on Southern Life-Writing*. Ed. Carmen Rueda-Ramos and Susana Jimémez Placer. València, Spain: Universitat de València, 2018.

McHaney, Thomas. "The Modernism of *Soldiers' Pay*." *William Faulkner: Material, Studies, and Criticism* 3 (1980): 16–30.

McHaney, Thomas. "*Sanctuary* and Frazer's Slain Kings." *Mississippi Quarterly* 24 (Summer 1971): 223–45.

Meriwether, James B., and Michael Millgate, eds. *Lion in the Garden: Interviews with William Faulkner 1926–1962*. New York: Random House, 1968.

Millgate, Michael. *The Achievement of William Faulkner*. Lincoln: University of Nebraska Press, 1978.

Millgate, Michael. "Faulkner in Toronto: A Further Note." *University of Toronto Quarterly* 37 (January 1968): 197–202.

Millgate, Michael. "Starting Out in the Twenties: Reflections on *Soldiers' Pay*," *MOSAIC* 7 (1973): 1–14

Millgate, Michael. "William Faulkner, Cadet." *University of Toronto Quarterly* 35 (January 1966): 117–29.

Mitchell, William. *Winged Defense: The Development and Possibilities of Modern Air Power—Economic and Military*. 1925. Mineola, NY: Dover, 1988.

Montross, Lynn. *War Through the Ages*. Revised and Enlarged Third Edition. New York: Harper & Row, 1960.

Morgan, Speer. Afterword. "Love." By William Faulkner. *The Missouri Review* 11 (1988): 148–50.

Mortane, Jacques. *Guynemer: The Ace of Aces*. Trans. Clifton Harby Levy. New York: Moffat, Yard & Company, 1918.

Mudge, Jean McClure. *The Poet and the Dictator: Lauro de Bosis Resists Fascism in Italy and America*. Westport, CT: Praeger, 2002.

Murphet, Julian. *Faulkner's Media Romance*. New York: Oxford University Press, 2017.

Murray, D. M. "Faulkner, the Silent Comedies, and the Animated Cartoon." *Southern Humanities Review* 9 (Summer 1975): 241–57.

"Nazis Pile Books for Bonfires Today." *New York Times*. May 10, 1933.

Overy Richard. *The Birth of the RAF, 1918: The World's First Air Force*. London: Allen Lane, 2018.

Overy, Richard. *The Bombing War: Europe 1939–1945*. London: Penguin Group, 2013.

Parini, Jay. *One Matchless Time: A Life of William Faulkner*. New York: Harper Perennial, 2004.

Payne, Stanley G. *A History of Fascism, 1914–1945*. Madison: University of Wisconsin Press, 1995.

Polk, Noel. "William Faulkner's *Marionettes*." *Mississippi Quarterly* 26 (Summer 1973): 247–80.

Price-Stephens, Gordon. "Faulkner and the Royal Air Force." *Mississippi Quarterly* 17 (Summer 1964): 123–8.

Proceedings of The International Helicopter Safety Symposium, Montréal, Québec, Canada, September 26–29, 2005. https://www.h-a-c.ca/IHSS_Helicopter_Safety_History_05.pdf

Pynchon, Thomas. *The Crying of Lot 49*. New York: Harper and Row, 1966.

Rascoe, Lavan. "An Interview with William Faulkner, 1947." *Conversations with William Faulkner*. Ed. M. Thomas Inge. Jackson: University Press of Mississippi, 1999. 66–72.

Reid, Panthea. "William Faulkner's 'War Wound': Reflections on Writing and Doing, Knowing and Remembering." *Virginia Quarterly Review* 74 (Autumn 1998): 597–615.

Richthofen, Manfred von. *The Red Baron*. 1917. Spitfire Publishers, 2019. First published in German as *Der Rote Kampfflieger* in October 1917 by Ullstein & Company and in English as *The Red Battle Flyer in 1918 by Robert M. McBride & Co, New York*, and as *The Red Air Fighter* also in 1918 by the Aeroplane and General Publishing Ltd, London.

Rickenbacker, Capt. Edward V. *Fighting the Flying Circus*. New York: Frederick A. Stokes and Company, 1919.

Rieff, Philip. *Freud: The Mind of the Moralist*. Third edition. Chicago: University of Chicago Press, 1979.

Rollyson, Carl. *The Life of William Faulkner: The Past Is Never Dead, 1897–1934*. Vol. 1. Charlottesville and London: University of Virginia Press, 2020.

Roosevelt, Kermit, ed. *Quentin Roosevelt: A Sketch with Letters* New York: Charles Scribner's Sons, 1921.

Saint-Exupéry, Antoine de. *Southern Mail and Night Flight*. Trans. Curtis Cate (with acknowledgments to Stuart Gilbert's translations). London and New York: Penguin, 2000. 1929. 1933.

Saint-Exupéry, Antoine de. *Wind, Sand and Stars*. Trans. Lewis Galantiére. 1939. New York and San Diego: Harcourt, Inc., 1992.

Salaris, Claudia Salaris. "Aerial Imagery in Futurist Literature." *Futurism in Flight: "Aeropittura" Paintings and Sculptures of Man's Conquest of Space (1913–1945)*. Ed.

Bruno Mantura, Patrizia Rosazza-Ferraris, and Livia Velani. Published to accompany the exhibition at the Accademia Italiana delle Artie delle Arti Applicate, London, September 4–October 13, 1990. London: Aeritalia, Societá Aerospaziale Italiana, 1990. 27–32.

Salinger, J. D. "For Esmé—with Love and Squalor." *Nine Stories*. New York: Little, Brown and Company, 1953a. 87–114.

Salinger, J. D. "The Laughing Man." *Nine Stories*. New York: Little, Brown and Company, 1953b. 56–73.

Sassoon, Siegfried. *Memoirs of an Infantry Officer*. 1930. New York: Penguin, 2013.

Sassoon, Siegfried. *Sherston's Progress*. London: Faber and Faber, 1936.

Sensibar, Judith L. *Faulkner and Love: The Women Who Shaped His Art*. New Haven and London: Yale University Press, 2009.

Sheehan, Neil. *A Bright Shining Lie: John Paul Vann and America in Vietnam*. New York: Random House, 1989.

Simpson, Lewis. P. "Foreword: Yoknapatawpha and the World of Murry Falkner." *The Falkners of Mississippi: A Memoir*. By Murry C. Falkner. Baton Rouge: Louisiana State University Press, 1967. vii–xv.

Smith, Dean C. *By the Seat of My Pants*. Boston: Little, Brown, 1961.

Smith, Henry Nash. "Interview with Henry Nash Smith, 1932." *Lion in the Garden: Interviews with William Faulkner 1926–1962*. Ed. James B. Meriwether and Michael Millgate. Random House, 1968a. 28–32.

Smith, Marshall J. "Interview with Marshall J. Smith, 1931." *Lion in the Garden: Interviews with William Faulkner 1926–1962*. Ed. James B. Meriwether and Michael Millgate. Random House, 1968b. 5–15.

Smith, Phil. "Faulkner and 'The Man with the Megaphone': The Redemption of Genre and the Transfiguration of Trash in *If I Forget Thee, Jerusalem*." *Faulkner and Film: Faulkner and Yoknapatawpha, 2010*. Ed. Peter Lurie and Ann J. Abadie. Jackson: University Press of Mississippi, 2014. 169–96.

Snell, Susan. *Phil Stone of Oxford: A Vicarious Life*. Athens and London: University of Georgia Press, 1991.

Solomon, Stefan. *William Faulkner in Hollywood: Screenwriting for the Studios*. Athens: University of Georgia Press, 2017.

Spratling, William. "Chronicle of a Friendship." *Sherwood Anderson and Other Famous Creoles*. By William Spratling and William Faulkner. 1926. Austin and London: Humanities Research Center of the University of Texas, 1966. 11–16.

Springs, Elliott White. "Foreword." *War Birds: Diary of an Unknown Aviator*. By John MacGavock Grider. New York: Grosset & Dunlop, 1926. v–ix.

Stallings, Laurence. "Faulkner in Hollywood." [From *New York Sun*, September 3, 1932]. *Conversations with William Faulkner*. Ed. M. Thomas Inge. Jackson: University Press of Mississippi, 1999. 27–9.

Stein, Jean. "Interview with Jean Stein Vanden Heuvel, 1956." *Lion in the Garden: Interviews with William Faulkner 1926–1962*. Ed. James B. Meriwether and Michael Millgate. New York: Random House, 1968. 237–56.

Stevens, Wallace. "The Death of a Soldier." *Harmonium*. New York: Knopf, 1931. 120.

"Stunt Flier Burns to Death in South." *New York Times* February 15, 1934: 11.

Sullivan, Alan. *Aviation in Canada 1917–1918*. Toronto: Rous & Mann Limited, 1919.

Swope, Herbert Bayard. "Boelcke, Knight of the Air." *World War I and America: Told by the Americans Who Lived It*. Ed. A. Scott Berg. New York: Library of America, 2017. 254–60.

Theweleit, Klaus. *Male Fantasies: Volume 1: Women, Floods, Bodies, History*. Trans. Stephen Conway in Collaboration with Erica Carter and Chris Turner. Minneapolis: University of Minnesota Press, 1987.

Towner, Theresa M. and James B. Carothers. *Reading Faulkner: Collected Stories*. Jackson: University Press of Mississippi, 2006.

Trevor-Roper, H. R. *The Last Days of Hitler*. 1947. London: Pan Books Ltd., 1973.

Trotter, David. *Cinema and Modernism*. Malden, MA: Blackwell Publishing, 2007.

Tuchman, Barbara W. *The Guns of August*. 1962. New York: Ballantine Books, 1990.

"Two Fliers Killed at New Orleans." *New York Times*. February 18, 1934.

Urgo, Joseph. *Faulkner's Apocrypha: A Fable, Snopes, and the Spirit of Human Rebellion*. Jackson and London: University Press of Mississippi, 1989.

Virilio, Paul. *Ground Zero*. Trans. Chris Turner. London: Verso, 2002.

Virilio, Paul. *The Original Accident*. Trans. Julie Rose. Cambridge, UK: Polity Press, 2007.

Virilio, Paul. *Speed and Politics: An Essay on Dromology*. Trans. Mark Polizzotti. 1977. Los Angeles: Semiotext(e), 2006.

Virilio, Paul. *War and Cinema: The Logistics of Perception*. Trans. Patrick Camiller. 1984. New York: Verso, 1989.

Volpe, Edmund. *A Reader's Guide to William Faulkner*. New York: Noonday Press, 1964.

Waid, Candace. *The Signifying Eye: Seeing Faulkner's Art*. Athens: University of Georgia Press, 2013.

Wasson, Ben. *Count No 'Count: Flashbacks to Faulkner*. Jackson: University Press of Mississippi, 1983.

Watson, James G., ed. *Thinking of Home: William Faulkner's Letters to His Mother and Father, 1918–1925*. New York: Norton, 1992.

Watson, James G. *William Faulkner: Self-Presentation and Performance*. Austin: University of Texas Press, 2000.

Watson, Jay. "Under the Spell of a Generator's Thrum, a Faulkner Masterpiece Was Born." *The Conversation*. (January 14, 2016). theconversation.com/under-the-spell-of-a-generators- thrum- a-faulkner-masterpiece-was-born-51712.

Watson, Jay. *William Faulkner and the Faces of Modernity*. Oxford, UK: Oxford University Press, 2019.

Weber, Kenneth Lewis. "Aviation in the Fiction of William Faulkner." M.A. Thesis, Ohio State University, 1964.

Weinstein, Philip. *Becoming Faulkner: The Art and Life of William Faulkner*. Oxford and New York: Oxford UP, 2010.

Wells, Dean Faulkner. *Every Day by the Sun: A Memoir of the Faulkners of Mississippi*. New York: Crown Publishers, 2011.

Weston, Jesse. *From Ritual to Romance*. 1920. New York: Doubleday, 1957.

Wilde, Meta Carpenter and Orin Borsten. *A Loving Gentleman: The Love Story of William Faulkner and Meta Carpenter*. New York: Simon and Schuster, 1976.

Williamson, Joel. *William Faulkner and Southern History*. New York: Oxford University Press, 1993.

Winslow, Carroll Dana. *With the French Flying Corps*. London: Constable & Company, 1917.

Wise, S. F. *Canadian Airmen and the First World War: The Official History of the Royal Canadian Air Force*. Vol. I, Toronto: University of Toronto Press, 1980.

Wittenberg, Judith. *Faulkner: The Transfiguration of Biography*. Lincoln: University of Nebraska Press, 1979.

Wohl, Robert. *A Passion for Wings: Aviation and the Western Imagination, 1908–1918*. New Haven: Yale University Press, 1994.

Wohl, Robert. *The Spectacle of Flight: Aviation and the Western Imagination, 1920–1950*. New Haven: Yale University Press, 2005.

Wright, Stephen. *Meditations in Green*. Toronto: Bantam, 1983.

Wulfman, Clifford E. "Sighting/Siting/Citing the Scar: Trauma and Homecoming in Faulkner's *Soldiers' Pay*." *Studies in American Fiction* 31 (Spring 2003): 29–43.

Yeates, V. M. *Winged Victory*. 1934. London: Grub Street, 2004.

Yonce, Margaret J. "The Composition of *Soldiers' Pay*." *Mississippi Quarterly* 33 (1980): 291–326.

Yonce, Margaret J. "'Shot Down Last Spring': The Wounded Aviators of Faulkner's Wasteland." *Mississippi Quarterly* 31 (1978): 359–68.

Zeitlin, Michael, "Bodies, Injury, Medicine." *War in American Literature and Culture*. Ed. Jennifer Haytock. Cambridge and New York: Cambridge University Press, 2021. 57–70.

Zeitlin, Michael. "'An Entirely New Way of Conducting War at a Distance': The First World War and the Air War of the Future." *Remote Warfare: New Cultures of Violence*. Ed. Rebecca Adelman and David Kiernan. Minneapolis and London: University Press of Minnesota, 2020. 31–52.

Zeitlin, Michael. "Faulkner, Adorno, and 'the Radio Phenomenon,' 1935." *William Faulkner in the Media Ecology*. Ed. Julian Murphet and Stefan Solomon. Baton Rouge: Louisiana State University Press, 2015. 115–30.

Zeitlin, Michael. "Faulkner and the Royal Air Force Canada, 1918." *The Faulkner Journal* XXX (Spring 2016) [March 2018]: 15–38. Special Issue: "Faulkner and the North." Ed. Robert Jackson.

Zeitlin, Michael. "Faulkner's *Pylon*: The City in the Age of Mechanical Reproduction." *The Canadian Review of American Studies* 22 (Fall 1991): 229–40. Special Issue, "Urban Studies." Ed. Bruce Tucker.

Zeitlin, Michael. "*Pylon* and the Rise of European Fascism." *The Faulkner Journal* 27 (Spring 2012): 97–114. Special Issue: "Faulkner and the Metropolis." Ed. Peter Lurie.

Zeitlin, Michael. "Pylon, Joyce, and Faulkner's Imagination." *Faulkner and the Artist: Faulkner and Yoknapatawpha 1993*. Eds. Donald Kartiganer and Ann J. Abadie. Jackson: University Press of Mississippi, 1996. 181–207.

Zeitlin, Michael. "War, Labor, and Gasoline in 'Carcassonne.'" *Faulkner and Money: Faulkner and Yoknapatawpha 2017*. Ed. Jay Watson and James G. Thomas, Jr. Jackson: University Press of Mississippi, 2019. 15–30.

Zender, Karl F. *The Crossing of the Ways: William Faulkner, the South, and the Modern World*. New Brunswick and London: Rutgers University Press, 1989.

Zischler, Hanns. *Kafka Goes to the Movies*. Trans. Susan H. Gillespie. Chicago: University of Chicago Press, 2003.

Žižek, Slavoj. *Looking Awry: An Introduction to Jacques Lacan through Popular Culture*. Cambridge: MIT, 1991.

Index

Printed in the USA
CPSIA information can be obtained
at www.ICGtesting.com
LVHW011923091223
766049LV00003B/100